BELONGING
AND
ALIENATION

Belonging And Alienation

Religious Foundations for the Human Future

Edited By

Philip Hefner and W. Widick Schroeder

C
S
S
R

Center for the Scientific Study of Religion

Chicago, Illinois

STUDIES IN RELIGION AND SOCIETY

Center for the Scientific Study of Religion

For a complete list of the publications in the
series, see the back of the book.

Center for the Scientific Study of Religion
5757 University Avenue
Chicago, Illinois 60637

I S B N: Cloth   0-913348-07-4
           Paper   0-913348-08-2

Library of Congress Catalog Card Number: 75-30254

PREFACE

The idea of establishing a Center for the Scientific Study of Religion evolved following an annual meeting of the American Sociological Association in the early 1960's. Gibson Winter and one of the co-editors of this volume, W. Widick Schroeder, were conversing about the meetings and about the paucity of ontic interpretations of reality among the participants in that assembly. Both of them had done substantial work in sociology but neither of them shared the foundational presuppositions predominant in that discipline.

As they reflected on their convention experiences, they considered the development of a research facility to provide a context to facilitate the work of people interested in relations between theology and the social sciences. Mindful of the need for interdisciplinary and interfaith focuses and of the emerging Cluster of Theological Schools in the Hyde Park area of Chicago, they felt the time was propitious to establish a center to facilitate the mutual interests of a number of people. Several faculty and graduate students in the theological schools in Hyde Park and in other institutions in the Chicago area expressed an interest in participating in the work of such a center, and the non-profit interfaith and interdisciplinary center was formally constituted in 1965. The Center has minimal physical facilities, and all of the participants contribute their time. Consequently, it has been able to develop several substantial studies with minimal resources.

In its early days, much of the efforts of participants in the Center was focused on studies incorporating new and original empirical data. Several of the volumes in the "Studies in Religion and Society" series reflect these interests. Most of the participants in the Center have some interest in the development of these types of studies, but they also have interests in developing interpretative studies utilizing the empirical work of others. In recent years, the participants in the Center's colloquium have focused more directly on interpretative issues and issues of public policy. The essays in this volume reflect these later interests, for interpretative motifs are salient.

For three years, the contributors to this volume have met regularly in a Center colloquium on religious foundations for the human future. The essays presented here are the outgrowth of these sessions.

The movement of thought in the seminar sessions over several years focused on issues in American life, as the various members found their lives and study grasped by those issues. It became increasingly clear, however, that the basic concern of the seminar was not to catalogue the issues in American society as such. Rather, we had the sense that as we probed our own questions about America, something that lay deeply entwined

in the fabric of American life and in our own experience of that life was
being unveiled to our gaze.

It was not a simple matter to perceive or to understand just what
was unfolding in our considerations. At one level, we focused on current
problem areas, generally from a stance that is critical of what is happening
in our society today. At another level, some of the causes of these problems
came to the surface. The dominance of instrumental reason, the technolog-
ization of the American spirit, and the desire to manipulate all things natural and social--these and related themes consumed our interests for a
time.

In the final months of our discussions, we realized that we were
wrestling more profoundly with the question of the fundamental nature of
human beings and their world. The diversity of perspectives, assumptions,
and methodologies was unified in a concern for the fundamental character
of the relationship between human beings and their world and the way in
which an understanding of this relationship throws light on illness and health,
givens and imperatives, that permeate our common life as Americans.

The essays that comprise this volume indicate how diverse the
opinions in the seminar have been, but they also reveal how fundamental
the question of humanity and world is to our reflections. This question
finally focused for us as the issue of belonging. The breadth and the detail
of the essays demonstrate how basic belonging is to the human situation--
ranging from the details of ecological concerns to social analysis, the educational process, to the farther reaches of philosophical and metaphysical
reflections. If the volume says anything at all, it insists firmly that nothing
less than a range of reflection that extends from a consideration of human
beings and their physical and natural environment to an examination of social
institutions and metaphysical and theological foundations is adequate to probe
the significance of belonging for our human future.

The contributions of W. Alvin Pitcher and Gibson Winter to this
volume should be especially noted, for the CSSR colloquium evolved out of
a seminar on Religion and the American Future they were conducting in the
Ethics and Society field of the Divinity School of the University of Chicago
several years ago.

The Center wants to acknowledge with appreciation a grant from
the Community Renewal Society to help defray the costs of publishing this
volume.

Philip Hefner
W. Widick Schroeder

TABLE OF CONTENTS

vii

BELONGING
AND
ALIENATION

Part One

THE INTERRELATEDNESS
OF HUMANITY AND NATURE

CHAPTER I

THE NATURE OF MAN AS A NICHE IN NATURE AND AS AN IMAGE OF GOD

by
Ralph Wendell Burhoe

In times of rapid transformations, the strains and stresses upon individuals and groups often exceed the power of the cybernetic or controlling responses that keep life in healthy order. On the surface of the earth there has been no period of more rapid transformation for living systems than that which has been produced by the scientific-technological revolution that started about the time America was settled by Europeans. We can get some measure of the radicalness by some comparative numbers.

First for the scientific aspect[1] of this revolution, the well-known estimate that modern science doubles its information every ten or twenty years means that only a century ago there was less than three per cent of the scientific information that has accumulated since then.

The second or technological aspect of this revolution also did not amount to much until a little over a century ago. While the ways of knowing (epistemology) and conceptions of the known ("ontology" and "metaphysics") of modern science are commonly considered to have been on their way by the time of Copernicus and Galileo in the middle 1500's and 1600's, their application to the several arts of human living (such as agriculture, building, clothing, communication, energy handling -- including food and heating and refrigeration --, manufacturing, and transportation) began to be significant only in the 1800's.[2]

Of course, an earlier stage of science that had begun to flourish during the previous major explosion of man's knowledge in classical Mediterranean civilization--including astronomy and geometry--had already been applied to give us our arts of timekeeping and navigation. But most of our common, essential, and practical arts did not reach the stage of their development found in 1800 by the application of any theoretically formulated and empirically verified science. Rather, those technologies were a result of an earlier mechanism of cultural evolution that has prevailed for hundreds of thousands of years and had produced primitive man's arts of fabrication, tool making, fire making, cooking, linguistic communication, economics, religion, education, and government.[3]

3

Religion, in this list, is somewhat anomalous, because, millennia before modern science, it was a pioneer in the development of imaginative hypotheses (the invention of hypothetical entities, that account for the otherwise inexplicable nature of life and the world, often called myths when they are no longer seriously believed). Moreover, religions have antedated science even in the modern scientific methodology of empirical verification.[4] But in recent centuries the situation has become quite different, and the consequent failure of religious hypotheses to fit with those of the modern sciences needs to be noted for our understanding of the present crisis of history.

The differences in civilizations and sociocultural systems are shaped primarily by differences in the cultural rather than the genetic information that is transmitted from generation to generation. Moreover, when one portion of the cultural transmission is radically altered, it usually implies radical changes in other aspects of the system. The tremendous change in American patterns of belief and behavior wrought by science and technology during the past century alone is greater than the greatest changes previously brought even to the most primitive tribal cultures by the most advanced civilizations at any time before 1875. The changes in behavioral patterns of the West Indians from the time of the arrival of the then great, compass-guided, Christian-culture-bearing, three-masted Santa Maria in 1492 until 1592 seem relatively slight in comparison to the changes in believing and behaving of the average American between my grandmother's youth and my later adulthood.[5]

Not even the mightiest conquest of barbarians by the civilized, or of the civilized by the barbarians, has ever wrought such a magnitude of change in human thinking and behaving as the relatively quiet labors of a few hundred men in Christendom who in the nineteenth and early twentieth century discovered the conceptual schemes of the modern sciences including electromagnetism, the atomic and molecular basis of physical and chemical, and more recently of biological, psychological, and sociological phenomena; the universal laws of behavior like those of thermodynamics; the geological and biological history that multiplies Bishop Ussher's time scale of creation by millions of times and extends our knowledge of space beyond our solar system by equal magnitudes; and the analysis of the nature and history of man as a part of this complex, including his brain, culture, and the bio-chemical-neurophysiological sources of his willing, feeling, thinking and behaving--all as a natural dynamic program designed by the total being or reality system of which man is a creature. A few of those revealers of these new horizons and inner secrets of the vast system in which we live and move and have our being were Americans, like Josiah Willard Gibbs or Joseph Henry. Like Gibbs, the name and significance of many of them were hardly known in their own towns or universities. The names of many of them--these relatively few who have changed our ways of thinking and our standards and patterns of living far more than Napoleon, Hitler, Lincoln, or Churchill--are still not widely recognized except when other scientists have made them the technical terms--like the <u>gibbs-helmholtz equation</u>, the <u>henry</u>, <u>hertz</u>, or <u>mach</u>--to represent common measures necessary for living in our scientific-technological culture. [6]

The basic value-generating core of any sociocultural system or civilization is religion, according to growing scientific evidence, some of which I shall give later. Without effective religious systems, societies fade and die. Let us, therefore, look more carefully at the relation of religion to this explosive expansion of new knowledge and new technology.

From the times of Copernicus and Galileo until today, the radical transformations of our understanding of nature brought about by the sciences--both the external nature in which we live and the innermost nature of ourselves--have left in another world the classical and medieval metaphysics in which religion is communicated. Religion thus is often incongruous with the scientific worldview. The general credibility and omnicompetence of the natural-science worldview, and the relative incredibility and insubstantiality of other worldviews, have brought some professional theologians in the last two or three decades to declare that God is dead.

At the time the United States was being organized two hundred years ago, there was a noble attempt to be rational about God in the context of the Newtonian worldview. This permitted the dawning psychosocial and established physical science of the Enlightenment to cooperate with a mixture of liberal, often deistic theology, to forge a new nation under God fairly rationally, as Sidney Mead and others have pointed out. [7] Sidney Ahlstrom and Gibson Winter have shown how more traditional and Judaic elements of the Protestant reformation provided a deeper and recurrent nourishment of the American civil, or common, religious culture to give it more of the ever-needed moral motivation and spiritual courage needed to reduce the inequities in the body politic and keep up the morale. [8] But though the early efforts at yoking religion and scientific reason made the founding of the United States an historic landmark, and a monument to the possibility of the symbiosis of religion with reason and freedom, the capacity of its religious leaders to keep the basic wisdom of the Judeo-Christian tradition intellectually and motivationally compelling tended to weaken; and in less than 200 years the religious core of the culture had so eroded that faith in the nation and its erstwhile divine destiny was fading from the minds and hearts of the people. Morals and morale were crumbling. Leaders in national bureaucracies in the 1960's began to see this and to be aware of the impotence of traditional religion to restore the public morals and morale; and they began to explore governmental ways to fill the breach. [9]

But America was not the only state where the backwardness or impotence of religion was causing problems. Modernized and "scientized" programs of salvation grew up out of such parareligious reform movements as Marxism and various kinds of nationalisms. [10]

By the 1970's the institutions of civilization around the world were so unable to control themselves in the face of internal and external realities that Robert Heilbroner's Human Prospect might be summarized: Science (and, he would add, free government) killed religion; the death of religion threatens man's prior successful adaptation to the requirements of his combined ecological and social system; hence the ultimate controlling forces of history will have to kill free government and science to save man, meanwhile exacting from him a terrible price in widespread violence, agony, and death. [11]

Thus, the twentieth century finds us in the midst of the most drastic transformation of living systems in all of evolutionary history thus far. The strains upon human individuals and institutions are tending to produce expectable distress and dismay. There is an increase in the sense of alienation and estrangement, of meaninglessness and confusion that from time to time crosses the threshhold into rage, fear, and despair. Here and there the disruptions may blow up into world wars with mushrooming powers of destruction. In between the more violent flurries of destruction and mass murder, the psychological and social fabric rots, leading to the threshhold of new breakdowns. Many wonder whether they belong in this world, in this nature, whether this is a proper, rightful, or fitting place.

While to some degree the evolving systems of life on earth have always faced crises, we are today haunted by well-grounded suspicions that modern scientific technology creates a novel and perhaps totally lethal crisis. It is a technology that has put all our eggs in one basket, all the sacred genetic pool of living systems into a single habitat. Man is walking unstably in emotionally treacherous terrain, holding in his hand a fantastic new bomb. If he trips and lets it fall, it could trigger others with radiations to wipe out the whole genetic heritage of his own and many other species.

This horror of the possible end of all life on earth is only the last of a large number of possible errors or sins. During the past century, in the absence of a guiding higher wisdom, man has greedily grasped at the magic offered him by scientific technology, remaining quite naive about the responsibilities for the control of his own destiny that the magic lays upon his own shoulders. Towards the end of the twentieth century man is waking up in the kind of nightmare portrayed by the sorcerer's apprentice. His errors of commission or omission are producing mushrooming chaos. If he does not have the eyes to see directly the fearful potentialities, their mounting pressures increasingly seep into his dreams and his moods.

In this situation, many sensitive souls are grasping at straws for salvation--straws ranging from suicide and schizophrenia to running back to the safety of mother's skirt, whether the mother be the symbol systems of eternal values of yesterday (nineteenth-century Christian theology), of the day before (some more primitive and esoteric faith from Astrology to Zen), or of a few days before that (the genetically programmed, instinctual aims or goals, including the famous trilogy of eat, drink, and be merry, for tomorrow . . . .)! Rushing from one unrequiting savior to another, these poor people do not yet know that yesterday's mother cannot provide guidance in the world of scientific technology until she is taught to speak credibly in terms of scientific concepts.

Less sensitive souls, particularly those whose welfare is not immediately threatened, are given a less stressful passage on spaceship earth as it rolls along. They are like passengers on the Titanic, who may have remained blissfully asleep in her cabins just before she foundered upon the iceberg. Not so the guardians of the ship who know the perils of the sea. They must be anxious. It is for this reason that the past century has been flooded by an outpouring of prophets and poets of tragedy and doom --of man's meaninglessness, despair, and absurdity. But where are the guardians who truly know our real perils or what we can do to be delivered of them?

As Engel's paper in this volume suggests, not every prophet is truly salvatory. Much of our running back to mother's skirts is, indeed, childish primitivism. Even if it can provide man with some temporary emotional buffers, some temporary islands of safety in a rising flood, these are not likely to give a solution to the long-range problem of what can provide man with the wisdom, moral motivation, courage, and hope to act in ways that will permit life in the context of modern science and technology. Engel writes that

> a more adequate statement of the problem of nature and culture is needed:. . . . how to understand man's special relationship to nature in such a way that the unique values of both nature and society are affirmed within the character of the relationship itself. [12]

It is to this task that I address myself in this paper but in ways different from those referred to in the concluding section of his paper. My approach requires a more inclusive, contemporary, and scientific understanding of the term nature.

Nature

Since the term nature or natural is understood quite differently by different people and in different contexts, it is important for clarity that I state how I am using the term. I wish to use it in the most universal and general sense in which I find it used by scientists and systems theorists to include the complex totality of everything that enters into the makeup of the structures and evolutionary dynamics of total systems--and not to the more popular and restricted senses of common speech or recent romantic "ecology" referring to sylvan and bucolic simplicity or urban and economic tidiness. Hence my use of "nature" refers to the Oxford English Dictionary definition I, 1: "The essential qualities or properties of a thing; the inherent and inseparable combination of properties essentially pertaining to anything and giving it its fundamental character." This suggests that "nature" is connected with the metaphysical essence of a thing. While "nature" derived its meaning from the "innate" characteristics present at birth, it has absorbed a much wider meaning by analogy with the wider processes of creation. It may denote the "inherent dominating power by which action or character is determined" (Oxford no. 9); or "the inherent power or force by which the physical and mental activities of man are sustained (sometimes personified)" (Oxford no. 10); or "the creative and regulative physical power which is conceived of as operating in the material world and as the immediate cause of all its phenomena. . ." (Oxford no. 11); and, in a wider sense still, "holding nature to represent the whole cosmos, and to include both the physical and the spiritual" (Oxford no. 13b).

In this usage of the term, we find Nature to be the name of the British analogue of Science, the weekly journal of the American Association for the Advancement of Science. The term as well as the journal embraces the whole network of logically articulated and tested conceptual models of science that have been accumulated for understanding the phenomena of human experience. Included is a realm of invisible and intangible entities, such as electrons, fields of force--a hierarchy of hidden dynamic structures --as well as the general rules or laws that have been discovered to explain the temporal sequences (history) and relationships of all kinds of events that may be discovered to be taking place anywhere and anytime. These events may be as vast and distant as the birth and death of stars we cannot see or as close and complex as why I or my neighbor is behaving, feeling, or thinking in ways I could not earlier understand. Within the "nature" of modern science, these very different systems of events may be interdependent--not in the simplistic or absurd relations of astrology, but in the evolutionary sense of my behavior being the natural product of several billion years of history of events produced by the natural forces around the star we call the sun.

While scientists know they could never know or explain the full story of how the sun produced what I am now doing, feeling, or thinking, the presently extended scientific conceptual system in this century has become so successful and so well confirmed by evidence that this general model or scheme of explanation has become accepted and useful as a fantastic advance in man's capacity to explain or understand. The new conceptual system shows how nature is a hierarchically ordered, organized, evolving system within which new levels of interacting subsystems emerge to create such ranges of dynamic structures or entities as atoms, molecules,

living cells, organisms, and civilizations. Plausible and partially validated
explanations have been developed of how chemical evolution can produce
cells of living matter; how the evolution of cells can produce organisms
including man; and how in the new level of human cultural evolution there
are produced religions, civilizations, and science.

The whole multidimensional network of the hierarchical structures
of nature is found to be governed at all levels and in all dimensions by
certain universal principles, such as the laws of thermodynamics, which,
for the scientifically informed mind, illuminate and explain the unity or
interconnectedness of the spiralling hierarchies of evolving complex systems as stable or metastable dynamic states at successive new levels of
remove from thermodynamic equilibrium for prior stages. As J. Bronowski
has put it, it is as if there are in nature a succession of hidden but empirically real preferred configurations that become the successive steps on the
ladder of the metastable states in evolution as events climb from one level
to those above. Our current vision of this ladder starts on steps below the
level of the atom and continues up through our own awareness of ourselves
and our civilization. Bronowski writes:

> So, contrary to what is usually said, the Second Law of Thermo-
> dynamics does not fix an arrow in time by its statistics alone.
> Some empirical condition must be added to it before it can describe
> time (or anything else) in the real world, where our view is finite.
> When there are hidden strata of stability, one above another, as
> there are in our universe, it follows that the direction of time
> [history] is given by the evolutionary process that climbs them
> one by one. [13]

When scientists undertake the analysis of ecosystems, it is
ultimately this total system of nature that may be involved, and not simply
the material and energy balances within some fractional segment of it. In
the other direction, toward smaller size, systems analysis may study and
describe the inputs, transformations, and outputs of entities as complex
and small as a brain or as tiny as a molecule or atom. As becomes clear
in reading some of the materials of the Club of Rome or Robert Heilbroner's
Human Prospect, or Roger W. Sperry's "Science and the Problem of Values,"
the operations of the human brain or of human feelings, thinkings, and be-
havings--as products of a sociocultural system--are interacting elements
no longer negligible in the analysis of the larger ecosystem of the world's
matter-energy balances. [14]

Nature--including the totality of all phenomena that man can experience or properly project or infer (infer, that is, without disconfirmation
by evidence to the contrary)as entities and their behavior or processes--
then, is what the physical sciences have sought to describe and explain as

far as they can. In the past few centuries this effort has been immensely
successful in providing explanations of ever wider ranges of phenomena by
using an ever more tightly knit and relatively small system of postulates
or logical presumptions. This hypothecated symbolic network as the
ground for describing and explaining more and more of what really or
actually happens in human experience appears to be a growing or evolving
storehouse of information (information in the technical sense), akin to the
evolution of information found in socioculturally evolved linguistic symbol
systems and akin to the evolution of the biogenetically evolved information
in the gene pools of species and ecosystems.

This vast conceptual system of the sciences describes a nature
or system of entities such as electrons and electromagnetic fields that are
not directly visible or tangible to common human sense. One could say
that contemporary physics has fabricated its own metaphysics or system
of underlying realities that are universal characteristics of the cosmos
anywhere and anytime. These "foundations" of modern science, this new
or "meta physics," provide us today with what we may call the essence of
nature. This is very different from the essence of nature found in the barn-
yard or forest by common sense.

This "metaphysics" or trans- or super-commonsense natural of
the modern physical sciences is commonly conceded to manifest certain
general characteristics that are remarkably close to what philosophical and
theological metaphysicians since Plato and Aristotle have used in describing
the deity or first cause and final end, the alpha and omega.

For instance, the nature of the cosmos or the totality of nature is
by most scientists held to be a single, interconnected whole, a monistic
picture. At least this has been a central and fruitful hypothesis and has led
to increasing junctions of the previously disjoined conceptual fields, such
as biophysics, biopsychology, and now even "psychobiophysics"! One can
successfully search and be rewarded in finding ever more detailed connections among the events of human experience in which they all cohere in the
basic conceptual scheme or symbol system of the sciences. This can include some studies of the most intimate phenomena of what has previously
been called "private" or subjective human experience involving the subtle
shades of aesthesias, conscious "mind," logic, culture, and even the
phenomena of religion in its psychological as well as sociological aspects.[15]

I shall discuss later some generalizations of the important attributes
or characteristics of this total system of nature, but what has been said thus
far may be sufficient basis for proceeding to use this physics or new metaphysics as the basis for an inquiry into anything into which the human mind
can inquire. I propose we now use this new light for examining that area,
sector, or domain of total nature that seems so important to us: man.

Man's Nature

Here we shall find that an illuminating scientific account of the nature of man emerges when we see him as an integrated system or whole which has been organized and constituted by the interweaving and selection of elements from three sequentially emergent stages or domains of the total nature or reality of events on earth as recently revealed by the physical sciences: (1) the original ground of being--the prebiological, physicochemical ecosystem; (2) the biogenetically structured stage or domain, whose emergence goes back a couple of billion years; and (3) the sociocultural stage or domain whose emergence goes back only a couple of million years. In the contemporary scientific history of nature, these three successively emerging stages in the hierarchy of life on earth represent widely separated domains. But in the past few decades the expansion of the scientific pictures has begun to fill in the innumerable detailed steps that have produced the evolution from lower levels of each domain through to the level of the next gross stage above and to show that higher stages exist only when grounded on those below.

As Engel correctly points out in his paper, there is a good deal of confusion in our language today concerning the cultural domain and its relation to "nature," which for many is a term that applies only to the first two of these three domains. [16] My analysis aims to dissolve the estrangement and alienation of man's contemporary schizophrenic dualism, which sees man and his culture or mind as distinct from and embattled against nature. I shall attempt to show how culture and mind are indeed found within the total nature embraced by the modern sciences. It is an attempt to provide again what Eliade asserts the more rational religions have lost: the sense of what is sacred for man in the midst of the world. [17]

Since our task is to show where man belongs in the scheme of things, what is sacred there for him, and thus to reduce his alienation and estrangement from the ground of his being in the world, we shall focus our examination upon those aspects of man's three natures which are pertinent for understanding the religious or sacred and salvatory concerns of man. For special reasons I shall begin my analysis with man's middle or biogenetic stage.

The Biogenetic Stage of Man's Nature and Ground of Religious Experience

I am using the term "biogenetic" to denote biological phenomena insofar as they are shaped by genetic information, by the DNA codes accumulated in gene pools of species and ecosystems. We shall see that religion has deep biological roots.

From a scientific perspective today we can see that religion has biological roots in ancient, genotypically programmed patterns of the central nervous system, traceable back more than a hundred million years. Hudson Hoagland, founder of the Worcester Foundation for Experimental Biology, summarized a wide field of biological evidence when he suggested that religion is an inevitable result of the way the brain has evolved to provide viable organic responses to internal and external conditions. The brain is an organ of survival established by biological evolution. Its main function has been to enable the organism to integrate sensory information into configurations that will enable the organism to adapt and remain viable or in being.

> The ability to form meaningful configurations that encompass large segments of the environment is a property of the more highly developed brains, and a good case can be made for the view that man's concerns with science, philosophy, political ideologies, and theologies are a reflection of a basic property of his nervous system to integrate extensive configurations relating himself to his environment. [18]

Many have suggested that the gods are projections or symbols naturally produced by the human brain to fill the gaps in our understanding of cause-and-effect in vital areas of our experience. [19] These symbols, elaborated and selected as lasting social memories in cultural evolution, represent the vital but often hidden aspects of the "super-powers of nature" (an interesting translation for "supernatural")[20] that determine human destiny. In origin and in their explanatory function, the stories or myths of the gods are essentially primitive scientific hypotheses, imaginative projections of the brain to provide suitable "initial causal termini" that enable logical or cause-and-effect statements of explanation. In the sciences such hypotheses may become so well confirmed, like "atoms," that they become "facts" from which science then moves up the ladder to new levels of its conceptual system. [21]

But, in addition to the cognitive functions akin to scientific hypotheses, religious beliefs have provided--through the now partially explained natural interactions in the neocortices of a network of brains--the necessary symbolic and cognitive extensions of the feelings: emotions, fears, desires, and hopes, which are largely generated in and mediated by man's lower and more ancient paleomammalian brain level, the limbic system, which was developing more than 100,000,000 years ago. These vital lower-brain functions operate to orient and motivate animals (including Homo) adaptively, giving them proper fears and proper courage, providing directions and hope concerning the most sacred ultimacies for their lives so that their behavior will be directed to these ends even in the midst of seemingly overwhelming threats to life.

To those not familiar with biological and evolutionary mechanisms, the description of religion in terms of biological theory may seem rather indirect, unconvincing, alien, or irrelevant, particularly to those who associate religion with personal experiences of deep feeling which they often suppose are not expressible in rational language at all. However, these and other recent scientific revelations have begun to provide more rational explanations of the dynamics of the brain, its evolution, and its role in producing human conscious awareness--including perceptions, feelings, reasonings, and even the seemingly irrational decisions that men experience themselves making.

Recent findings, such as those of Paul D. MacLean, have clarified the roles for human nature and religion of three phylogenetic levels of our brains: (1) the very old reptilian level which generates our <u>instincts</u> including those involved in ritual and religion, (2) the limbic system of our old mammalian brain which is involved in generating deeply religious feelings and emotions, and (3) the human neocortex, which can associate diverse elements from several sensory modalities into <u>symbols,</u> and then associate the symbols and establish symbols of symbols of symbols in systematic hierarchies.

The neocortex makes possible symbolic abstractions (including language and linguistic logic) and their projection in <u>dynamic models</u> of self and its world in dreams and linguistic symbols, motivated and fed by input from the "instincts" and "feelings" of the lower two brain levels as well as by input from the sensory modalities commonly "cross-referenced" and integrated to produce the "things" (the beings, existents, or entities of ontology) and our feeling-tones about them that are characteristic of what we call consciousness, conceiving, willing, etc. These dynamic models are the stuff out of which are formed such things as religious myth, philosophy, theology, and science. Operations by the brain tend to integrate necessary elements from all three levels of the brain for complex understandings, decisions, and motivations that adapt our behavior adequately to our sociocultural ecological niche and to the ultimate reality system around us.[22]

These functions of the brain provide new grounds for understanding the reality of religion, the usefulness and validity of deep religious feelings and emotions. They give a tangible basis for the power of religion to motivate morals as well as provide hope and courage. They give a clue on how the brain may mediate to us the rare spiritual mixtures of the combined products of all three of these genetically given levels of our brain, programmed from the outside by combinations of high cultural, genetic, and environmental information, to produce in conscious self-awareness the idealistic rapture and vision of deeper reality known in the mystical experience of the love of God and beatific vision. That is, they allow us to account for religious experience. It also becomes clear how such projections may reflect validly not only man's needs but also a picture of the "objective reality" that is sacred for him and to which he must adapt.

Genetic programming alone of the brain's behavioral patterns cannot produce social behavior and human society, even though genetically programmed brain structures and functions are essential for our knowing, feeling, and behaving. Geneticist George C. Williams has given strong evidence that "the natural selection of alternative alleles [can never] foster the production of individuals willing to sacrifice their lives...for mere friends," only for close genetic relatives, such as offspring.[23] If true, this forces us to explain the social motivation and altruism necessary for human societies (those extending beyond the range of close relatives) on grounds that transcend the information inherited from our gene pool. Williams himself seeks to explain this in terms of the expansion of brain capacity in recent mammalian evolution so as to provide for the discrimination that extra-familial friendship and devotion may be of value for one's own future viability.

Ethologist Konrad Lorenz has outlined the phylogenetic evolution of ritual by means of processes of variation and selection of animal behaviors that gradually become functional as symbols for communicating certain messages to other animals so as to produce useful responses by them for one's own life.[24] Both the senders and the receivers of these messages have been attuned by natural selection in their central nervous systems to respond in ways that enhance probabilities for life. Higher animal and human social life are founded on the programming of brains by the communication powers of such ritual behavior.

This is in contrast to insect societies and societies of cells (including organisms), where the social norms and motivation are programmed directly by genetic information. This is possible with them because in those cases there is no violation of the rule of genetics that prohibits the selection of self-sacrificial social altruism beyond very close relatives. The cellular societies that constitute organisms have identical genotypes. The large populations of diversely specialized and functioning individuals in insect societies are genetically very closely related, sometimes closer then siblings.[25]

Since the biogenetic stage or domain of man's nature, although essential for his being and his religious experience, nevertheless by itself is insufficient for the evolution of complex mammalian societies and civilizations, we shall now turn to the stage of man's nature whose emergence in the past million years has produced a "new being" in the evolution of life on earth, giving man a "soul" essentially different from all previous creatures.

The Sociocultural Stage of Man's Nature

I am using the term "sociocultural" to characterize social phenomena insofar as they are shaped by culturally encoded and transmitted information. Although selected by nature, as is genetic information of genotypes, the patterns of cultural information (which I have called "culturetypes") are collected, stored, and operative through very different mechanisms from those of genotypes.

Lorenz points out,

> the properties of any human group which make it coherent . . .
> are norms of behavior ritualized in cultural development. . . .
> Without traditional rites and customs representing a common
> property valued and defended by all members of the group,
> human beings would be quite unable to form social units exceed-
> ing in size that of the primal family group.[26]

Lorenz points out something further which is of importance to our understanding how "wisdom" is accumulated in cultural evolution of religions without any such wisdom necessarily being developed consciously by the participants.

> It is quite certain that it hardly ever was insight into a valuable
> function that gave rise to traditional norms and rites, but the age-
> old process of natural selection. Historians will have to face the
> fact that natural selection determined the evolution of cultures in
> the same manner as it did that of species.[27]

I presume that Lorenz, in using the term "same manner" is speaking of the cultural analogue of genetic selection, where the cultural transmission and selection processes are focused in the neocortex of the brain rather than the gonads, even though the same general program of (at least partially random) variation and the retention or memory of stable patterns carries out the task.

We move now from the biological grounds of and necessity for ritual up to its role in religion as noted by cultural anthropology. Anthropologist A.F.C. Wallace of the University of Pennsylvania pointed out to the first symposium of the Center for Advanced Study in Theology and the Sciences of the Meadville/Lombard Theological School in January of 1966 that "the primary phenomenon of religion is ritual. Ritual is religion in action. . . . It is ritual which accomplishes what religion sets out to do."[28] This analysis of the nature of religion, which was first published in Zygon, was later incorporated in Wallace's Religion, an Anthropological View, which Margaret Mead in her review called

> an impressive attempt to bring the entire history of all human
> religious experience, past, present, and future under one
> rubric. . .certainly the most brilliant and ambitious treatment
> of religion in this generation,

although she finds the book inadequate on many counts and "essentially
a book for the specialist sophisticated in the study of religion."[29]
But it is exactly for his remarkable scientific specialization that
I have chosen to use Wallace's insights into a unifying theory of religion
under a contemporary scientific rubric that seems to draw things together
as it ranges from thermodynamics through psychology to cultural anthropology. It provides a link between the biological mechanisms of ritual and
the socialization of the only mammal that has been significantly socialized:
Homo sapiens. This link is the capacity of ritual behavior through its
neurological contacts with deep-seated feelings and motivations to become
the communications channel between the two distinct heritages of man's
nature: biogenetic and sociocultural. I should indicate that there is a whole
school of psychoanthropological interpretation of religion growing out of
Wallace's insights. Some of these are significantly convergent with those
of Anton T. Boisen, the curious genius who was basic to the clinical pastoral
education movement.[30]
Wallace and others also have pointed out that, in human life, ritual
necessarily becomes intertwined with systems of belief, ranging from
primitive myths to advanced theologies and sciences. "Belief, codified in
linguistic structures, rationalizes ritual and renders it more effective than
it would be by itself. . . . A myth can be defined as a transformation of
ritual."[31] According to Wallace, "the goal of science and the goal of ritual
and myth are the same: to create the image of a simple and orderly world."[32]
Religious rituals and beliefs, then, are outgrowths from very ancient roots
of rituals as primitive, genetically programmed communications directly tied
to genetically programmed motivations or response patterns in order to provide adaptive or viable behavior relative to fellow creatures and the larger
environment.
In addition to the evolution of ritual, myth, and belief by the pre-
rational and prescientific kinds of variation and selection in the brains of a
population as noted by Lorenz, in recent millennia the cumulative store of
cultural information shared through language and the critical tools of the
logic of language and the brain's capacity therewith to project future states
have provided new levels for the evolution of knowledge about the sacred as
well as about the profane.[33] Tradition and myth began to be explained and
reformed by theology. Wallace noted that "religious propositions are a
product of human cerebration; they are, often, defended (as well as attacked)

by reasonable argument; and they invariably appeal to experience for validation. " He then noted that in the reformation of the Seneca Indian religion the Prophet Handsome Lake proposed an experiment with "sophisticated concepts of sampling and control" as evidence to test or prove his religious propositions. [34]

This kind of approach indicates the closeness of theology to the sciences and the use of theology in improving religion as akin to the use of science to improve technology. As are scientific hypotheses or theories, religious myths and theologies are efforts to reduce cognitive dissonance, and

> religion can be seen as a general rationalizer for all those inescapable contradictions of expectation and experience with which even the best of all possible worlds must confront its most trusting traveler. [35]

Wallace's theory of religion includes an accounting for what it is that generates it, which is very close to that of Boisen. [36] Moreover, we find the brain dynamics akin to those that generate science and technology, although in religion at a much higher level of concern.

> Religious belief and practice always originate in situations of social and cultural stress and are, in fact, an effort on the part of the stress-laden to construct systems of dogma, myth, and ritual which are internally coherent as well as true descriptions of a world system and which thus will serve as guides to efficient action. [37]

Here is Wallace's classic theory of religion, which was presented to the 1961 Star Island Conference of the Institute on Religion in an Age of Science, and which embraces vital information from a wide range of the sciences to show religion's relation to the evolution of living systems of increasing order or organization (in a universe subject to the entropy of the second law of thermodynamics) and its relation to man's primary psychobiological needs.

> In view of the near-universality of religion among men, its antiquity, and the multiple functions which it seems to serve, it would seem that we may speak of "the religious process" as a type of event which occurs among human beings under very widely varying conditions. The essential theme of the religious event is, nevertheless, definable: it is the dialectic of disorganization and organization. On the one hand men universally observe the increase of entropy (disorganization) in familiar systems: metals rust and corrode, woods and

fabrics rot, people sicken and die, personalities disintegrate, social groups splinter and disband. And on the other hand, men universally experience the contrary process of organization: much energy is spent preventing rust, corrosion, decay, rot, sickness, death, and dissolution, and indeed, at least locally, there may be an absolute gain of organization, a real growth or revitalization. This dialectic, the "struggle" (to use an easy metaphor) between entropy and organization, is what religion is all about. The most diverse creeds unite in the attempt to solve the sphinx-riddle of the relationship between life and death, between organization and disorganization; the ideas of the soul, of gods, of world cycles, of Nirvana, of spiritual salvation and rebirth, of progress are all formal solutions to this problem, which is indeed felt intimately by all men.

But religion does not offer just any solution: it characteristically offers a solution which assures the believer that life and organization will win, that death and disorganization will lose, in their struggle to become the characteristic condition of self and cosmos. And religion further attempts to elucidate and describe the organization of self and cosmos. Religion then may be said to be a process of maximizing the quantity of organization in the matrix of perceived human experience. Religion maximizes it, perhaps, beyond what rational use of the data of this experience would justify, but it thereby satisfies a primary drive. We must, I think, postulate an organization "instinct": an "instinct" to increase the organization of cognitive perception. Religion and science, from this point of view, would seem to be direct expressions of this organizational "instinct."[38]

This "organizational instinct" is, of course, another way of saying what Hoagland said about the genetic proclivities selected in brains to provide order. It is, at the sociocultural level in religion and science, the operation of the basic characteristic of life in the universe pointed to by Erwin Schrödinger and many others since, and most beautifully explained by Bronowski: "an inherent potential for large-scale order to act as a sieve or selector on the individual chance events."[39] Bronowski's full paper is a rich resource for all theologians who would understand this fundamental problem of life's relation to the nature of the universe.
    A number of anthropological, psychological, and biological scholars as well as physical systems analysts have in the past two decades shown important evidence for the hypothesis that there is a natural selective process operating in the evolution of human sociocultural patterns, even in individual psychological development, analogous to the well-known mechanisms of

biogenetic selection.[40] This natural selection of human culture operates under nature's requirements for stability or viability of the system, regardless of what human conscious choices may be. For certain very long-range and complex problems, human choices may be considered for all practical purposes to be random mutations. (This may help revive our religious humility before the real gods.)

However, we must note that in cultural evolution, the unit of selection no longer is an individual body; a sociocultural system is the larger unit or phenotype selected. In cultural selection the heritable information is stored not only in the DNA gene pool but also in a "culture pool," in such coded memory patterns as the mores-informing, behavioral and verbal rituals, which are transmitted by a sociocultural system and inscribed in the neurological patterns of brains. The feedback insemination of this information to shape the next generation of new "culturetypes" (analogues of genotypes) does not require a biological generation, but may even be instantaneous in verbal response, or it may be held "in vitro" for millennia as in the discovery of a non-living artifact of a previous culture which may immediately change a present culture. For the past five thousand years or more, written languages have been increasingly important among such non-living artifacts and have made possible significant new stages of cultural evolution.

It must never be forgotten, however, that cultural evolution is only a superficial modification of biogenetically transmitted forms. As George Gaylord Simpson has pointed out, culture in the end is a biological property -- a property of living people -- and, if a culture's evolved patterns do not produce viable organisms or phenotypes, natural selection in the biologic gene pool will soon obliterate that cultural pattern. E.O. Williams' Sociobiology comes to a similar position.[41]

Yet central to understanding the difference between men and other animals is to understand this emergence of cultural codification and transmission of information that shapes man's central nervous system and behavior. The input of cultural information in the brain is an essential overlay and a transformation of the genetic heritage in order to make us human. The emergence of variant cultural patterns in variant groups or units of the human population is what enabled selection by natural processes to create a social animal out of a mammalian population of species-wide genetic variability, thus overcoming the in-species barrier to genetic selection of altruism pointed out above by Williams.

One could say that this overlay of cultural information in symbiosis with genetic information in the hominids of the past million years was an emergent that can be ranked in total evolutionary history in a class with the emergence, some billion years ago, of the symbiosis of the information in ribonucleic acids (genetic DNA) with the information in the then existing phenotypes as that was shaped by the dynamic chemical patterns of amino

acids in a very narrow and specialized habitat of energy-dissipation flows
in the earth's tidal pools. This thousand times older symbiosis provided
for the internalization of the latest and best selection of the remembered
patterns or recipes for how to live that became the basis of biogenetic
natural selection and evolution. The mechanisms for cultural memory and
transmission provide analogous mechanisms for cultural evolution.

After the emergence of either of these symbioses of information
systems, the rapidity and effectiveness of evolution was raised to a new
level. During less than a million years of cultural evolution, new levels of
complexity, with adaptation to wider ranges of habitat, could be evolved at
rates a thousand times as fast as previously. Man thereby could become
and was indeed transformed into a social animal capable of a self-consciousness of himself as more than his own body.

To understand this miracle of a culturally generated social and
spiritual animal, of which Homo sapiens seems to be the only existing species
on earth, we need to understand the role of ritual and belief in shaping man's
overall or primary adaptations to his environment and to his fellow men.
This role of ritual and belief is the supreme art or technology in any sociocultural system because it deals in man's long-term values or man's motivations with regard to his ultimate concerns. This art or technology of
enculturating the human brain with culturally accrued information on top of
the existing genetically accrued information to provide viable concerns and
behaviors for life, or survival of the system in the long-range future, is
what men commonly have called religion. It is a social art or technology
that has to be practiced if the primate Homo is in fact to continue to be
human. It would seem that the evidence is overwhelming that religion is a
part of man's basic and perennial nature, biogenetically and socioculturally.
It seems clear that the perennial necessity for Homo to produce adaptive
behavior for a sociocultural life in the real world is assurance that religious
rituals and beliefs will continue to evolve with man so long into the future as
he himself survives as a sociocultural animal. Homo sapiens is by nature
Homo religiosus, as Eliade notes.[42]

There must be in every viable culture some institution or institutions that carry on now, as in the past, these functions of religion: to
transmit to each individual man the information that will generate in him
the proper attitudes or values toward himself, toward his fellow men, and
toward the larger environing world, in ways that fulfill the needs of the life
of his sociocultural system as well as his present bodily needs. It is a
scientific fact that in men, as in no other animals, basic attitudes of normative value (of how to distinguish right from wrong) and basic beliefs or
convictions that generate a desire to respond in ways that are right or good
are programmed through cultural conditioning of the basal, genetically
patterned mechanisms of the central nervous system.

Feral or wild or "natural" children do not develop the basic attitudes and skills necessary for human sociocultural life. The various cultural traditions such as language and mores must be transmitted from one brain to another in processes such as imitation, conditioning, reinforcement, ritual, learning, stories, myths, symbol systems, dramas, poems, education, books, TV, etc.

As we have indicated, the human brain is not genetically programmed sufficiently to produce human life. Life that is human also requires the input of various channels and levels of cultural reinforcements of certain behavioral patterns that constitute an overlay and refinement essential for converting the rough, genetically given tendencies or values into patterns adaptive to individual man's sociocultural ecological niche. In this way we acquire our adult phenotype of languages, technologies, and general social mores. Thus sacred and moral values and motivations do not come out of the thin air, even though the naive often suppose so; but are dependent on the sociocultural transmission of religious and theological components of culture. This transmission enculturates in the outer fringes of the brain an overlay of circuits that harmonize the genetically programmed values or behavioral tendencies with those necessary for viable symbiosis of a man in his environing sociocultural habitat.

The Ecosystemic Stage of Man's Nature and the Ultimate Source of His Being

At the end I take up the first and most fundamental stage or domain of human nature. It should be clear that the trinity of domains of nature under which I am describing man are indeed distinct realms but of one nature. They originate at different points in the evolutionary sequence and are made up of different levels of structuring the same atoms.

The third or sociocultural stage, which began only a few million years ago, is structured by the biochemical boundary conditions inscribed in men's outer brains, but these in turn are shaped by physical artifacts outside of organisms in the habitat, such as chemical, sonic, and light wave patterns, and a wide variety of other unconsciously and consciously produced dynamic or fixed artifacts that inform or structure the cultural environment and hence the behavior of the populations that inhabit it. These boundary conditions (both inside and outside the head) are memory traces selected to produce socially organized behaviors and structures.

The second or biogenetic dimension, which began a few billion years ago, is structured inside the membrane of each cell of our bodies, which cells in turn shape our basic brain mechanisms. The structure of the genes is a memory store of the environment and ecological niche of man in the form of an internalized representation of what is meaningful for life

in these boundary conditions in history up to the present. This memory then
structures the behavioral patterns of the materials in the current dissipative
flow patterns of the world so as to constitute a living organism. [43]
    These two sets of information sacred for life are what nature has
culled from the significant acts of a very long history of several billion years.
The patterns in the genetic and cultural pools of information are literally
reflections or images of that natural history or nature. What is important
for us to note is that the sociocultural stage piggybacks upon the biogenetic,
in fact emerges out of it as a special elaboration of it, in a continuing cosmic
program of an emerging hierarchy of levels of organized complexity of metastable patterns of dissipative energy flow where each level exhibits a higher
degree of order than its predecessor.
    The first or basic domain or stage of human nature we may take
to be the solar system, at least as a first approximation. Our particular
ecological niche is within this representative particularity of an infinity of
stars and other unknowns in a universe or reality system about which at
least some theologians and scientists properly admit they can know only a
finite portion. Ultimately, of course, my god-symbol must be cosmic. I
have speculated about life in a transmundane and trans-solar context elsewhere. [44] But for our present purposes we have a large enough frame of
reference in our scientific pictures of the solar system as the ecosystem
whose natural evolution or course in time has been the creator and sustainer
of our being at every step during the past five billion years until the present
moment and probably will continue to be for about as far in the future as we
now need to take thought.
    It should be at once noted that the solar system includes the earth
and all the biological and human life upon it, not only as of now but also in
a four-dimensional space-time "solid" where cross sections along the time
axis show us the stages of evolution of these three hierarchical levels of
increasingly complex order that we call human nature. I am not merely
saying that the solar system is a spatial boundary within which exist increasingly complex living systems, as we find that fleas, dogs, and children live
within a house. I am saying that it is as if the house itself generated or
created the fleas, dogs, children, and parents--and also built the house.
It is that kind of solar system in which we live, according to recent science.
This is the nature (the ultimate dynamism of substance and form) in the
context of which man lives and moves and has his being. This is the nature
that created, guides, nourishes, and selects or judges all things, all creatures,
all men, all societies of men, and all things men do even in the innermost
secret places of their hearts or brains.
    I return now to my earlier promise to discuss further some of the
significant attributes of this all-encompassing habitat or ecosystem, the
totality of the nature within which we dwell--the cosmos of the new physics
which is a vast extension and improvement of the hidden or underlying

realities formerly presented as metaphysics. In the same stroke I am
returning to my still earlier promise to discuss further the unique character of religion's kinship to the sciences as a source of truth, even a salvatory
truth, a logos or light, to guide man in the way to life and away from death.
     The nature of the solar system is not indifferent to the nature of
man, as has been erroneously concluded by many scientists and clergymen
during the past couple of centuries. The new picture suggests that this large
bit of cosmic nature by its very nature was determined or destined to create
life, and man, and to guide this negentropic trend to ever higher levels of
complex, dynamic flow patterns that are in the technical language of today's
cybernetics most properly called information. [45] Moreover, this information
has been correctly referred to as an image of its creator. The DNA of
living organisms is a reflection or image of its evolving ecological niche
and ultimately of its habitat or the general system we call nature when we
refer scientifically to the totality of the solar system.
     It should be clear that this primary stage or domain of the trinitar-
ian hierarchy of domains necessary for understanding human nature is not
only inclusive of the other two domains, if one examines the system far
enough in time and space, but that it is indeed kindred to the first person
of the Christian trinity or to the sovereign creator or ultimate reality that
determines human destiny in the other religions. If one accepts the new
physics in place of the old metaphysics, one has no question about the reality
of the sovereign Lord of History hailed in the Old and New Testaments of the
Judeo-Christian tradition. The more a man meditates upon the evidences
of the larger reality system that created and sustains him the more convinced
that man becomes of his creatureliness, his finitude, and his utter dependence
upon the nature that determines, or Lord of, History.
     Further, one becomes clear that life is more than the body, more
than this present stage of evolving life, and much more than meets the eye.
One becomes impressed with one's continuity as an immortal element of
God's kingdom, a kingdom which is no longer a wishful fancy of a well-
meaning idealist but is the more realistic or true vision of what is really
going on within us, of something closer to the ultimate concern of our larger
soul. The kingdom of heaven is right here, and nothing happens that is not
of the making or "will" of the Lord of History. The primary problem of man
is to be given the eyes to see and the ears to hear the new revelations about
his role or niche in the total nature as an immortally developing structure
of complexity ever more fully reflecting the glory of his creator.
     This same revelation also shows man is not a separate individual,
alienated and estranged from the larger sociocultural system or from the
still larger solar ecosystem. Man is the creature, son, and heir of the
supreme Lord of History and a brother not merely to his close genetic
brothers but a creature whose life and meaning is embedded in the interlaced structures of the sociocultural system and ecosystem in which he lives

and moves. But he is such a son and heir only to the extent that he actually
incarnates the will of the father, the supreme creator, and serves the needs
not merely of his temporal body but his immortal soul which is his true
nature and ties him in love and service to his brothers and father who is
sovereign Lord of all events and processes of the cosmos of the new physics.

A correction on the mistaken dualistic interpretation of the "other"
world of religious tradition is to understand it as the real or true character
of the world that we live in, but which is "other" than or different from
what our primitive common senses can reveal to us without supplementary
cultural revelation. "Heaven" is the good news of the reality of a world
that makes much more sense for us than the commonsense view, afforded
by only genetically programmed mechanisms and illumined only by primitive
belief structures. These limit the unillumined and unenculturated individual
to life at a more primitive level. It is our God-given task to spread the
good news as it is now newly revealed as the still-valid picture of ourselves
as the son and servant of the sovereign creative power of all nature, our
souls immortally interlaced with our brothers' and all evolving patterns of
God's kingdom. From this reality we can never be separated or alienated.
Estrangement is the product of a phase of our inadequate understanding of
our original sin or our perennial evolutionary incompleteness before we
learn that by the grace of God, in which we participate, our incompleteness is
continually in process of being overcome.

Salvation is to perceive the glory of God's kingdom and to glory in
participating in its continual building. God's kingdom is the succession of
actual or real states of the world, among which are the actually selected
or ordained ecological niches of life. Man's nature could be likened to an
infinite, inverse river bed in time, a niche in nature through which course
God's ever given dissipative streams of energy destined by God's nature
ever to form more complex structures higher above the previous levels of
thermodynamic equilibrium. At least that seems to be the trend one sees
in trying to read the lesson of the past few billion years of history and pro-
jecting it to guide our future for as far as we can see. Beyond that, in
scientific as well as traditional theologies, sure knowledge fades and all
creatures can do no better than trust the nature that is the Lord of History.

NOTES AND REFERENCES

[1]Only in the past century has the term "science" come to imply
"physical and experimental science, to the exclusion of theological and metaphysical." The year 1867 is the date given in the Oxford English Dictionary
for this. But such usage by specialists occurred about a century earlier.
The American Philosophical Society established by Benjamin Franklin about

1763 was given that name because at that time natural philosophy was more readily thought of as what we now mean by science. But in 1779 the naming of the American Academy of Arts and Sciences represented the transfer that was to take the Latin rather than the Greek term to represent the new tradition for seeking true knowledge of the nature of things. In this connection it is interesting that "arts" in the name of the American Academy implied the practical arts or technology, not fine arts which the term has now come to signify. It is also interesting that at about the same time (1850) the British named their scientific journal Nature while the Americans called theirs Science. "Science," of course, was the Latin for knowledge of any kind, and up until one or two centuries ago was used that way in the English and other European languages.

[2]A recent summary of the nature of science and of technology, the relation between them, and how it was not until the nineteenth century that the sciences had reached the point where they became significant in improving technology and generating new technologies that "never would have been invented had it not been for scientific investigation, " is provided by R.B. Lindsay, a creative physicist and technologist as well as historian and philosopher of the field, in "The Scientific and Technological Revolutions and Their Implications for Society, " Zygon 7 (Dec. 1972):212-243. More details and fuller bibliography are given in Lindsay's The Role of Science in Civilization (New York, Harper & Row, 1963).

[3]Technology, defined as "human activity directed toward the satisfaction of real or imagined human needs by appropriate manipulation and more effective use of the environment" (Lindsay, Zygon 7 : 222), not only evolved for millennia prior to science, but it evolved among our ancestors as ways of meeting their needs in several stages of evolution going back to the first genetic programming of a cell on how to get nourishment and to defend itself. This kind of learning how to meet the needs of living systems and remembering how to build and operate the machinery is involved in the unconscious learning of the gene pool on how to do such things as utilize solar energy (plants), farm (e.g., the social insects), fly and navigate (bees, birds, bats). Further unconscious learning in the central nervous systems of animals began to participate in such technological advancement more than a hundred million years ago. Significant cultural transmission of unconscious learning with the addition of some conscious learning was taking place in our ancestors a few million years ago (See E.O. Wilson, Sociobiology (Cambridge, Harvard University Press, 1975). There were several stages of this kind of acquisition of technology up to and including the very special addition of the application of the modern sciences. Some of this history of prescientific evolution of learning of the technologies for living is briefly summarized in my "Five Steps in the Evolution of Man's Knowledge of Good and Evil, " Zygon 2 (Mar. 1967) : 77-95; "The Control of Behavior: Human and Environmental, " Journal of Environmental Health, 35 (Nov.-Dec. 1972) : 247-258;

and "The Civilization of the Future," Philosophy Forum 13:149-77 (June 1973). In much contemporary interdisciplinary research developing new frontiers of understanding, major contributors of hypotheses to theories (such as of cultural evolution and its non-genetic selective and retentive mechanisms) are often from other disciplines. As well as cultural anthropologists one will find in the citations in the above-noted papers a chemist, biologist, or psychologist to be a significant contributor to this exciting field of research that was almost uncultivated a couple of decades ago.

[4]The biblical account of the test for the true god on Mt. Carmel is well known (I Kings, 18) as one case of this. See the generalization on page 17 for anthropologist Wallace's generalization on this as a characteristic of religions.

[5]The change in behaving (vocational and living styles) is so obvious as to need no comment beyond mention of the contrast between 1875 and our present use of electricity, telephone, automobile, airplane, radio and television and the transformation and decimation of the rural population by farming by machinery. The radicality of the change in believing is not so easy to verify, although one could safely presume that the statistical norms of belief about the sociocultural system have changed to correspond with the changed character of the sociocultural system--including the nature, use, safety, propriety, etc. of electrical apparatus, the telephone, etc. It has been quite clear to me from the sample of the population two or three generations older than I, with whom I talked at great length on these matters in the 1910's and 1920's, that they lived with a radically different view of the nature of man and the world from that which I had by 1930 as the result of Harvard College courses in physics, biology, anthropology, psychology, history, and philosophy. Of course, still in the 1970's one runs across those prescientific views of man and world. As they were congealed in the general philosophical or religious value stereotypes concerning man's duties and hopes in the scheme of things, they still dominate contemporary culture. As the incongruities between the new scientific views and the earlier philosophical and religious metaphysics seep into the thinking of people, we find in the twentieth century the rampant growth of the phenomena of alienation, estrangement, anomie, and existential absurdity. These incongruities of belief and hence of meaning are the heart of our problem to be resolved if man and civilization are to become healthy and whole again. I have sought to document this incongruity of belief systems in different ways in most of my papers and books of the past decade.

[6]We could not use or enjoy many of the products of modern chemistry and electrical engineering, or radio and TV, or air flights approaching the speed of sound, if there were not some people in our culture who understand and apply these particular technical terms--or the concepts and realities for which they stand--in these technologies.

[7]Mead, Sidney E., <u>The Lively Experiment: The Shaping of Christianity in America</u> (New York: Harper & Row, 1963).

[8]Ahlstrom, Sidney E., <u>A Religious History of the American People</u> (New Haven: Yale University Press, 1972). Winter, Gibson, "Symbol and Society," Chapter IX of this volume.

[9]I am not certain of the extent to which this is recognized or documented, but I am a personal observer of it in a number of instances. The delicacy of the problem of religion and moral values in the context of a government based on the separation of church and state stands in the way of full publicity concerning such matters. But I can testify to the already published results of two conferences in which I have been an invited member to help develop for government bureaucracies an understanding of what it is that produces morals and morale in the public. The first was held by the National Institutes of Mental Health on May 15-17, 1968, on Studies of the Acquisition and Development of Values, and published reports can probably still be obtained from the NIMH. The second was called by another branch, The Administrator of Health Services and Mental Health Administration of the National Institutes of Health in 1972 and published in the <u>Journal of Environmental Health</u>, 35(3) (Nov.-Dec., 1972) : 220-304.

[10]Many historians and social scientists have recognized the religious and moral nature of Marxism and various nationalisms, including Gibson Winter in his chapter in this volume. From the French Revolution to the Maoist, nation after nation has bypassed its no longer effective traditional religion and sought to espouse a new, modern, scientific "Enlightenment" faith because new leaders and their followers felt that the traditional religions were standing in the way of proper adaptation to the new worldview and conditions of life with the modern sciences and technologies. Why this has not happened in the English-speaking world and how the separation of church and state or something else there may have allowed at least a vestigial common public faith or civil religion to evolve and survive with a modest power until this date in some areas is something to be explained. I would hypothesize that a major factor has been the freedom of religion and its necessity to compete for public acceptance in an "open market" of ideas. I also would hypothesize on why this freedom alone has not been sufficient, and why even in the English-speaking world the vestiges of civil religion in its Judeo-Christian form are dissolving and how this may be revitalized even more powerfully than in the earlier Great Awakenings. This paper is a partial statement of that hypothesis.

[11]Robert L. Heilbroner, <u>An Inquiry into the Human Prospect</u> (New York: W.W. Norton & Co., 1974). For an extensive analysis of this see the <u>Zygon</u> issue for September 1975, which is given over to papers of the Symposium on the Human Prospect of the Institute on Religion in an Age of Science.

[12]J. Ronald Engel, "The 'New Primitivism'," page 56 of this volume.

[13]J. Bronowski, "New Concepts in the Evolution of Complexity: Stratified Stability and Unbounded Plans," Zygon 5 (Mar. 1970) : 18-35. Just to indicate that this is not the animadversions of one esoteric poet, but a consensus in a broad community of scientists backed by widespread empirical evidence, I would cite a few other books or papers which present essentially the same picture. The explanation of the transition from chemical to biological evolution was pioneered by A. I. Oparin in his Origin of Life (New York: Macmillan, 1938); supplemented by E. Schrödinger's What Is Life? (Cambridge, England: Cambridge University Press, 1944); Norbert Wiener's Cybernetics (1948) and The Human Use of Human Beings (Boston: Houghton Mifflin, 1950); and Francis Crick's Of Molecules and Men (Seattle: University of Washington Press, 1966), A. Katchalsky's "Thermodynamics of Flow and Biological Organization," Zygon 6 (June 1972) : 99-125, and many others. The passage from biological to sociocultural human evolution has been treated by Konrad Lorenz in On Aggression (New York: Harcourt Brace, 1966); Hudson Hoagland and Ralph W. Burhoe in Evolution and Man's Progress (New York: Columbia University Press, 1961); Julian Huxley in Religion Without Revelation (New York: Harper, 1957); J. Z. Young in An Introduction to the Study of Man (Oxford: Oxford University Press, 1971); Donald T. Campbell in his presidential address to the American Psychological Association, "On the Conflicts between Biological and Social Evolution and between Psychology and Moral Tradition," American Psychologist, Dec. 1975; Herbert A. Simon in The Sciences of the Artificial (Cambridge, Mass.: M. I. T. Press, 1969); George E. Pugh, The Origin of Human Values (New York: Basic Books, 1976); Harold J. Hamilton, "The Evolution of Societal Systems," pamphlet of The Center for Futures Research, Graduate School of Business Administration, University of Southern California, Los Angeles, September 1974.

[14]See particularly R. W. Sperry, "Science and the Problem of Values," Zygon 9 (March 1974) : 7-21: "The human brain is today the dominant control force on our planet: what moves and directs the brain of man will, in turn, largely determine the future from here on."

[15]This does not imply that the sciences can explain all things or even very much of the phenomena of human experience. The Gödel theorem in mathematics is a proof of why this cannot be done by any finite system of learning and knowing. The implication is only that in evolving systems of life the process of information accrual has been shown to be a real and accelerating process.

[16]J. Ronald Engel, "The 'New Primitivism' "in this volume, page 34.

[17]Mircea Eliade, The Sacred and the Profane (New York: Harcourt Brace, 1959): "The sacred is equivalent to a power, and, in the last analysis, to reality" (p. 12). "It does not devolve upon us to show by what historical

processes and as the result of what changes in spiritual attitudes and behavior modern man has desacralized his world and assumed a profane
existence" (p. 13). I am suggesting in this paper that, contrary to what
even Eliade suspects, that the modern sciences provide the best route back
to the true reality or power in the world that is sacred to man.

[18]Hudson Hoagland, "The Brain and Crises in Human Values, "
Zygon 1 (1966) : 140-57. The quotation is from p. 155.

[19]Gods, as names of the hidden, unknown, or ultimate causes of
the phenomena of human experience are common hypotheses. Such hypotheses are given new illumination by recent views of the way the brain or a
computer works in making decisions by analyzing or deducing conclusions
from premises. Eugene G. d'Aquili and Charles Laughlin, Jr., have
provided an interesting picture of the brain's "initial causal termini of
strips of observed reality" in their "Biopsychological Determinants of
Religious Ritual Behavior, " Zygon 10 (Mar. 1975) : 32-58, esp. p. 55.

[20]In addition to the brief indications above in this paper of how
modern physical sciences have become the contemporary account of the
realities that are beyond or above ordinary commonsense experience and
hence "meta-physical, " I have in a number of other papers set forth this
general clarification of what has become a confusing element of our language
and a barrier between theology and the new sciences, particularly in "Natural
Selection and God" Zygon 7 (Mar. 1972) : 30-63 and on pp. 423-24 of "The
Concepts of God and Soul in a Scientific View of Human Purpose" Zygon 8
(Sept. -Dec. 1973) : 412-442, and "The Human Prospect and the 'Lord of
History' " Zygon (Sept. 1975) : 299-375.

[21]The intertwined character of facts (what is actually perceived or
observed) and hypotheses (or theoretical and conceptual systems) is widely
recognized in the literature of and about the sciences (see Thomas S. Kuhn,
The Structure of Scientific Revolutions (Chicago: University of Chicago
Press, 1962). A clear source for nonscientists would be Henry Margenau,
The Nature of Physical Reality (New York: McGraw-Hill, 1950), or Richard
von Mises, Positivism: A Study in Human Understanding (Cambridge, Mass.:
Harvard University Press, 1951), or Karl R. Popper, The Logic of Scientific
Discovery (New York: Basic Books, 1959). Popper says,

> We may distinguish within a theoretical system, statements belong-
> ing to various levels of universality. The statements on the highest
> level of universality are the axioms; statements on the lower levels
> can be deduced from them. Higher level empirical statements have
> always the character of hypotheses relative to the lower level state-
> ments deducible from them (p. 75).

[22]For a discussion of man's brain levels and their functions, see
Paul D. MacLean, "The Brain in Relation to Empathy and Medical Education, "

Journal of Nervous and Mental Disease 144 (1967) : 374-82 . A later paper
on the importance of the various brain levels in man for understanding
motivation and the grounds and reasons for religious ritual and enculturation
is "The Brain's Generation Gap: Some Human Implications, " Zygon 8
(1973) : 113-128.

[23]George C. Williams, Adaptation and Natural Selection (Princeton,
N. J.: Princeton University Press, 1966), esp. pp. 93-95. "Allele" in this
quotation refers to a particular form or pattern of a gene, distinct from
other patterns that might exist in the same place. It is as if in a loose-leaf
cookbook you could insert one of several possible recipes for apple pie,
except that we are not here dealing with a menu but with DNA-encoded
recipes for characters or traits of structure or behavior of a living creature.

[24]Konrad Lorenz, On Aggression (see n. 13). The original title
in German is a better characterization: Das sogennante Böse, which might
be translated So-Called Evil.

[25]For the genetic problems of selecting social norms, see
Williams, n. 23 above, esp. Chapter 7. A classical paper of some twenty
years ago, but still essentially valid, is Alfred E. Emerson's "Dynamic
Homeostasis, a Unifying Principle in Organic, Social and Ethical Evolution, "
which was reprinted with some changes in Zygon 3 (1968) : 129-168. A new
and comprehensive synthesis is Edward O. Wilson, Sociobiology (Cambridge,
Mass.: Harvard University Press, 1975).

[26]Lorenz, n. 24 above, p. 256; italics added.

[27]Ibid., p. 251.

[28]Anthony F. C. Wallace, "Rituals: Sacred and Profane, " Zygon 1
(1966) : 60-81, p. 61. Most of this paper was later published in Wallace's
Religion, an Anthropological View (New York: Random House, 1966).

[29]Margaret Mead, Review of Religion, an Anthropological View,
Zygon 2 (1967) : 418-31.

[30]For Boisen, see n. 36. Younger men who are carrying forward
some of Wallace's insights into religion include Eugene d'Aquili (see his and
Charles Laughlin's "The Biopsychological Determinants of Religious Ritual
Behavior, " Zygon 10 (1975) : 32-58) and Solomon D. Katz (see his "Evolutionary Perspectives on Purpose and Man, " Zygon 8 (1973) : 325-40).

[31]Wallace, Religion, an Anthropological View (see n. 28 above),
pp. 243-44.

[32]Ibid., p. 239.

[33]For a quick evolutionary picture of the evolution of knowledge or
information from genetic to scientific levels, see my "Five Steps in the
Evolution of Man's Knowledge of Good and Evil, " Zygon 2 (1967) : 77-95.

[34]Anthony F. C. Wallace, Religious Revitalization: A Function of
Religion in Human History and Evolution (Brookline, Mass.: Institute on
Religion in an Age of Science, 1961, 24 pp.), p. 4. I have already pointed
to a Judeo-Christian "scientific" approach to religion in n. 4, above.

[35]Wallace, Religion, an Anthropological View (see n. 28 above), p. 29.

[36]Anton T. Boisen, Religion in Crisis and Custom (New York: Harper & Bros., 1955) presents a theory and confirming data to show the generation of religious novelty and reform during periods of group stress.

[37]Wallace, Religion (n. 28 above), p. 30.

[38]Wallace, Religious Revitalization (n. 34 above), pp. 9-10, or Religion (n. 28 above), pp. 38-39. For a physicist's statement about the role of entropy as a guide for human values, see R.B. Lindsay, "The Scientific and Technological Revolutions and Their Implications for Society," Zygon 7 (1972) : 212-43, esp. pp. 235-37.

[39]For probably the primary document on living systems and their relation to entropy, see Erwin Schrödinger, What Is Life? (see n. 13 above). J. Bronowski's "New Concepts in the Evolution of Complexity" provides a more recent and clearer solution. It was first published in Zygon 5 (1970) : 18-35, and the quote is on p. 29.

[40]A committee of the American Academy of Arts and Sciences in 1960 brought together a few dozen pioneers to assess the relation of theories involved in biological, social, and personal development, some of the papers from which were published in the Summer 1961 issue of Daedalus and in 1962 by the Columbia University Press as Evolution and Man's Progress, ed. by Hudson Hoagland and Ralph Wendell Burhoe. Zygon contains numerous papers by many authors on this topic. Theodosius Dobzhansky in Mankind Evolving (New Haven, Conn.: Yale University Press, 1962) provides a good summary in his first chapter on cultural and biological evolution; and see also the citations in n. 13 above. My "Civilization of the Future" (Philosophy Forum 13 (1973) : 149-177) provides a useful review of some of the story.

[41]The Simpson communication is private, on tape; although he may well have said the same sort of thing in some publications. The most comprehensive text on Sociobiology is E.O. Wilson's book of that title (Cambridge, Mass.: Harvard University Press, 1975).

[42]Eliade (n. 17 above), p. 17.

[43]Aharon Katchalsky-Katzir in his "Thermodynamics of Flow and Biological Organization" Zygon 6 (June 1972) : 99-125 provides a good account of this not-so-well-known link between chemical thermodynamics and living systems (including religions).

[44]For instance, see my "A Cosmic Perspective on Man's Future," pp. 182-192 in Images of the Future, the Twenty-First Century and Beyond, edited by Robert Bundy, (Buffalo, N.Y.: Prometheus Books, 1976).

[45]Early accounts of life as moving in the opposite direction to the trend produced by entropy, and hence being information or negentropy, were those referred to above by Schrödinger and Wiener in n.13. George Wald in his "Origins of Life" (Proceedings of the National Academy of Sciences 52(2): 595-611, August 1964) is one of a number of scientists who have

pointed out that, given the nature of hydrogen and what is more or less
bound to happen in the course of time and circumstances, the system is
bound to produce other elements, various molecules, and various living
species. Such men presume by their same vision of the nature of molecules that similar patterns of life have been produced on other planets
based on the same kinds of forces and circumstances. He points out that
the nub of his argument "is to bring life within the order of nature, to see
its development as an orderly process, everywhere affording full play to
chance, but not in any important degree accidental" (p. 609).

CHAPTER II

THE "NEW PRIMITIVISM"

by
J. Ronald Engel

I

The Problem of Nature and Society

Recent consideration of the global ecological crisis and the capacity of industrialized societies, such as the United States, to address it, has renewed discussion of a theme as old as the beginnings of Western civilization: the normative relationship of nature and society. So far discussion has proceeded on the premise that reevaluation of the relationship between nature and society is long overdue in the West because of an inherited predisposition to separate one from the other. The modern disjunction between the natural sciences and the social sciences, and the lack of attention by normative ethical and religious traditions to human-nature relations are considered symptomatic of a fundamental societal disregard for the organic and inorganic matrix of human life. The "ecological crisis," it is generally agreed, is a mandate for reexamination of Western cultural self-understanding in order to newly appreciate the interdependencies of humanity and nature.

There is reason to think that such a statement of the problem, while truthful, is nonetheless inadequate because incomplete. The relation of nature and society is a complex subject and generalization is very difficult. But there is historical warrant to assert that alongside of traditions that have separated nature and society in the West there are others, often equally as strong, that have sought the very opposite: to found society in conformity with nature. I am not now referring to the whole of the natural law tradition, but to that specific, yet immensely influential, variant within the tradition known as "primitivism." One reason the problem of nature and society as stated above is inadequate is that Western thought has at least a double perspective on the relationship.

This extension of the problem is important to make because "primitivism" -- as I hope to demonstrate -- is currently appearing in the context of the ecological crisis as the "answer" to the problem of society and nature. This should not surprise us. "Primitivism" is often associated

33

with a literature of cultural protest. Furthermore, due to the continuity and
finite number of basic ideas in human history, there is a tendency in periods
of reexamination such as the present for inherited notions submerged in
recent understanding to find new viability. Yet because any new formulation
seems inherently novel, the continuity of old and new is often obscured.
The widespread recurrence of primitivism at the present time is an example
of this. Just as the "ecological crisis" is not altogether new, but only the
latest and most virulent chapter in the story of humanity's swift and dramatic
modification of its earthly habitat, so contemporary responses to the relation
of society and the environment are not thoroughly "new" either. Unless we
appreciate the continuities between the "old" and "new" primitivism, and
recognize that it is a deep-seated Western attitude and mode of cultural
criticism, any definition of the problem of nature and society in the context
of the ecological crisis must be misleading.

One value, then, of an attempt to identify and analyze the "new
primitivism" lies in developing an awareness of certain unconscious presuppositions permeating current debate. This will help clarify the discussion
of the relation between nature and society.

But the value of describing the "new primitivism" rests, fundamentally, on the assumption that there is danger in either a radical separation or naive equation of nature and society, and that the heart of the
problem lies in humanity's connection with nature.[1] The constructive
position from which I approach the problem is neither that of man in nature
("primitivism") or man over nature ("progressivism") but of man and nature
together creating a new level of reality -- unforeseen and unrepeatable.
There is critical value, from the standpoint of this third constructive perspective, in understanding the positive reasons for the reappearance of
primitivism at this time, as well as exposing the unsatisfactory character
of the "new primitivism" as a basis for human social action. The principal
task of this essay therefore is to identify the contribution as well as the
concealment of the "new primitivism." In the final section, I will make a
suggestion as to how we might move beyond the impasse of a dialectic
limited to primitivism and its historical antithesis -- progressivism.

We should be especially alert in America to primitivist modes of
thought reappearing in new guises in response to new occasions. A substantial body of scholarship over recent decades has focused upon the nature
and function of the myth of "America" as a recovery of earthly paradise, or
its rationalistic equivalent, a nation founded upon "natural" principles.
Some aspects of this myth, but by no means all, may be considered
"primitivist" in expression. For example, Howard Mumford Jones, in
O Strange New World, a study of the European sources of the double image
of American nature as both Arcadia and threatening wilderness, cites the
following passage written by one Andrew Burnaby in the mid-eighteenth
century.[2] I quote it here as one expression, among thousands, of the

primitivist image of mankind living in simplistic harmony with nature in the New World.

> I could not but reflect with pleasure on the situation of these people; and think if there is such a thing as happiness in this life, that they enjoy it. Far from the bustle of the world, they live in the most delightful climate, and richest soil imaginable; they are every-where surrounded with beautiful prospects and sylvan scenes; lofty mountains, transparent streams, falls of water, rich valleys, and majestic woods; the whole interspersed with an infinite variety of flowering shrubs, constitutes the landscape surrounding them: they are subject to few diseases; are generally robust; and live in perfect liberty: they are ignorant of want, and acquainted with but few vices. Their inexperience of the elegancies of life precludes any regret that they possess not the means of enjoying them: but they possess what many princes would give half their dominions for, health, content, and tranquillity of mind.

While I cannot hope to do justice to the scope and penetration of this literature here, I will draw upon it in what follows for two purposes: to help establish the special character of modern, especially American, primitivism; and in order, at the conclusion, better to define the problem of nature and society in America.[3]

That Robert Heilbroner is correct in speaking of the pervasive "mood of our times" as one of fear of progressive deterioration of modern society due to alienation of humanity and nature is indicated by the fact that what I am here calling the "new primitivism" has appeared widely among both popular and academic publics in the United States and elsewhere.[4] What is common to all manifestations is the sense of a decline of Western civilization because it has over-reached certain "natural" limits, and the hope of reestablishing the structure of society on the basis of some original "state of nature."

Of the many examples that could be drawn from popular culture, perhaps the most striking is the message common to the recent spate of "disaster" films. According to critic Carole Stanley Gill, "The Poseidon Adventure," "Juggernaut," "Towering Inferno," "Earthquake," all portray society as a whole caught in the throes of massive upheavals due to the illusory triumphs of "artificial" civilization over nature.[5] "It is unnatural man facing natural power and finding that his synthetic life is not only dangerous, but that nothing he has created can surpass or oppose natural power." In most of these films, a strong natural leader appears, and the few survivors who follow him are able to assure the perpetuation of the species by facing life and nature directly and learning once again to work together for the common good.

Within humanistic academic circles, probably the most important example of contemporary enthusiasm for the "new primitivism" is provided by the swiftness with which the thesis of Lynn White's essay, "The Historical Roots of Our Ecological Crisis," first published in 1967, was adopted by architects, literary critics, ecologists, historians, and theologians. The significance of this immense popularity is apparent when it is recognized that it was not the thesis, but its evaluation, which was new:

> White's earlier essays, then, contain most of what is in "Historical Roots" . . . . The important difference is that in his earlier work White almost uniformly put the Christian contribution to science and technology in a positive light as democratizing and humanizing. The uniqueness of "Historical Roots," and the ironic source of its fame, is that here White turns pessimistic and makes a sour face at what up till now has afforded him much pleasure.[6]

Insofar as White's remedy for the ecological crisis is a return to the values, if not the technology, of the pre-modern era, implying the abandonment of two thousand years of "Christian" reflection on the relation of society and nature, he is an exemplar of the "new primitivism" which is the mood of so much current reflection.[7]

However, the social critics who are doing most to mold contemporary opinion on the ecological crisis, and the kind of cultural transformation required to meet it, are not historians such as White, but natural and social scientists who speak out of an alleged foundation of hard factual data. It is their implicit perspective which it is most important to analyze if the reappearance of "primitivist" attitudes at the present time is to be effectively identified. To this end the following influential documents are chosen for analysis here: the first two Reports to the Club of Rome -- Limits to Growth, and Mankind at the Turning Point; An Inquiry into the Human Prospect, by Robert Heilbroner; and The Future of Technological Civilization, by Victor Ferkiss.[8] Limits to Growth, the First Report to the Club of Rome, was written by a team of experts in the natural and social sciences gathered under the direction of systems analyst Dennis Meadows at MIT. It purports to carry forward to a higher level of sophistication earlier systems dynamics modelling of Jay Forrester as reported in his book, World Dynamics.[9] Mankind at the Turning Point, the Second Report to the Club of Rome; was written by systems analysts Mihajlo Mesarovic and Eduard Pestel with collaboration from experts in a wide variety of sciences. It seeks to correct the shortcomings of the Meadows world model by the use of a multi-level, regionalized World System Computer Model which allows qualitative and logical relationships in addition to numerical ones. Robert Heilbroner is an economist at the New School for Social Research and Victor Ferkiss is a political scientist at Georgetown

University. It is important to acknowledge that almost all of the scientists involved in these statements are Western, and most are American.

While the specific scientific disciplines, purposes, and methods of these works differ, it will be my argument that they agree on a fundamental "primitivist" orientation to nature-society relationships. In varying degrees, each work alleges to base its claims on an appeal to empirical data and trends involving the interaction of economic forms, social systems, natural resources, and human values. The reflections that follow in no way take issue with the estimate these books share regarding the critical global situation that now pertains as a result of the interaction of these factors. Nor do they seek to take exception to the empirical data or special scientific methodologies upon which their conclusions purport to be based. Such a task is beyond the competence of the author and at least in certain respects has already been undertaken by competent critics.[10] The concern here is with a cluster of Western and American cultural symbols and values to which these books bear eloquent contemporary witness. In spite of their attempt to set society and nature on a new, trans-historical footing, these works in fact constitute strong evidence for the resiliency and continuity of historical cultural patterns. They are evidence that old ideas and reactions can have an unanticipated relevance and empirical warrant in new situations. But it is important to realize that they are old ideas, and because they are such they may both obscure as well as reveal directions for the future.

II

The Old Primitivism

Nor think in Nature's state they blindly trod;
The state of Nature was the reign of God:
Self-love and Social at her birth began,
Union the bond of all things, and of Man.
Pride then was not; nor Arts, that Pride to aid;
Man walk'd with beast, joint tenant of the shade;
The same his table, and the same his bed;
No murder cloth'd him, and no murder fed.

-- Alexander Pope, An Essay on Man

The attempt to ground society directly in nature appears to be a recurring phenomenon in the history of Western ideas and to be correlated in some measure with fundamental crises of confidence in the viability of inherited modes of civilized life. Robert Nisbet's study on the influence of the metaphor of "growth" on theories of social development and change in

the West documents the use of organic analogies such as "degeneration,"
and "birth" at key turning points in cultural self-understanding.[11] A.O.
Lovejoy, in his classic Primitivism and Related Ideas in Antiquity, the
major source for the categories of the analysis that follows, describes
the transformation in the relations between physis (nature) and nomos (law)
that occurred in Greece in the fifth century B.C. coincident with the loss
of faith in traditional cultural norms.[12] Whereas nomos took on the connotation of "subjective," "erroneous," "various," physis became identified
with "objectivity," "health," "universal," and "the cosmic system as a
whole." In such fashion the attempt was made to refound society on that
which was "according to nature." Similar dynamics were at work in the
Stoic-Christian synthesis of the third century A.D.,[13] and in the Enlightenment of the seventeenth and eighteenth centuries.[14] While attempts to found
society upon some prior normative understanding of nature are by no means
confined to periods of experienced social stress, and indeed constitute, in
the words of Lovejoy, "one of the strangest, most potent, and most persistent factors in Western thought," nonetheless it cannot be gainsaid that they
are likely to occur at such times.

    The phase of this larger tendency with which I am concerned was
clearly identified and documented by A.O. Lovejoy, George Boas, Gilbert
Chinard, and others associated with the History of Ideas Club at Johns
Hopkins University.[15] In a series of related works these scholars sought
to show how "primitivism" is a complex of ideas with a long genealogy in
Western thought stemming from the twin sources of classical antiquity and
Christianity. Except for the work of James Baird on Melville, and the
recent study of the Cult of Childhood by Boas, however, this particular
school of scholarship did not pursue the subject into the nineteenth and
twentieth centuries. In fact, Boas has speculated in a recent summary
article on "primitivism" prepared for the Dictionary of the History of Ideas
that while evidence for the attitude may be found in such diverse places as
modern painting (Klee, Miro, Picasso), in Freud and Jung, in Fascism, in
extreme forms of progressive education, and in the adoption of certain
animalistic types of explanation for the behavior of civilized nations, as a
major motivating structure of thought primitivism has been superseded by
progressivism in the twentieth century:

> Primitivism now seems to exist mainly in the arts, perhaps be-
> cause it is no longer reasonable to deny the benefits of scientific
> discovery and technological inventions. It appears as if modern
> man were committed to civilization with all its weakness and lack
> of picturesqueness.[16]

In this judgment he is at odds with Lovejoy who in his introduction to
Primitivism and Related Ideas in Antiquity in 1935 expressed the hope that

a retrieval of the classical background could be a resource for the clarification of the "manifold expressions of primitivism . . . in modern literature, early modern historiography, and modern social philosophy and ethics":

> Since the beginning of the present century, Western man has become increasingly sceptical concerning the nineteenth-century "myth of progress," increasingly troubled with misgivings about the value of the outcome of civilization thus far, about the future to which it tends, and about himself as the author of it all; and similar doubts and apprehensions found expression two millennia and more ago . . . . This volume, then, has been planned chiefly to be of convenient use to those whose primary interest is in the history of ideas in modern times.[17]

Unfortunately, Lovejoy did not live to see these implications of his project realized.

Building on the work of Lovejoy and his associates, I would propose the following general definition of "primitivism:" Primitivism is the view that a way of life based on humanity's commonality with the rest of nature is superior to any distinct social creation that diverges from or adds to it, and that men can find harmony with one another and with their own "natures," by following this way of life, which is simple, and clear to everyone. The great objective of primitivism is to overcome dualism between man and nature by conformity to the over-arching unities which nature provides and which humanity shares by virtue of its essential identity as a part of nature.

There is a variety of ways in which the primitivist viewpoint can be manifested. The basic conceptual framework which Lovejoy used to define primitivism involved its sub-division into two distinct, yet closely related, aspects: the first, "chronological primitivism," a philosophy of history, and the second, "cultural primitivism," a theory of the value of human institutions and accomplishments. It is also possible to find bases in his work for other types, viz. primitivist views of human nature, practical reform, and epistemology. The outline below seeks to summarize and extend Lovejoy's conceptual schema. The two elements marked with a single asterisk constitute, in my opinion, contributions of modern, especially American, primitivism. The element of "sociological primitivism," marked by a double asterisk, was suggested by William Burch in his work on the sociological aspects of the environmental crisis.[18]

Aspects of Primitivism

I.   Chronological Primitivism

    A. Definition:

        The highest excellence was at the "beginning." The earliest stage of human history was the best; the earliest period of national, religious, artistic, or any strand of history was better than the periods that have followed. Childhood is better than maturity. Hence the recent past is the story of "fall" from the original harmonious state. The future may be radically better than the present but at best it is a <u>recovery</u> of an integrity that has been lost.

    B. Theories of decline:

        1. Theory of the Fall

            Since the original fall from happiness, there has been no further serious decline.

        2. Theory of Progressive Degeneration

            Since the original fall from happiness, there has been, and will continue to be, steady decline.

        3. Theory of Decline and Future Restoration

            Since the original fall from happiness, there has been general decline, but at a future time there will be a restoration of the harmonious state.

      *4 Theory of Paradise Regained

            Since the original fall from happiness, there has been a period of general decline, but the present constitutes a time of restoration and renewal.

II.   Cultural Primitivism

    A. Definition:

        Cultural primitivism is the discontent of the civilized with society, or some conspicuous and characteristic feature of it, because of its departure from the "natural" condition of mankind. It is the belief of persons living in a relatively highly evolved and complex culture that a life <u>simpler</u>, less artificial, more "natural, " in some or in all respects, is a more desirable life. It may or may not be combined with chronological primitivism. The model of human individual and social excellence and happiness is often perceived to reside in the present mode of life of distant, exotic (especially "Eastern") or primitive peoples.

B. General types:

   1. Hard (reductive) cultural primitivism:

      a. Society is too hedonistic, luxurious, wasteful, comfortable, driven by insatiable individual needs and desires.

      b. Nature is hard, physically vigorous, disciplining moral virtue through poverty, renunciation, austerity.

   2. Soft (expansive) cultural primitivism:

      a. Society is too burdened with apparatus, restrictive rules, complexity, labor, injustice, oppression.

      b. Nature is free, spontaneous, leisurely, self-expressive, simple, harmonious, egalitarian, fraternal.

C. Expressions:

   1. Technological primitivism

   The best human society is one most free from the "intrusion" of "art, " in which only the simplest and most rudimentary of the practical arts are known. Often associated with an anti-intellectualism holding that the progress of knowledge has not added to human happiness.

   *Under the conditions of modern natural science and technology, an extension of technological primitivism has been made to include those practical processes and kinds of theoretical knowledge which lead "automatically, " "naturally" to an increase in the conformity of human society to natural patterns.

   2. Economic primitivism

The best human society is one without private property, and in particular, without property in land; in other words, economic communism.

3.   Juristic primitivism

The best human society is one with the least organized political government, or without any government except the "natural" government of the family or clan. Direct person-to-person relationships ought to take priority over organized political entities. "Humanity" ought to constitute one natural political body.

4.   Ethical primitivism

The control of human life ought to be by "natural" impulses without entanglements by rules, deliberate self-conscious effort or reflection, or sense of sin. Man ought to act in unity with himself as a natural being.

III. Supplementary Primitivist Views

A.   On human nature:

Because of the necessity to account for the fall out of harmony with the "state of nature, " primitivism is as apt to stress the shortcomings as the goodness of humanity. Hence, man may be perceived as a creature alienated from nature, with an unnatural craving for distinction, pride, self-assertion; or he may be considered naturally good and led astray by cultural artifice.

B.   On practical reform:

1.   Theory of reversion:

Reform ought to be undertaken through elimination of accretions of past history, by undoing the work of the past. The perfect model of social organization, simple, complete, lies in plain sight. Social problems are essentially simple once one sees them in the "light of nature. "

2.   Theory of oppression:

Since history shows the fall or decline of humanity and its sinful or weak nature, since the "law of nature" no longer controls human behavior, strong, organized governmental action is required with stern, punitive laws unknown in the "state of nature." It is necessary to repress anti-social, anti-natural human conduct.

C. On epistemology:

True knowledge is that which is or can be known universally and without special revelation, that which was known in the primitive age, that which is uncomplicated, easily intelligible, that which is evident to the untutored, unsophisticated mind (yet often dim to the learned mind). There is an appeal to the "consensus gentium."

**D. Sociological primitivism:

The "state of nature" is appealed to as a way of ordering the meanings of freedom, equality and fraternity within three basic patterns: "(1) the management of problems of a social class in its struggle with other classes, (2) the attempt to link super-ordinate and subordinate classes through identifying their natural commonality, and (3) to purify and move beyond class patterns."

Because of their importance as immediate background to the literature under examination below, it will be helpful to discuss at this point the first two additions to Lovejoy's schema: the first in the area of chronological primitivism; the second in the area of the technological expression of cultural primitivism.

In the first case, the discovery and settlement of America, and the subsequent interpretation of this event in a primitivist frame, resulted in the addition of what amounts to a fourth major theory of chronological primitivism. Not until a virgin continent, inhabited only by primitive peoples, was opened to European settlement, did the possibility seriously arise that a recovery of primitive man-nature harmonies could be regained on a large scale on this earth in human history. Of course, there are many sources for the idea of the sanctification of this world, but insofar as it appeared within a primitivist orientation, it constituted a novel expansion of the thought forms of that tradition in the direction of the passage quoted earlier from Andrew Burnaby: the New World as the temporal, geographical recovery of Eden. It makes an immense difference, ideologically as well as emotionally, if instead of looking backwards or forwards to Eden, one believes that it is present here and now. The emphasis shifts from nostalgia or expectation to preservation of what is now enjoyed. Only on such a basis can we appreciate the full motivational power of those primitivist symbols of our culture documented by Henry Nash Smith, W. R. B. Lewis,

Arthur K. Moore, and others. Such an attitude also helps explain "the peculiar virulence of the American ecological movement and its religious crusading spirit."[19] But there is a possibility for a more enduring consequence which takes us beyond specifically American history, although not necessarily beyond the "idea" of "America." In the context of other aspects of primitivist thought, especially what Lovejoy refers to as the "uniformitarian" premise of Enlightenment epistemology,[20] and with the aid of such recent influences as evolutionary biology, the idea of the New World as Eden recovered could pass into the notion of the whole earth as Eden and the whole species of "humanity" as living -- if it would but recognize the fact! -- in the midst of a natural paradise.

The second case is an expansion in the cultural meaning of "technological primitivism" to include the applications of the natural sciences in modern technology. It builds upon and reinforces the chronological primitivism of paradise regained.

Frequent reference is made in the literature to Ortega's discussion of the Western industrial Naturmensch as the prototypical adherent of this attitude:

> The meaning is that the type of man dominant today is a primitive one, a Naturmensch rising up in the midst of a civilized world. The world is a civilized one, its inhabitant is not: he does not see the civilization of the world around him, but uses it as if it were a natural force. The new man wants his motor car, and enjoys it, but he believes that it is the spontaneous fruit of an Edenic tree. In the depths of his soul, he is unaware of the artificial, almost incredible, character of civilization, and does not extend his enthusiasm for the instruments to the principles which make them possible.[21]

By this definition, material progress is not anti-primitivist. Insofar as it is based on a sense of everflowing Edenic abundance, through an innocent use and enjoyment of scientific technology, it does not require, in Ortega's analysis, an understanding or appreciation of the immensely complex and artificial "principles" of civilization, among which are the historically precarious, and highly specialized, principles of experimental science.

Perhaps the best discussion of modern American technological primitivism is found inter alia in Leo Marx's The Machine in the Garden.[22] In his analysis, all aspects of American society are constantly subject to the tendency to veer in the direction of primitivism. Technology and natural science and industry are no exception and historically this has occurred in the guise of the "technological sublime." Often technology was perceived, along with its immediate progenitor, the Newtonian "mechanistic sciences," as revealing the innermost "laws of nature" and thus as an extension of the

virgin creation directly into human society. It was therefore a means, not
a deterrent, to the fulfillment of the promise of America as paradise regained. For example, much was made in the early nineteenth century over
the distinction between the machine in its European form as an urban factory
system, and the machine in America as the "way of nature" beneficial to an
agricultural nation. It is apparent we are talking here not about the crafts,
or the civil, fine, or creative arts, in which the distinctive human contribution is apparent, but about the peculiarly modern phenomenon of
impersonal machine technology which is adopted ready-made by the user.
Such technology, like the most "cosmic" of the natural sciences, can provide an illusion of "detachment" from human interference in natural
processes -- an objective "model" of the natural unities to which, in the
primitivist frame, human society ought to conform. Hence modern science
and technology perpetuate in a new guise an "imitative" philosophy of nature
which has deep roots in Western thought:

> In such a philosophy (Lucretian-Epicurean) . . . man achieves
> his place in nature, not by sharing the attributes of a divine
> artisan, but by imitation of natural processes and learning from
> them or by working hard to supply his needs on the principle that
> necessity is the mother of invention. [23]

This mode of technological primitivism finds renewed expression in the
"new primitivism" examined in the next section.

III

The "New Primitivism"

The enlightened and liberated man is "one with cause and effect"
-- From a Zen Buddhist parable

None of the documents under examination here are pure examples
of primitivism. Heilbroner, for instance, poses as a reluctant primitivist.
He wishes it did not have to be so that humanity will lose its social and
cultural freedom. But nonetheless, "nature," including "human nature,"
requires it. The authors of the Club of Rome Reports disclaim any illusions
about the complexity of the elements they are seeking to bring together in
unifying world-models and the need for more knowledge which is dependent
on the most sophisticated scientific techniques. Yet, somehow all the
acknowledged complexity adds up to one grand organic simplicity which
anyone can see, and understand. Ferkiss is perhaps the most internally
contradictory of all. While arguing for an "ecological humanism" by extolling

the unique freedom of mankind to make itself and re-make nature, he nonetheless equates this freedom with processes of information input-output,
for the sake of society's survival through system equilibrium.

        This contradictory character of the documents before us should
not come as a surprise since they were written in each case by scientists
with deep roots in Western scientific culture suddenly disillusioned with
major aspects of Western society and searching for some way to come to
terms with failure. The mind-set of the authors is suggested by the
quality of "new discovery" that marks their writing. They communicate
the impression that they have just awakened from the idyllic assumption
that man and nature <u>are</u> in harmony (Heilbroner calls it the "fortifying
view that history was working like a vast organic machine"[24]) to discover
the ecological crisis, that they alone grasp its deadly implications, that
they must speak quickly and change everything immediately. Ferkiss
clearly identifies himself with the "noted scientist," the hero, who he
describes in the opening chapter of his book as the "only one . . . aware
of desperate peril when virtually everyone else sees nothing unusual and
no one will listen, of sounding the alarm when the established rulers of
society are secret agents of the enemy."[25] There is no more telling
primitivist attribute that Ferkiss' insistence that "there is no historical
precedent." No wonder that metaphors should be mixed!

        In spite of this ambiguity, each of the documents gives evidence of
chronological, cultural, and other forms of primitivism. I would like in
this section to discuss the common traits which link this literature with the
thought forms of the past. Those characteristics which set it apart as in
some ways unique will be considered in the following section in the context
of evaluation of the primitivist contribution.

        In the first place, there is evidence of a resurgence of <u>chronological</u>
<u>primitivism</u>, mostly of the type identified by Lovejoy as "Theory of Decline
and Future Restoration." In each case there is the assumption of a past
stage of human evolution in which humanity lived in organic harmony with
nature, a present, "modern" period of degeneration in which humanity
separated itself from nature with consequences destructive to both, and the
possibility for a recovery of harmony in the future. Heilbroner's "negative"
primitivism is probably the clearest example of this:

>   In these half-blind gropings there is, however, one element in
> which we can place credence, although it offers uncertainty as
> well as hope. This is our knowledge that some human societies
> have existed for millenia, and that others can probably exist for
> future millenia, in a continuous rhythm of birth and coming of
> age and death, without pressing toward those dangerous ecological
> limits, or engendering those dangerous social tensions, that threaten
> present day "advanced societies." In our discovery of "primitive"

cultures, living out their timeless histories, we may have found
the single most important object lesson for future man.[26]

For Heilbroner the image of the primitivist origins and future restoration
of humanity in nature is best reflected in the myth of Atlas "bearing with
endless perseverance the weight of the heavens in his hands." It is an
image of servile labor appropriate to a traditional, static society organized
around problems of survival. Such a society is placed by Heilbroner's
chronology before and after the present, destructive, Promethean industrial age.

The authors of the two Club of Rome Reports express a more
optimistic chronological primitivism. The image advanced in Limits to
Growth is of a golden age to be ushered in at the point at which exponential
growth ceases and humanity returns to equilibrium with nature. At such a
time, justice, equality, leisure, and the arts will likely flourish. The
present decline, the time of the "human problematique," was ushered in
when humanity separated itself from natural restraints and it will end when
those restraints are reinstated. Although such a reversal of history will
require a "Copernican" revolution of the human mind, a radical break with
the values of the past, it will usher in a new Eden:

> An equilibrium could permit the development of an unprecedented
> golden age for humanity. Freedom from ever increasing numbers
> of people will make it possible to put substantial effort into the
> self-realization and development of the individual.[27]

Mankind at the Turning Point is less given to descriptions of future
bliss contingent upon a recovery of "organic growth" or equilibrium but the
position is equally clear. Modern history has meant a loss for man of a
"sense of his destiny and at the same time that of his communion with
Nature and with the transcendent" but this loss may be restored at such
time as we pass through the "most awesome test" in our history and return
to an attitude based on harmony rather than conquest of nature:[28]

> The transition from the present undifferentiated and unbalanced
> world growth to organic growth will lead to the creation of a new
> mankind. Such a transition would represent a dawn, not a doom,
> a beginning, not the end.[29]

A return to origins will mean new identity for humanity. Instead
of concerns with personality and social classes, the focus will be on use of
resources and survival of the human species. Distinctive human concerns,
in other words, will be replaced by those which we share with all creatures
of nature.

Ferkiss follows more closely the imagery of The Limits to Growth although he claims a closer affinity to Heilbroner's chronological scenario of piecemeal collapse if humanity remains on its present course. However, should we change, accept his postulates of holism, naturalism and immanentism, summarized in the single principle that "mind and matter are really the same thing" and create a steady-state world in keeping with this principle, then "we can enter into the kingdom of freedom, " and break the bonds of "space and time. " "The true approach to Eden may be through the future."[30] Ferkiss calls himself a "Utopian" which suggests that he might more appropriately belong in the tradition of thought which rests its hopes for human transcendence in the distinctive powers of human mind and spirit. But this is misleading. His real sympathies lie with a form of "Christian" primitivism in which the universe conceived as a whole has a directionality well beyond human intention or control. This was made clear in a recent speech which he gave at a conference on Heilbroner's work:

> Like everyone else, including Heilbroner, I do not know what is
> going to happen in the next year or the next one hundred years.
> More than that, unlike Heilbroner, I am not sure, speaking as a
> Christian, that it makes any difference . . . . Maybe all sorts of
> things are happening to the world that we cannot now predict and
> would not like, and maybe this is God's will for us. He may want
> the world to be saved or He may not, or most likely, He may con
> ceive of the salvation of the world in other terms than we do . . . .
> What distinguishes the Christian from the non-Christian may be a
> willingness to accept even Heilbroner's most gloomy view of the
> future as something which may be God's will and therefore some
> thing which we will also. [31]

An incredible statement! In spite of all the "ecological humanist" fanfare, Ferkiss' real commitments are such as to lead him to effectively renounce human responsibility for the world! In keeping with this a-moral "Christian" primitivism, Ferkiss closes The Future of Technological Civilization with the statement that "to believe in a green tomorrow is an act of faith" best expressed in such epic fables as that of C.S. Lewis in which the "Lion will return and redeem his kingdom. "[32]

All of the documents under consideration postulate, in summary, a time of harmony between humanity and nature from which there was a "fall" (into modernity, exponential growth, undifferentiated growth, or liberalism), and to which there may (will) be someday a restoration.

In the second area of cultural primitivism, differences between Heilbroner and the other authors are also apparent. Heilbroner tends towards what Lovejoy calls a "hard" cultural primitivism. He is critical of capitalism for its wasteful, insatiable hedonistic drive for material

abundance through industrial technology which has out-stripped mechanisms
of social and environmental "control." The attempt to provide more for
everyone has resulted in a loss of morale and a spiritual emptiness.
Heilbroner includes in his catalogue of present cultural forms that are
unsatisfactory because of their lack of contact with the hard realities of
human and environmental nature his own liberal individualism and privileges
as a scientist. Such liberties are expendable; in fact, they are "luxuries"
which a society in harmony with nature could ill afford. What is necessary,
in contrast to the superfluity of contemporary life, is a society attuned to
the disciplines of nature itself perceived as scarcity rather than abundance.
Hence the species of society with greatest survival value will be like a
"monastic barracks." Sacrifice, self-discipline, austerity, are the virtues
required by a culture in conformity with the "state of nature." Most important of all, industrial technology will be vastly reduced or eliminated.
Heilbroner is therefore a technological and economic cultural primitivist
in the ancient sense of these terms. And as we might expect, the contemporary "model" for such a primitive culture is Eastern and exotic --
China. [33]

In contrast, The Limits to Growth, and Future of Technological
Civilization offer an expansive, "soft" cultural primitivism. The trouble
with modern culture lies not in its comfort and luxury but in its repressive
complexity. For example, both texts hold that once the mentality and
economy of unbridled growth is replaced by equilibrium a great simplification of the problems of mankind will have been effected with the consequence that there will be more leisure and opportunity for all persons
for meaningful personal pursuits. Ferkiss goes so far as to claim that
once scarcity is eliminated by the steady-state economy "most human conflict can be eliminated or at least mitigated"! [34]

The basis for this form of soft primitivism is the perpetuation
within the limits of equilibrium of technological modes of relationship to
nature. Contrary to Heilbroner, the Meadows Report to the Club of Rome
and Victor Ferkiss perpetuate the modern technological form of primitivism
in their assumption that technology is an extension of natural processes into
human life in such a way as to eliminate the differences between society and
nature: that it is the adaptive mode of human behavior. Although Ferkiss
refers to the need for "control" of technology, his basic point is that control
in the modern bourgeois sense of direction from without will no longer be
necessary once technology is understood as a "merely instrumental" extension of human-natural powers. "Control" will then be automatic because
technology will be but an aspect of man's participation along with the rest of
nature in the self-consistent whole of monistic process. Ferkiss develops
his primitivist notion of technology most explicitly in his earlier work,
Technological Man, where he defines technology, in contrast to "technique"
or "art," as a "self-conscious organized means of affecting the physical or

social environment, capable of being objectified and transmitted to others, and effective largely independently of the subjective dispositions or personal talents of those involved."[35] Technology, in other words, is impersonal, a dimension of the essential unity of process in the organic and inorganic realms. It is increasingly analogous to biological and electro-chemical processes which are gradually leading to the elimination of the age-old distinction between the natural and artificial. To "control" technology means that technology as an extension of humanity will take its harmonious part within the "seamless process" of the whole of nature shaping itself by interactions among its elements.[36]

While Mankind at the Turning Point avoids more than a suggestion that leisure and meaningful self-expression will arrive with the new beginning of mankind in the state of organic growth, it joins with the first Report to the Club of Rome in its dependence upon the technology of world-system computers to simplify the burden of complexity of the modern world and lead us in a return to elemental harmony. The world-system computer models are able to perform this feat because they accurately reflect the "natural whole" within which humanity fits. Although Mankind at the Turning Point makes some show about the importance of taking into account human choices and values through "man-machine symbiosis, " the policies suggested by a comparison of scenarios in each area of ecological stress are predictably the same: the way of "organic growth" whereby through differentiated modes of "cooperation" everyone gives a little and gains a little. The dependence on computer modeling in the Club of Rome Reports is eloquent testimony to epistemological primitivism: true knowledge is that which can be known universally, without individual revelation, without the complications of subjectivity and circumstance. Both reports are, in fact, surprisingly simple in their basic arguments. It is as if they were saying: beneath all "appearance" of a complex "human problematique" is a simple situation which everyone can recognize and a simple remedy everyone can agree upon -- because they are obvious to even the most untutored mind.[37]

IV

The "New Primitivist" Contribution and Concealment

When you come, as you soon must, to the streets of our city,
Mad-eyed from stating the obvious . . .
Spare us all word of the weapons, their force and range,
The long numbers that rocket the mind . . .
Nor shall you scare us with talk of the death of the race.
How should we dream of this place without us --

The sun mere fire, the leaves untroubled about us,
A stone look on the stone's face?
Speak of the world's own change.
            - - Richard Wilbur, Advice to a Prophet

It is not easy to dismiss the reappearance in the late twentieth
century of the primitivist mode of thought. In spite of its simplistic approach, its disregard of history, its tendency to collapse any meaningful
distinction between human aspirations for community and organic health
and survival, its danger of sidetracking the practical economic and political
changes which the environmental crisis requires, and its latent and sometimes overt authoritarianism, it can be argued that this time around the
primitivist perspective has got hold of a basic truth. While some of the
"peculiar virulence" of these expressions of the ecology movement may be
traceable to the reaction which only representatives of a culture that believed it was already in harmony with nature could feel upon the "discovery"
of an "ecological crisis, " nonetheless the fact remains that humanity is
destroying its environment on a scale and at a rate unequaled in history.
A protest in response to this fact must be considered a positive contribution
almost regardless of the ideological perspective that accompanies it.
        "Almost" -- for in this case the perspective may be as concealing
of the situation as it is revealing.
        The contribution of the "new primitivism, " its revelatory power,
lies in its new application of primitivism. It brings an ancient perspective
to bear in a new way upon a new situation. The new situation -- "new" in
its intensity and scope -- is the present impact of society upon the natural
environment to the point that the environment is itself destroyed and human
civilization jeopardized. One "new" factor which sets the new primitivism
off from the old is that it has a peculiar sensitivity to this situation. It
"sees" the extreme qualitative diminution of the environment in the late
twentieth century.
        The MIT Systems Dynamics Group, authors of The Limits to
Growth, is aware of this function of its perspective in enabling it to "see"
the world in a way in which alternative perspectives do not see it. Writing
in response to criticisms from the project team at the University of
Sussex, the MIT Group concludes:

> We see no objective way of resolving these very different views of
> man and his role in the world. It seems to be possible for either
> side to look at the same world and find support for its view.
> Technological optimists see only rising life expectancies, more
> comfortable lives, the advance of human knowledge, and improved
> wheat strains. Malthusians see only rising populations, destruction

of the land, extinct species, urban deterioration, and increasing
gaps between the rich and the poor.[38]

What is here identified as a "Malthusian" view, the self-confessed view of
the MIT Group, is earlier described in the same article in terms which are
clearly descriptive of primitivism. In contrast to what it perceives as the
concept of man of the Sussex Group, which is rooted in the Judeo-Christian
tradition, and which holds that man is "essentially omnipotent," the MIT
Group identifies itself as holding the following view:

> The opposite concept of man is also an ancient one; but it is more
> closely related to the Eastern religions than to the Western ones.
> It assumes that man is one species with all other species embedded
> in the intricate web of natural processes that sustains and con-
> strains all forms of life. It acknowledges that man is one of the
> more successful species, in terms of competitiveness, but that
> his very success is leading him to destroy and simplify the natural
> sustaining web, about which he understands very little. Subscribers
> to this view feel that human institutions are ponderous and short-
> sighted, adaptive only after very long delays, and likely to attack
> complex issues with simplistic and self-centered solutions . . .
>
> They would also point out that much of human technology and
> "progress" has been attained only at the expense of natural beauty,
> human dignity, and social integrity, and that those who have
> suffered the greatest loss of these amenities have also had the
> least benefit from the economic "progress."[39]

In keeping with its cultural primitivism, the MIT Group identifies humanity's
distinctiveness with its capacity to compete rather than create, and its own
view with Eastern rather than Western thought.
    The contribution of the new primitivism, as the passage above
suggests, lies in its sensitive awareness of the seriousness of the contemporary impact of humanity upon nature and the fact that such impact is
destructive of the quality as well as viability of both natural and human
communities.[40] This is well illustrated in the literature under examination
and takes two forms -- qualitative and quantitative. The first form is
evident in how each text involves graphic descriptions of immediate, empirical deprivations of contemporary life due to the loss of continuity with
nature. The Limits to Growth, for example, begins with the announcement
that the intent of its project "is to examine the complex of problems troubling
men of all nations."[41] Almost every example of the complex of problems
which it then cites can be construed as a loss directly or indirectly in the
qualitative relationship between humanity and nature: "poverty in the midst

of plenty, degradation of the environment, loss of faith in institutions, un-controlled urban spread, insecurity of employment, alienation of youth, rejection of traditional values; and inflation and other monetary and eco-nomic disruptions." Heilbroner's list of contemporary crises includes these of the Club of Rome but is longer and more explicit with regard to the qualitative dimension. He is concerned with "brooding doubts, " the "mood of our times, " "oppressive anticipation of the future, " "civilizational malaise." These various attitudinal motifs are traced finally to "our startled awareness that the quality of our surroundings, " of "life, " is worsening. For "of all the changes in our background awareness, perhaps none is so important as this." It is our felt incapacity to deal with this "possibly disastrous decline in the conditions of existence" which leads to our recognition of the "ultimate inadequacy of material possessions, " the loss of confidence in the values of an industrial civilization. [42] Ferkiss, too, is most patently concerned with a "crowded, ugly, mechanized, reg-imented, and totally dehumanized world, " which exists in such contrast to scenes where "hawks still wheel in the sky, lovers' pulses quicken at the sight of the beloved, men and women still feel awe at the sacred, children still marvel at the sea and the sky."[43] These are all authentic statements of the contemporary imagination.

The second form of awareness of the new primitivism is quanti-tative. This introduces a further factor in the configuration of notions which sets the "new primitivism" apart from the old. The new factor is the premise that the contemporary situation may be best understood in terms of the quantitative generalizations of the modern physical and bio-logical sciences. Whereas the old primitivism expressed its analysis of how conformity to nature was lost in imagery roughly continuous with its description of human experience (and such imagery as that of "hard" or "soft" primitivism, for example, lives on in the new literature) in the new primitivism there is a heavy dependency upon indirect, unseen, factors for explanations of our plight and guidance to new ways of harmony. Even the modern impersonal primitivism of the "technological sublime" is closer to tangible human emotion, manipulation and purpose than the "objectified" scientific findings which dominate the new perspective.

Of course, it is not this scientific material itself, but its use, which is distinctive in the new primitivism. Whereas alternative per-spectives, especially progressivism, use similar data and generalizations as part of their prescription for human action, the new primitivism uses it as the substance of what is meant by conformity and non-conformity of humanity with nature. The concealment of the new primitivism occurs at this point: with the movement from a qualitative, experiential description of the situation to an analysis of the whole "system" of nature in terms of quantifiable equilibria and then back again to experiential consequences. This double transition could not occur as abruptly as it does except in the

framework of the primitivist ideal of <u>imitating</u> nature. The movement is
reductionistic, primitivist, concealing because the assumption is made that
the hidden abstract necessities of macro-cosmic equilibria, if conformed
to as a supreme law, will result in specific qualitative harmonies; because,
in other words, the qualitative distinctiveness of both society and nature
is obliterated by an equation on an abstract level of brute existence and
value. [44] (This equation, of course, is of negative value by Heilbroner,
positive value by the <u>Club of Rome</u> and Ferkiss).

Put another way, there can be little doubt that in respect to the
value of the sheer survival of the human species the gross quantitative relationships so acutely perceived in these tracts must be taken with the utmost
seriousness as necessary tools of understanding, and that in respect to the
value of a variety of abundant, diverse, healthy natural environments, such
relationships are also necessary (if less direct) conditions. But there is
room for considerable doubt that they are <u>sufficient</u> for the attainment of
either of these ends. Yet it is precisely this equation of theoretical scientific "necessity" with practical sufficiency which the new primitivism pro-
motes.

There is no discussion in the works under consideration to the
effect that the very capacity to attend to the chains of cause and effect un-
covered by the natural sciences might require a renewal of those unique
<u>cultural</u> capacities of humanity which when exercised give rise to society
as distinct from nature. Any hint of the importance of a renewal of the
humanistic disciplines -- esthetic, political, moral, social, philosophical,
religious, or scientific -- by which humanity displays appreciation and
exercises choice and purpose among the plurality of natural ends and means
is missing. To be sure, it is suggested that political, moral, social, and
religious changes must be made, but these activities are perceived as
instruments to a pre-established goal, or an efflorescence which will appear
after the goal is reached. The new primitivism <u>contributes</u> an awareness of
the value of nature, especially its "limits," in concrete human life. But it
<u>conceals</u> the creative role of human culture in affirming and perpetuating
that value.

It may be that the issue can be summarized in the proposition that
the authors propose a particular cultural definition of the art or <u>technē</u>
necessary for man-nature harmony. Heilbroner reluctantly argues for an
inevitable return to the authority of "tradition and ritual" of primitive religion. Ferkiss and the <u>Club of Rome</u> consider the technology of world-
system dynamics to constitute the authoritative basis for society in the late
twentieth century. But these are primitivist reductions of culture to its
pre-historical, or narrowly scientific phases of development. They omit
entirely the place of the liberal arts in the normative definition of the relationship of nature and society.

A Restatement of the Problem

This music crept by me upon the waters,
Allaying both their fury, and my passion,
With its sweet air: thence I have follow'd it.
          -- Shakespeare, The Tempest

It is not that the primitivist mode of thought, in either American or Western culture generally, has gone uncriticized that points to the need for a more adequate definition of the problem of nature and society. In fact, most of the recent literature on primitivism, and especially that which is devoted to the history of ideas and symbols in America, is forcefully critical of the Edenic myth for its perpetuation of a view of man and nature which is lacking in realism, sense of tragedy, and appreciation of time and history. While most of this literature appeared prior to the recent recognition of a "global ecological crisis," the substance of criticism still holds. For example, the observation that primitivism is responsible for distortions in the American psyche through an assumption of innocence and the quest for human community on the basis of natural abundance is pertinent to our discussion above. So is the criticism, frequently voiced, that the myth of America as paradise regained is a way of achieving security in the face of the anxiety occasioned by the radical character of human freedom.

Perhaps David Noble has been most vocal among American historians in his critique of what he terms the "Jeffersonian covenant with nature:"

> The Puritans of the seventeenth century reacted to the disintegration of the medieval community by reaching out for a covenant with God that would provide them with earthly security . . . . Our historians from Bancroft to Beard asserted that the reality of the American experience was this Puritan covenant translated into the material form of the Jeffersonian republic. Americans, they wrote, live not as members of a historical community with its inevitable structure of institutions, but as the children of nature who are given earthly definition by the virgin land that had redeemed their ancestors when they stepped out of the shifting sands of European history. [45]

But, as important and relevant as the major force of this body of criticism remains, it has nonetheless had the unfortunate effect of setting up a dichotomy between primitivist and historical realist perspectives and thus, in my opinion, perpetuating the problem of society and nature in

America rather than constructively addressing it. The alternative Noble
recommends is to deny the "immutable time of origins in 1776 or 1789"
and embrace a "civilization of the sinful brotherhood of mankind. "[46]
Ironically, by failing to assume the burden of identifying redemptive
possibilities within the American covenant Noble and others fall prey to
an anti-cultural viewpoint of their own. They pose for the American, and
indirectly, the Westerner with primitivist sympathies, an impossible
choice: demonic affirmation or soul-shattering rejection of one's own
cultural identity.

A more adequate statement of the problem of nature and society is
needed. It must be framed in such a way that justice is done to the truth
at the center of the Western Edenic myth -- the truth that humanity is a
participant along with other unique forms of life in a common world. It is
precisely a new perception of this truth that the primitivist response to the
ecological crisis has contributed to contemporary discussion. But the
acknowledgement of a shared world must be made in such a way that it does
not fall prey to an anti-cultural monism which only serves to strengthen
historicist or progressivist insistence upon a society-nature dualism.

The following restatement of the problem would appear to meet
these criteria: the problem of nature and society is how to understand man's
special relationship to nature in such a way that the unique values of both
nature and society are affirmed within the character of the relationship itself.

We are led to ask whether there is not a third alternative within
Western, or American thought which might hold the germ of such an understanding. Charles L. Sanford, in The Quest for Paradise, suggests that there
might be:

> In practice, Americans have consciously or unconsciously sought
> to establish a midpoint between savagery and civilization, to es-
> tablish a national identity which was neither primitive in the fron-
> tier sense nor excessively civilized in the European sense. [47]

Regrettably, due to his enthusiasm for his own psychologistic thesis, he
does not pursue the implications of this insight and closes with the stereo-
typical admonition that "more than anything else we need a tragic vision of
life in order to confront our problems more realistically. "[48] In a similar
vein, Henry Nash Smith closes his classical study, Virgin Land, with the
judgment that the American experience holds promise of a third alternative:

> But if interpretation of the West in terms of the idea of nature
> tended to cut the region off from the urban East and from Europe,
> the opposed idea of civilization had even greater disadvantages . . .
> For the theory of civilization implied that America in general, and

the West a fortiori, were meaningless except in so far as they managed to reproduce the achievements of Europe.

The capital difficulty of the American agrarian tradition is that it accepted the paired but contradictory ideas of nature and civilization as a general principle of historical and social inter-pretation. A new intellectual system was requisite before the West could be adequately dealt with in literature or its social development fully understood. [49]

Unfortunately, he does not suggest the sources of this "new intellectual system" that will mediate the dialectic of nature and civilization.

Leo Marx, however, has made a constructive effort in this direc-tion. In The Machine in the Garden and other essays, he argues that the "pastoral mode" constitutes a tradition of thought native to the West, es-pecially prominent in American literature, which seeks a "middle ground" between nature and society. [50] The pastoral form is defined as those works "whose controlling theme is a variant of the conflict between art and nature -- nature being represented by an idealized image of landscape, "[51] and whose aim is a reconciliation of this conflict in a synthetic "unity" that "binds consciousness to the energy and order manifest in unconscious nature. "[52] In this larger whole, the essential continuity of humanity and nature is affirmed by a reciprocal interaction between them -- an inter-action that stands in transcendent relation to either society or nature con-sidered alone. According to the pastoral mode of thought, "we can remain human, which is to say, fully integrated beings, only when we follow some such course back and forth, between our social and natural (animal) selves. "[53]

Since Virgil (pastoral) has advanced a vision of a whole life balanced, as it were, between two landscapes -- one identified with sophistication, art and the aspiring mind, and the other with simplicity, nature, and the strength to live without ambi-tion. [54]

Looked at from the side of society, the "pastoral impulse" is the urge, in the face of society's power and complexity, to "retreat in the di-rection of nature. " But this impulse is not "escapism. " It is a serious criticism of a society dominated by a mechanistic system of value. It aims at a contrast between the aggressive, expansionary dynamism of Western capitalism and industry, which depends upon highly manipulative techniques, and those aspects of life that are common to all men and which exemplify a more restrained, accommodating kind of behavior affirmative of both environmental and psychological balance.

At the highest or metaphysical level of abstraction, then, romantic pastoralism is holistic. During the more intense pastoral interludes, an awareness of the entire environment, extending to the outer reaches of the cosmos, affects the perception of each separate thing, idea, event. In place of technologically efficient but limited concept of nature as a body of discreet manipulatable objects, our pastoral literature presents an organic conception of man's relation to his environment. [55]

The pastoral perspective therefore embodies much of the strength of the primitivist contribution.

Looked at from the side of nature, however, the pastoral mode (unlike primitivism) acknowledges that nature in isolation from society is not an ideal place either! The wilderness destroys as well as supports human well being; it is a source of misery as well as felicity. There is no fact which makes this point more persuasively than humanity's mortality. In the past, pastoral literature has consistently reminded humanity of its natural finitude by the convention of placing a tomb or other token of death in the midst of an idyllic bower along with the phrase "et in Arcadia ego" (I am in Arcadia also). In addition to death, pastoral literature is rich with allusions to the dark side of nature's impact upon humanity: including labor, poverty, disease and natural disaster.

From the standpoint of pastoral, the idealization of either nature or society apart from one another, or apart from the threats that each uniquely poses to human existence, is unfounded illusion. The only ideal worthy of pursuit is one which includes the best of society as well as the best of nature, and it is this ideal which humanity comes closest to attaining in that unique interaction of natural grace and human discipline whose apogee is the fine arts. The classic "shepherd" figure of pastoral is the poet or homo artifex and he above all others is able to reconcile nature and humanity. In the words of Marx, "the woods 'echo back' the notes of his pipe." In pastoral, then, there is affirmed the possibility that the differences between nature and society may become reciprocally enhancing differences by reason of their mutual participation in a transcending "new creation." But this synthesis is never free from impingement from either the side of nature or the side of society.

Perhaps the most memorable literary work in the long history of the pastoral mode, which stems from Theocritus and Virgil and continues through Frost and Bellow, is Shakespeare's The Tempest. In this wondrous tale where the action moves back and forth between nature and civilization -- from the corrupt city to the wilderness to an idyllic integration and then back to a redeemed city, Gonzalo assumes the role of the primitivist, idealizing nature and repudiating calculating human efforts to master it, while Prospero (the "true" Duke of Milan) is the pastoralist, using the disciplines of the arts to transform a desert island into an idyllic garden and the ambitions of men into a harmony of personal desires. As Marx notes, Prospero's fusion of the mental and the objective through art makes love and power available to human community.

Heilbroner closes An Inquiry into the Human Prospect with a rejection of Prometheus (the progressivist) as an adequate guide to the future and the recommendation that Atlas (the primitivist) may better serve mankind in the face of the global ecological crisis. I would like to suggest that Prospero (the pastoralist) deserves consideration as our guide to the authentic belonging of humanity and nature.

NOTES AND REFERENCES

[1] Richard Means makes this point well in "Man and Nature," Chapter 5 of The Ethical Imperative: Crisis in American Values (Garden City: Doubleday, 1969), although he is principally concerned with the effects of separation. Kenneth Alpers argues that a typology limited to "inclusivist" (biocentric) vs. "exclusivist" (anthropocentric) positions needs to be augmented by the addition of a "verticalist" (theocentric) perspective in "Starting Points for an Ecological Theology: A Bibliographical Survey," Chapter VI of New Theology No. 8, edited by Martin Marty and Dean Peerman (New York: Macmillan, 1971). H. Paul Santmire makes the same point as Alpers in greater detail in "Historical Dimensions of the American Crisis," Chapter VI of Western Man and Environmental Ethics, edited by Ian G. Barbour (Reading, Massachusetts: Addison-Wesley Publishing Company, 1973).

[2] Howard Mumford Jones, O Strange New World (New York: Viking Press, 1952), 33.

[3] "Primitivism" in American history and literature has been discussed by James Baird, Ishmael (Baltimore: Johns Hopkins Press, 1956); Norman Foerster, Nature in American Literature (New York: Russell and Russell, 1923); R.W.B. Lewis, The American Adam (Chicago: University of Chicago Press, 1955); Perry Miller, "The Romantic Dilemma in American Nationalism and the Concept of Nature," in Nature's Nation (Cambridge: Belknap Press, 1967); Ralph N. Miller, "American Nationalism as a Theory of Nature," William and Mary Quarterly, XII (1955) 74-95; Arthur K. Moore, The Frontier Mind (Lexington: University of Kentucky Press, 1957); Roderick Nash, "The American Cult of the Primitive," American Quarterly 18 (Fall, 1966) 517-537; David Noble, Historians Against History (Minneapolis: University of Minnesota Press, 1965) and The Eternal Adam and the New World Garden (New York: George Braziller, 1968); Charles L. Sanford, The Quest for Paradise (Urbana: University of Illinois Press, 1961); Peter J. Schmitt, Back to Nature: The Arcadian

Myth in Urban America (Cambridge: Oxford University Press, 1969); Henry
Nash Smith, Virgin Land (New York: Random House, 1950).
    [4]Robert Heilbroner, An Inquiry into the Human Prospect (New
York: W.W. Norton, 1974), 20.
    [5]Carole Stanley Gill, "Is This What 'Disaster Movies' Are Really
Telling Us?" Chicago Sun-Times, Sunday, January 19, 1975, Section I-8, 2.
    [6]Thomas S. Deer, "Religion's Responsibility for the Ecological
Crisis: An Argument Run Amok," Worldview, January, 1975, 43.
    [7]Lynn White, "The Historical Roots of Our Ecological Crisis,"
Machina Ex Deo: Essays in the Dynamism of Western Culture (Cambridge:
MIT Press, 1968). Arnold Toynbee goes further and argues for a return
to a pre-Biblical paganism in which worship of nature can hold man's
greedy impulses in check. See for example, Arnold J. Toynbee, "The
Genesis of Pollution," The New York Times, Sunday, September 16, 1974.
    [8]Donnella H. Meadows et al., The Limits to Growth (New York:
Universe Books, 1972); Mihajlo Mesarovic and Eduard Pestel, Mankind at
the Turning Point (New York: Dutton & Co., 1974); Robert Heilbroner,
An Inquiry into the Human Prospect; Victor Ferkiss, The Future of
Technological Civilization (New York: George Braziller, 1974).
    [9]Jay W. Forrester, World Dynamics (Cambridge: Wright-Allen
Press, 1971).
    [10]See, for example, Robert Boguslaw, The New Utopians: A Study
of Systems Design and Social Change (Englewood Cliffs, N.J.: Prentice
Hall, 1965); H.S.D. Cole et al., Models of Doom, a Critique of the Limits
to Growth (New York: Universe Books, 1973); and Ida R. Hoos, Systems
Analysis in Public Policy (Berkeley: University of California Press, 1972).
    [11]Robert Nisbet, Social Change and History (New York: Oxford
University Press, 1969).
    [12]Arthur O. Lovejoy and George Boas, Primitivism and Related
Ideas in Antiquity (Baltimore: Johns Hopkins Press, 1935), 106-7.
    [13]See Ernst Troeltsch, The Social Teachings of the Christian
Churches, I (New York: Harper and Row, 1960 edition), 150 ff.
    [14]See George H. Sabine, "Modern Theory of Natural Law," A
History of Political Theory (Hinsdale: Dryden Press, 1973 edition).
    [15]In 1935 Arthur O. Lovejoy and George Boas published Primitivism
and Related Ideas in Antiquity, op. cit., which was Volume I of a projected
series entitled A Documentary History of Primitivism and Related Ideas,
under the general editorship of Arthur O. Lovejoy, Gilbert Chinard, George
Boas and Ronald S. Crane. Unfortunately, no further volumes appeared in
this series. However, a number of studies were published as parts of the
collateral series Contributions to the History of Primitivism, including
Lois Whitney, Primitivism and the Idea of Progress in English Literature
of the Eighteenth Century (Baltimore: Johns Hopkins Press, 1948). In
addition, several essays on primitivism and nature as norm in Arthur O.

Lovejoy, Essays in the History of Ideas (Baltimore: Johns Hopkins Press, 1948) are important background material for the topic.

[16]George Boas, "Primitivism," in Philip P. Wiener, editor, Dictionary of the History of Ideas (New York: Charles Scribners, 1968), III, 577.

[17]Lovejoy and Boas, Primitivism and Related Ideas in Antiquity, xi.

[18]William R. Burch, Jr., Daydreams and Nightmares (New York: Harper and Row, 1971), 73. Burch explicitly espouses the "primitivist" perspective as the basis for a constructive rhetoric of nature adequate to the environmental crisis.

[19]Cole et al., Models of Doom, 184. Donald Fleming traces the contemporary American ecology movement back to the transcendentalist "self-forgetfulness before nature." Donald Fleming, "Roots of the New Conservation Movement," Perspectives in American History, VI, 1972.

[20]Lovejoy, Essays in the History of Ideas, 86.

[21]Ortega Y. Gasset, The Revolt of the Masses (New York: W.W. Norton, 1932), 59.

[22]Leo Marx, The Machine in the Garden (New York: Oxford University Press, 1964). Charles Sanford, in an interesting account of the "intellectual origins of American industry" traces the origins to an anti-urban, moral faith in America as the locus of Edenic abundance. See The Quest for Paradise. Francis D. Klingender, in Art and the Industrial Revolution (London: Carrington, 1947) offers graphic portrayals of the esthetic celebration of machine technology in the 18th and 19th centuries.

[23]Clarence J. Glacken, Traces on the Rhodian Shores: Nature and Culture in Western Thought from Ancient Times to the End of the Eighteenth Century (Berkeley: University of California Press, 1967), 708.

[24]Heilbroner, An Inquiry into the Human Prospect, 17.

[25]Ferkiss, The Future of Technological Civilization, 4.

[26]Heilbroner, An Inquiry into the Human Prospect, 141.

[27]Jorgen Randers and Donella Meadows, "The Carrying Capacity of the Globe," Sloan Management Review, 13, No. 2, 11. Winter, 1972. Italics are mine.

[28]Mesarovic and Pestel, Mankind at the Turning Point, 152, 147.

[29]Ibid., 9. Italics are mine.

[30]Ferkiss, The Future of Technological Civilization, 286, 129.

[31]Victor Ferkiss, "Christianity and the Fear of the Future," Zygon, 10, 3 (September, 1975) 261-2.

[32]Ferkiss, The Future of Technological Civilization, 32.

[33]Heilbroner expanded his views on the "human prospect" in "Robert L. Heilbroner: Portrait of a World Without Science," Science, 16 August 1974, 598-99.

[34]Meadows, The Limits to Growth, 179-184; Ferkiss, The Future of Technological Civilization, 145.

[35]Victor Ferkiss, Technological Man (New York: George Braziller, 1969), 31. Italics mine.

[36]Ferkiss, The Future of Technological Civilization, 253.

[37]Other aspects of primitivism are evident throughout the several works under examination. Economic primitivism is present in the shared assumption of some form of economic communism. Ethical primitivism, the assumption that the moral act is the most natural act, is present in Heilbroner's argument that the basis for the choice of the survival of the species over present temporal benefits is to be found in the "furious power of the biogenetic force we see expressed in every living organism" ("What Has Posterity Ever Done for Me?" New York Times Magazine, January 19, 1975); in the Club of Rome's call for a new morality of environmental equilibrium or organic growth assumed as identical with the sacrificial norm of Christianity; in Victor Ferkiss' insistence that "there is no real difference between descriptive and normative statements" because all natural "facts" are statements of organic purposes of survival and health (The Future of Technological Civilization, 94). Contrasting primitivist views of human nature are held by Heilbroner, who argues for a politics based on humanity's natural weaknesses; and Ferkiss, who argues for a politics based on man's "essential goodness" because "human nature is a product of universal nature." Correlative with their respective views of human nature, Heilbroner and Ferkiss express differing primitivist understandings of practical reform. For Heilbroner, it is a theory of oppression. Since the ecological "laws of nature" no longer control human behavior, strong, organized governmental action is required to repress humanity's anti-natural conduct. For Ferkiss, it is a theory of reversion. By eliminating the accretions of past history -- in particular the history of laissez-faire liberalism (identified as the history of American society for the past two centuries!) -- the way will be cleared for a government which is really not a government because everyone will see social problems in the "light of nature." There is also a strong movement of sociological primitivism throughout these texts towards a collectivist society in which "fraternity" emerges as the dominant meaning of community. However, it is not a fraternal community that moves beyond class patterns. Rather, the assumption is that a managerial elite will have the power and authority to direct the larger society to environmental equilibrium. In Burch's terms, therefore, this literature could be understood as an apology for a structure of superordinate-subordinate classes linked by the common natural need for survival under ecological stress.

[38]Cole et al., Models of Doom, 240.

[39]Ibid., 226.

[40]By this analysis, the "new primitivism" is a peculiarly clear exemplification of the three characteristics of the unique twentieth century view of nature as outlined by Clarence Glacken: (1) a preoccupation with

the effect of present civilization on the natural environment, (2) a pessimistic evaluation of that effect, and (3) a lack of integration of this new
situation and its evaluation into either the history or philosophy of civilization. See Clarence Glacken, "Man's Place in Nature in Recent Western
Thought, " in Michael Hamilton, editor, This Little Planet (New York:
Scribners, 1970).

[41]Meadows, The Limits to Growth, x.

[42]Heilbroner, An Inquiry into the Human Prospect, 13-27.

[43]Ferkiss, The Future of Technological Civilization, 4, 293.

[44]Samuel Z. Kausner describes the difficulties facing research on
environmental problems due to the combination of physical and social factors in any environmental issue. He is perceptive with regard to the temp-
tations for "reductionism" in current literature on ecology but his own
position is that "the development of an overarching theory in which both man
and environment may be treated seems to be utopian at this point. " He consequently argues for the necessity of alternating between terms appropriate
to social and physical realms. See "Some Problems in the Logic of Current
Man-Environment Studies, " Paper 16 in William Burch, Neil Cheek and Lee
Taylor, editors, Social Behavior, Natural Resources, and the Environment
(New York: Harper and Row, 1972).

[45]Noble, Historians Against History, 176.

[46]Ibid., ix, 226.

[47]Sanford, The Quest for Paradise, viii.

[48]Ibid., 264.

[49]Smith, Virgin Land, 305.

[50]Marx has been accompanied in his analysis of the "pastoral mode"
by a plentiful variety of recent scholarship, ranging from the thematic "genre"
approach of Harold E. Toliver in Pastoral Forms and Attitudes (Berkeley:
University of California Press, 1971) to the Marxist analysis of William
Empson in Some Versions of Pastoral (New York: New Directions Publishing Corporation, 1960). Brian Dibble, in A Theory of the Pastoral and a
Study of American Pastoral Poetry (Unpublished Ph.D. Dissertation, University of Chicago, 1971), documents the revival of interest in the theory of
pastoral in the last decade and presents an original theory of American urban
pastoral literature. The pastoral mode, as a third fundamental perspective
on nature-society relationships in the history of Western ideas, finds its
locus in Lovejoy's writings in what he terms "semi-primitivism" or the
"ethic of the middle link, " best described in The Great Chain of Being
(Cambridge: Harvard University Press, 1936). In this perspective, especially prominent in the eighteenth century, man occupies a middle place between the animal and the intellectual or angelic forms of being.

[51]Marx, The Machine in the Garden, 25.

[52]Ibid., 66.

[53]Ibid., 70.

[54]Leo Marx, "Pastoral and Its Guises," Sewanee Review, 82, Spring 1974, 363.

[55]Leo Marx, "American Institutions and Ecological Ideals," Science, 1970, 27 November, 1970, 949. In this article, Marx argues for a convergence between the American pastoral literary and ecological scientific critiques of dominant Western civilization. Joseph W. Meeker, however, is highly critical of the pastoral literary mode and unfavorably contrasts it with the idea of comedy in The Comedy of Survival: Studies in Literary Ecology (New York: Charles Scribner's Sons, 1972). In the terms of this essay, Meeker is best classified as a "primitivist." Paul Shepherd provides insight into the evolutionary emergence of the pastoral mode in Man in the Landscape: A Historic View of the Esthetics of Nature (New York: Alfred Knopf, 1967), and while in his most recent work he is critical of the pastoral economy, he nonetheless advances a normative conception of the relation of society and nature which is expressive of the pastoral metaphor. See The Tender Carnivore and the Sacred Game (New York: Charles Scribner's Sons, 1973).

CHAPTER III

ENERGY: TECHNICAL, ECONOMIC, POLITICAL, MORAL AND RELIGIOUS ISSUES

by
W. Alvin Pitcher

The Energy Situation in the United States

The issues surrounding the production, distribution, and consumption of energy provide an occasion for considering our relation to nature and to each other. They provide an opportunity to reflect on the meaning of the modern West. They compel us to ask some questions about where we are, whither we are tending, and what is at stake in our present situation. In this essay, I consider first the general energy situation in the United States, conservation as a moral imperative, a technical possibility, and a political improbability and use the issue of conservation to illustrate some different approaches to energy issues. This is a kind of case-study approach, rooted in the contemporary discussion. I use it to bring out the religious issue, the structure and content of meaningful action or being.

Secondly, in this essay I use the materials of the first part to indicate how there are technical, economic, political, moral and religious issues involved and how they are generally related to each other.

Finally, I indicate how the issues involved raise questions about the underlying American faith, about the symbols we use to delineate and to deal with what is at stake.

We are becoming painfully aware of a new situation in our economy: natural gas and oil will not be available abundantly and cheaply for long. Some respond to this awareness by advocating a frenzied search for and development of new natural oil and gas resources. Government reserves should be leased for development, objections or cautions about off-shore leases should be disregarded, and prices and profits should be maximized in order to encourage exploration and development.

Others respond to the forecast of our running out of natural gas and oil by pressing for the expansion of our coal industry and for public support for technological developments that will provide for the liquefaction and gassification of coal as well as for the regular use of more coal with high sulfur content.

Some have chosen nuclear power as the alternative, an alternative available in the light water fission reactor in the short run and in the liquid metal fast breeder fission reactor in the long run.

Some, in the light of risks involved in fission reactors prefer nuclear fusion processes or some non-nuclear source of energy such as solar. Along with solar energy which seems to get most support, auxiliary sources are advocated, such as wind, organic wastes, tides, waves, sea thermal gradients, and the growing of trees and plants for fuel.

Running through much of the contemporary discussion is a consideration of more efficient use of energy (conservation) and here and there a question is raised about a culture which uses so much energy, sometimes in relation to what is used by other people and sometimes as a serious question about industrial civilization itself.

The immediate cause for widespread concern about energy is the awareness of the power of OPEC (Organization of Petroleum Exporting Countries) to control the supply and the price of oil. The underlying cause is the growing awareness of the limits of energy resources and the public discussion regarding "the limits to growth," a discussion centering around the first Club of Rome report. In spite of all the differences in projections about future discoveries I think that we can assume that supplies of natural gas and oil will be exhausted within fifty years, if they continue to be used at the present rate, and sooner if their use continues to grow at rates comparable to those of the last few years. One might debate the judgment about when supplies will run out and argue that prices are bound to rise and that consumption will fall as the end of the supply gets in sight. New sources of supply will be discovered. Estimates of their amount vary. But the facts remain, tremendous amounts of oil and gas are being used; the rate of growth in the use of oil and gas is about 6 per cent (this means that the amounts used double about every twelve years); there are real limits to the supply; consumption even at current rates cannot continue for many years; substitutes for natural gas and oil must be found if the present energy use pattern is to continue.[1]

Everyone agrees that the United States has considerable supplies of coal. Why not use them? Why not substitute coal for gas and oil or use coal to produce gas and oil?

The United States has consumed about one-half billion tons of coal per year during the last few years. The estimates of reserves vary, chiefly depending on what one means by reserves, from about 1200 billion tons to 3000 billion tons. The annual consumption of one-half billion tons represents about 15 per cent of the national energy consumption; natural gas represents 30 per cent and oil 50 per cent. The future growth in coal production and consumption depends on many factors; among them are the substitution of coal for oil in electrical power generation (utilities now use about 28 per cent of the oil, the equivalent is about 343 million <u>tons</u> of coal per year) the development of liquefaction and gassification processes for producing synthetic oil and gas, the availability of imported oil, and the way in which coal technology and public concern for the societal costs of coal production and consumption are related.

Without elaboration[2] I want to indicate what some of the factors are; societal costs, about which there is a growing concern include: the effects of subsidence (the damages resulting from the sinking of land that has been mined); acid drainage, (about one ton of sulfuric acid is produced for every ton of coal mined); mine fires; soil erosion; and land reclamation. In addition there are the unusual personal costs of producing coal-- fatal accidents, non-fatal accidents, and black lung disease. The societal costs in connection with the use of coal, sulphur oxide pollution, nitrogen oxide pollution, particle pollution, mercury pollution, radiation from coal ash, and thermal pollution, all raise further questions about the use of coal and about the bearers of the costs. The cost of removing the pollution by sulphur oxides has been estimated to be 6 mills per kilowatt of electrical energy developed. It is difficult to understand how such costs can be estimated accurately, but one cannot but wonder about the present use of coal and the extended use of coal in the face of the alleged societal cost of about 10 mills per kilowatt of electricity produced, assuming that each ton of coal is converted into 2200 kilowatt hours of electrical energy.

The United States has extensive oil shale deposits which could be developed to produce oil. In Colorado, Utah, and Wyoming the largest part of our oil shale can be found: the equivalent of 1000 to 2000 billion barrels of oil. If resources that would produce less than 15 gallons of oil per ton of oil shale are included, some estimates run as high as 20, 000 billion gallons of oil. Present estimates of costs run as high as $9.00 per barrel. This does not seem high compared to $13.50 per barrel paid for imported oil. Thus, with the rise in oil prices recovery from more and more of the oil shale resources becomes economically feasible. The chief long-run problems in the development of oil shale involve the environmental impact. Large quantities of water are needed, which can be secured, it is said, from underground water, but the desalinization of such water before discharge creates a major problem. The alternative is to use water from the rivers, but this is not available in the amount necessary for large scale development without great readjustments. The disposal of waste shale is also a problem of major magnitude. For every million barrels of oil there will be 1-1/2 million tons of shale, or for every barrel of oil 1-1/2 ton of shale will be processed, and if a feasible technology for underground processing is not developed this will leave thousands of acres covered with oil shale waste. All of the problems faced in reclamation of land after the strip mining of coal are magnified several times because of the size of the tailings (the piles of wastes).

There can be no doubt that a lot of oil is present in our oil shale deposits and given sufficient economic pressure to supply oil, ways will be found to develop them.

Thus far, however, we have developed nuclear fission processes as the chief alternative for fossil fuel in electrical power plants. Judgments about the wisdom of using nuclear fission power to produce electricity range from thinking it is the cheapest, cleanest, safest, most reliable fuel available to characterizing our use of it as a Faustian bargain in which we have sold our possibility of life on the earth for a few short years of energy.

The nuclear fission process uses uranium which is available in considerable supply. Here, as in all cases, the meaning of what is available depends in part upon what one is willing to pay to secure the supply and in part on the technology which is available for production and use. In the nuclear fission reactor now in use in the United States (the Light Water Reactor) uranium is available at "reasonable" costs to supply at least 5000 quadrillion BTU's of electrical energy.

The difficulty in knowing exactly where we are is suggested by an article in the December, 1975, edition of the Bulletin of Atomic Scientists by M. C. Day. He contends uranium is not as available for producing energy in the amounts generally anticipated, because we get less energy from each ton of uranium oxide than most estimates indicate, because it requires a great deal of energy to produce uranium oxide from low grade ore, because we have not developed the resources we have, and because of environmental problems with the handling of huge amounts of ore. One must read such articles to begin to appreciate the difficulty one faces in making assessments. If used in the Liquid Heavy Metal Breeder Reactor this same supply would produce about 500,000 quadrillion BTU's of electrical energy. Electrical energy consumption in 1973 was 6.4 quadrillion BTU's. At a growth rate of 6 per cent we would use about 13 quadrillion BTU's in 1985 and about 27 quadrillion BTU's in 2000. The possibility of using uranium to produce all of our electrical energy for some time to come if nuclear fission power plants are developed seems very real. The only question is, then, whether or not we should move in this direction.

I shall not try to answer this question. I will present briefly all of the arguments against the use of nuclear fission power with which I am familiar, then point to what seems to be a reasonable response to the objections, and then present a proposed policy statement by a National Council of Churches Task Force.

Arguments Against the Use of Nuclear Fission

It is argued that there is considerable danger of a serious accident in nuclear reactors in which many people will be exposed to radiation in lethal amounts. The system breaks down due to physical defects or human errors. If the risks are as small as it is suggested by Norman Rasmussen in his 3600 page report on nuclear reactor safety, why do the power companies insist upon the protection of the Price-Anderson Act which limits their liability in case of an accident to $550 million, most of which will be paid by insurance provided by the government at very low rates? There is also the possibility that natural occurences such as earthquakes will so disrupt the operation of plants that lethal amounts of radiation occur.

Furthermore, some acts of sabotage are very likely to occur with similar results.

Since very radioactive fuels are processed, transported to power plants, used in the plants, and transported to and from processing plants to be reprocessed there is considerable opportunity for terrorists to seize quantities of enriched uranium or plutonium and to use the materials as a threat either in the form of a bomb or in the form of particles that can be introduced into ventilating systems. It is claimed that the knowledge of what is required to make a nuclear bomb is available to everyone, and that the technical problems are not large.

The radioactive wastes from nuclear plants, some of which are dangerous for thousands of years, have been and will be permanent threats to life. There is no program for their permanent disposal and none is possible. There is no safe way to store them.

No adequate program has been devised to prevent serious pollution from the piles of waste products of uranium mining (the tailings). David Comey[3] estimates that for the 1000 nuclear power plants projected for the year 2000, 5,741,500 deaths will occur over the next 80,000 years due to radiation from the tailings.

The development of nuclear fission power in the United States leads to the development of nuclear fission power plants in other countries, and along with that go the materials, and the technology in some cases, to build nuclear bombs. India has two reactors and has the capacity to make nuclear bombs. Soon, it is claimed, many more nations will have the nuclear weapons capacity and will be able to use it to blackmail other countries.

Some claim that the radiation effects of normal operations are dangerous.

Pollution from the heat given off in the production of nuclear power in the long run represents a great risk. Since nuclear power plants run at lower temperatures than coal-fired stations, more heat is given off per kilowatt of energy produced.

Nuclear fission power plants are not dependable. They are more costly than coal plants because they are always breaking down. The amount of energy used in producing a nuclear plant is so large that it makes their net contribution much lower than other kinds of plants.

Finally, some argue that there are other much less dangerous or risky alternatives that could be developed and would turn out to be feasible and economic if even a part of what the government has spent in developing nuclear power were available.

In reply to these arguments against the use of nuclear fission power, I will use a very thoughtful study by Fred H. Schmidt and David Bodansky, The Energy Controversy: The Role of Nuclear Power. They do not see any really viable alternatives for the near future. They argue against the increased use of fossil fuels because of the possible danger due to the increase of carbon dioxide in the atmosphere. Assuming that all of the other dangers involved in using fossil fuels were surmounted, they believe that the effects of increased carbon dioxide are much more of a risk than is nuclear power production.

> We know of no atmospheric science experts who are certain whether increasing levels of carbon dioxide are harmless, beneficial, or disastrous. One can find arguments in support of each conjecture, but one thing remains clear: the time-scales for whatever the effects might be are long. Once the mistake (or the beneficial act) has been committed, the recovery-time of the atmosphere (if it recovers at all) must be very long. [4]

What these two physics professors have concluded after considerable attention to the arguments pro and con is that nuclear power is less of a risk. For nuclear power, they claim:

> Environmental impacts are small; radio-active emissions are negligible; the fuel does exist for everybody. Nuclear reactor technology, while more complicated than fossil plants, is already available. Moreover, we know how to teach those who desire to know how to handle the technology. The waste material in volume is very small, and we do know how to take care of it and store it. And the experimental test of a long term storage method (in case all else is deemed unacceptable) has been made for us by the ancient Egyptians: their elegant pyramids are still standing for all to see as convincing evidence of the durability of man-made structures. Were the interiors of similar structures filled with old radioactive debris, one could not care less! One would still climb their sides, for the shielding required for the residual debris is negligible. Could it be that one important legacy left to us by the great Egyptian civilization is the outcome of this unintended construction "experiment"? On the other hand, if we accept the judgment of expert geologists, deep salt deposits are even more durable.

Among the controversial questions swirling around nuclear power, uppermost in many people's minds is that of reactor safety. In our view, the Reactor Safety Study, the "Rasmussen Report," has put this worry to rest. . . . Unfortunately, however, but few people have time to pursue this sort of study, or even much more modest studies. Instead the issue is "settled" in the public mind by headlines, or, at best, brief news items and debate. Nuclear power, in such a climate, faces public rejection, so long as there is seemingly more news value in a nuclear power plant minor failure which injures no one than in, say, a natural gas explosion in which people are killed. In fact, it faces certain rejection if society adopts the tacit ground rules under which absolute perfection is demanded for nuclear power, while the consequences of not deploying nuclear power are ignored.

Alongside of the reasoned judgment by two concerned physicists, and one could find many informed persons who would agree with it, I will place exerpts from a report by a National Council of Churches Committee, The Plutonium Economy. The statement does not add to the issues already developed, but it indicates that very responsible persons make radically different assessments of what we should do.

We believe that the proposed "plutonium economy" is morally indefensible and technically objectionable. At many stages in the nuclear fuel cycle--including reactor operation, fuel transport, reprocessing, fabrication and waste management--opportunity exists for catastrophic releases of plutonium and other radioactive materials through accident or malice. There is no validated scientific basis for calculating the likelihood or the maximum long-term effects of such releases, nor for guaranteeing that risks will not exceed a particular level. All of the present or planned precautions intended to prevent releases are imperfect and, for fundamental reasons, are likely to remain so. We fear that the cumulative effect of these imperfections may well be unprecedented and irremediable disaster.

In a plutonium economy, moreover, nuclear theft and terrorism, weapons proliferation to both national and subnational groups, and the development of a plutonium black market seem inevitable. None of these problems will respect national boundaries, and the difficulties of international cooperation will complicate efforts to contain them.

In an effort to suppress nuclear violence and coercion, to limit
the spread of illicit nuclear weapons, and to encourage the needed
perpetual social stability, the United States and other countries
may have to undertake massive social engineering and to abrogate
traditional civil liberties. The drastic nature of the nuclear threat
is apt to elicit a drastic police response. Even these measures,
however repressive, might in the end prove ineffective.

There is additionally the fundamental ethical question of our right
to leave to countless future generations a permanent heritage of
radioactive waste products. In producing vast quantities of materials so deadly that they will require perpetual vigilance and
guardianship, nuclear power will inject into the future an element
of risk comparable to that of our vast store of nuclear arms.

These profound biological and social hazards, many without
present technical solutions, or easily foreseeable solution, would
be incurred in pursuit of small and possibly ephemeral economic
advantages. Decisions balancing the risks of the plutonium economy
with its benefits are now founded on self-serving economic and
technical assessments lacking in analytic quality. They are being
hastily made without the full and informed public discussion that
decisions of such unique importance require.

The controversy that rages over the use of nuclear fission power
will continue. But gradually, I predict, some objections will be overcome,
at least in part, by the introduction of precautionary practices. There is
a good deal of study of the possibilities for meeting the objections. In the
meantime nuclear fission plants will be built because we have the know-how,
because we are in need of short-run sources of energy before others are
developed, because we will not introduce a full-scale program of conservation, because we have not the will to move in other directions and support
alternatives, and because some people are convinced, just as Schmidt and
Bodansky are, that nuclear fission power is the best alternative we have now.
    There are several other sources of power, each of which presents
its own special possibilities and problems: nuclear fusion, solar, geothermal,
conversion of organic wastes, of algae, and of crops of plants or trees, wind,
waves, tides, and temperature gradients in lakes and oceans. Assessments
are not easy to make. Nevertheless, in order to develop our energy policy
someone must make some judgments about what is possible. In a very
preliminary way I will indicate what some of the possibilities and problems
are.
    According to the authors of <u>Energy and the Future</u>[5] depletable or
non-renewable resources are available in the following amounts for nuclear

fusion; deuterium-deuterium 63×10^9 quadrillion BTU's (enough to supply 1973 total U.S. energy use for 840 million years), deuterium-tritium, 63×10^6 quadrillion BTU's (enough for 840,000 years), geothermal (steam and hot water), 60×63 quadrillion BTU's or enough to supply total U.S. energy demands in 1975 for 50 years; geothermal (hot rock), 600×63 quadrillion BTU's or enough for 500 years at the 1975 rate of usage.

According to the same source renewable energy sources are available in the U.S. in the following annual amounts: solar radiation, 47,000 quadrillion BTU's; wind power, 315 quadrillion BTU's; thermal gradients in seas and oceans, 378 quadrillion BTU's; hydropower, 8.8 quadrillion BTU's; conversion of organic wastes, 6.3 quadrillion BTU's; conversion of plants or algae grown for fuel, 14.5 quadrillion BTU's; tidal energy, 6.3 quadrillion BTU's.

These estimates, of course, are based on what one might call very soft data. I use them only to indicate that there are a number of alternative sources of energy which would supply all or a significant part of our abstract energy demand if they could be developed and which might, provided they are not too costly, be substitutes for some uses of gas, oil, coal, and nuclear power. I have seen cost estimates which indicate that at least in the use of some of the resources -- wind, organic wastes, geothermal, and thermal gradients in sea and ocean -- costs are competitive. Solar energy is said to be competitive for space heating and cooling. Development of nuclear-fusion power is said to be decades away. Solar technology as yet does not seem to be developed to the place where it is competitive to produce energy for a large scale system. (It is now said to be two or three times as expensive as "ordinary" sources.) But no one knows what is possible. It is said, for example, that nuclear fission power resulted from the expenditure by the U.S. government of 60 billion dollars over the course of the years in which nuclear weapons have been developed. What would happen if solar energy research and development received that kind of money?

In some cases the problems posed by using the present sources of energy do not seem to be overcome or improved upon. The production of geothermal energy is attended by threats of changes in the earth's surface and by pollution from gasses and salts. Nuclear fusion power production is said to be accompanied by the emission of pollutions from gasses which are difficult to contain and to leave radioactive plants to be disposed of after about twenty years of service. The effects on the atmosphere of siphoning off the sun's energy are not known.

At this point I am convinced that among other things we should consider seriously a program of conservation or what might more precisely be called a program for the efficient use of energy.

Conservation: A Moral Imperative

A program of conservation or of more efficient use of our energy resources is an imperative for anyone who seeks to be responsible for life beyond very narrow limits in space and time.

First, fossil fuels, especially oil and gas, are in short supply. There is almost universal agreement that the gas and oil age is over. It makes good sense, then, to save gas and oil for future needs that cannot as yet be met by alternative fuels--for air travel, for example. Finite resources should be used carefully. What we do not use may be made available to other people.

Second, increased efficiency in the use of our present energy resources would lessen the growth in demand and thus postpone or slow down the building of the fission nuclear power plants which are very controversial. This at least provides time for the research and development which will reduce the risk which is said to be involved in the nuclear fission power industry.

Third, a program of energy conservation buys time for the research and development that may provide several alternative sources to replace oil and gas, such as solar, geothermal, wind, solid wastes, nuclear fusion, coal liquefaction and gassification.

Fourth, a program for the more efficient use of energy lessens the amount of pollution in the atmosphere and in the waters, particles, gasses, and heat.

Fifth, a program of energy conservation would reduce the environmental pressures on space, on the use of land for plants and for transmission mechanisms, on the wild life and recreation areas, and on the amount of reclamation required.

Sixth, a program to increase the efficiency in energy use would reduce the demand for energy and thus reduce the pressure for increases in the price of energy.

Seventh, an energy conservation program would give industry, the government, and the people time to consider policies in the public interest in the development of new sources for oil and gas, such as drilling in the Atlantic, and Pacific, sale or leasing of governmental reserves, and the building of new ports for the super tankers.

Eighth, a program for the more efficient use of energy would make us less dependent than otherwise on sources for oil and gas that are outside of the United States.

Ninth, an energy conservation program would reduce the pressure on the capital supply and make it available for use in industries that are more labor intensive. There is no doubt that conservation is a technical possibility.

I accept the conclusions of the report of the Ford Foundation's Energy Policy Project, A Time to Choose that an energy conservation program is possible in which (1) in due time we can save more than 40 per cent of the energy we might otherwise use, (2) in which the growth of the Gross National Product will not be affected significantly, and (3) which for those who introduce efficiency measures will save enough money to pay for the changes.

Conservation: A Political Improbability

Despite what seems to be the desirability of conservation and the technical possibility of conservation without undue cost to the conservers and to the productivity of the nation as a whole, a significant program of conservation does not seem to be very probable. There are many reasons for this.

First, with the exception of the effect of conservation on price, the interest in conservation involves long-range concerns. People, for the most part, are not moved to action by long-range concerns.

Second, to the extent that people might be moved by the long-run interests, a public is involved, a self-conscious group who see their common interest sufficiently clearly and strongly to be moved to action on goals that are clear enough to provide targets. That kind of public is a long way from being developed.

Third, there are powerful forces whose material interests are linked to the growth of energy use and to the growth of the economy which they link to the growth of energy use.

The energy industry is huge; the sales of the top four oil companies in 1973 were 57 billion dollars; these four companies are among the ten largest corporations in the United States. In 1971, the thirty largest companies had sales of 84 billion dollars and net income of 6 billion dollars. The electrical power industry predicts that in the next fifteen years one third of the capital investment in the U.S. will be in the electrical power industry (a total of 650 billion, four times the present investment). According to the Ford Study the officials of the ten oil companies, contributing most, gave Nixon $2,668,425 for the 1972 campaign, 70 per cent of which was given secretly.

If one adds to the production, processing, and distribution units directly involved in energy (in oil, gas, electricity, uranium, the builders of plants, and the equippers of plants) the industries of road construction and maintenance, automobile and truck manufacture and repair, and airplanes, and the suppliers of such industries, it is easy to see why growth in energy consumption has a priority.

Fourth, throughout the whole of our industry and our society economic growth functions both realistically and symbolically to indicate direction and meaning. Growth is identified with the health and fulfillment of human life. Growth functions as a way of dealing with inequalities and the frustrations of injustice. Therefore we look with suspicion upon those who advocate conservation or limited growth. The groups that have been excluded from full participation in the benefits of our society view advocacy of limitation as ideological, as an effort to perpetuate injustice, as protection for the haves at the expense of the have-nots.

Fifth, insofar as public policy and governmental intervention is involved we must recognize a built-in opposition to anything which does not use market mechanisms for arriving at decisions about what should be produced and consumed. At this time there seems to me more suspicion of government than usual. Even the asserted need for conservation is received with great skepticism.

Sixth, the social organization of our way of life requires or involves division of labor, shifting of population, reconstruction of communities, dispersion of families, separation of work and abode, and much travel for work and family relations as well as for transportation of goods. The forms of social organization assume or in part are a result of the existence of cheap energy.

Seventh, the spiritual climate of our times is such that meaning is associated with a way of life involving the use of energy. Having things (which require energy to make) and moving through space both to get places and to experience motion (requiring huge amounts of energy) are important both for instrumental and intrinsic reasons. The intrinsic motivation involves the need to fill a vacuum left by the evaporation of other more personal meaning and the symbolic meaning of things as an indication of success.

Energy Conservation: An Example of Different
Approaches to Energy Issues

While the interest in conservation varies from person to person and from group to group, most of those who are concerned about the energy crisis agree that conservation is to be a part of any future energy program.

There is, to be sure, a position which either by default or by intention focuses upon the provision of more energy. Many of the Advisory Board for The Energy Project of the Ford Foundation felt that the study neglected to emphasize the need for more energy. The study neglected the need for more exploration for oil and gas, for the leasing of more federal lands for the development of energy resources, oil, gas, coal and oil shale, for the relinquishment of policies holding prices down and thus preventing the accumulation of resources for development, for tax policies that did not encourage exploration of new resources, and for the relaxation of extreme precautionary measures involved in the development of nuclear fission power technology. What is needed is more energy and more energy from the resources of the United States. Environmental standards relating to fossil fuel involving pollution and reclamation should be relaxed until we are assured of sources of non-fossil fuels. Energy use will grow. Energy is crucial for the health and welfare of the nations. Everything possible must be done to insure a steady and plentiful supply of energy.

The Ford administration's position supports a program of conservation that uses the market system. A tax on imported oil of $2.00 per barrel is meant to discourage both its importation and use. The removal of controls from the price of old oil and of interstate gas would, in principle at least, lead to some price increases and to some decreases in demand. The argument in Congress is in part over the principle of using the market to influence consumption and in part over a technical matter, that is whether or not the demand for oil is elastic enough so that an increase in price would affect significantly the demand. Some argue that the demand for oil is so inelastic that it will require doubling or tripling of oil prices before consumption will be affected significantly. In the meantime, they argue, the poorer people will suffer significant reductions in real income since they spend a sizeable portion of their income on energy in one form or another. In California preferential rates for big users of gas and electricity have been discontinued. It is not clear how much this will affect energy use. It will, it is predicted, reduce the proportion of the energy bill paid by small users. If the effect of this policy is to reduce the peak load, it could reduce the need for plant, and hence of capital, that stands idle during off peak hours. It is not clear, of course, whether or not small users will respond by increased consumption.

What is clear is that the administration and many persons support a policy in which market mechanisms determine prices. At the same time they want tremendous infusions of government money for research, development, insurance protection, protection against sabotage, and continued provision of services. Billions of dollars from public resources are being poured into the Clinch River Breeder Reactor project. In comparison industry has provided about $500 million.

Another position, that advocated by the Energy Project Report of the Ford Foundation, advocates a vigorous governmental program of intervention. A tax on energy use, gradually increasing to 15 per cent, would provide resources for research and development, for public transportation systems, and for offsetting in other ways the hardships in lower income groups caused by higher prices. Legislation would require new automobiles to get a gradually increasing number of miles per gallon of gasoline, provide standards and incentives for the insulation of buildings, and encourage the development and installation of much more energy-efficient industrial technology. The magnitude of the program is suggested by the intention to reduce normal energy consumption at normal growth rates by 40 per cent by the year 2000. Such a governmental intervention would not only support conservation but would support the development of alternatives to fossil fuels and nuclear fission power.

There is another approach to the energy crisis, an approach which focuses upon our values, upon the meaning of life. This might be said to be the religious way of asking about the energy crisis. We begin by asking why we use so much energy.

First, we use so much energy because we live under the domination of an artificial necessity. The realm of necessity is the realm of the goods and services needed in order to sustain life. We live in a society in which the realm of necessity has been expanded until it is all out of proportion to our needs. The things and services that we think we need are so much a part of us, Herbert Marcuse contends, that they function almost like biological needs. We are so conditioned by our experiences in childhood that we think almost everything that is offered to us by our culture is necessary in order to be human.

The multiplication of things and of services creates expectations that drive us in all that we do. We live under this domination of artificial necessity. This domination is our chief problem. The first way to deal with the energy crisis or with most of our problems is to become free from the domination of artificial necessity. There is no limit to the possessions and services we seem to seek in order to be human. We use so much energy because we have allowed or have been enticed into allowing the realm of necessity to be expanded.

The second reason we use so much energy can be found in our preference for the new. We think that the new is better than the old. We live under the domination of the new. This is part of a cultural system. The new is not something we choose. The whole culture functions to emphasize the new. Our universities, for example, emphasize new knowledge almost regardless of the meaning of the new for the student or for anyone else. It is the same with regard to clothes and cars. The only people who have the strength to choose old clothes or cars and to keep them for a long time are the old line aristocratic families. Everyone else seeks the new in order to achieve the status he or she wishes to have.

The issue is not simply that the new is destructive and the old constructive. The issue lies in the role the new plays because it is new, regardless of whether or not it really is useful. The question here is like the question in the realm of necessity. What is the role of the new or of the necessary? What is the meaning attached to what we seek?

The third reason we use so much energy involves the notion of self-creation. We must be the creators. We sometimes dress this up and call ourselves co-creators. As over against using organic materials which participate in a natural cycle, in a natural rhythm, we create synthetic materials which cannot be absorbed back into nature. There seems to be an over-evaluation of our capacity to create an approach to life in which we are in control. Nature seems to be saying no to some of our self-creation. The environment cannot absorb the results of our creation. What is involved in this situation is the question of boundaries or limits. When we use the term co-creation we could mean that we are creating within the limits of a creator, or a given, of some boundaries, of some parameters, within which one has to function.

These three aspects of our lives, the domination of artificial necessity, of the new, and of self-creation are in part responsible for our large consumption of energy. They involve broad aspects of the meaning structure of our lives. But there are a number of supporting factors. One of these is the notion of freedom as self-initiation. This involves the freedom of the self to initiate. We think that if we initiate there is something good involved. This is set over against a notion of freedom in which the issue is more what is initiated than whether or not the self or another person initiates. In this second view of freedom it is important to initiate in relation to a whole, or the public interest, or destiny. In relation to the regulation of the number of miles a car will travel on a gallon of gasoline many will argue that we should be free to drive a gas guzzler if we are willing to pay for the gasoline. We should be free to choose.

We also invoke the notion of equality to justify producing more and using more energy. We do not really want to subject ourselves to the principle of equality if 800 million Chinese and 600 million Indians have to be taken into account. But the principle of equality functions within our own social system in such a way that we advocate equality regarding whatever there is to be had. By advocating equality and thinking that we are thereby moral we can avoid the question of the content of our lives or the substance of our culture.

The principle of equality of results provides a much more useful way to think about equality than does the principle of equality of opportunity, but in either case one avoids thinking about the content of equality.

Another aspect of our lives that results in high energy demand is the focus on the individual. It is related to the notion of freedom as self-initiation. The emphasis is upon the individual. This results in the atomization of life. Even the nuclear family is not the most significant unit. It is the individual who moves in and out of relations almost at will. But the family illustrates the movement in the direction of individualization. Every family has all its own gadgets. There are many experiments to move in the direction of community or of participation. The Kibbutz in Israel represents a significant move toward community. China is engaged in an experiment in which the community is the focus. We live, however, under the tyranny of the individual, as if the individual is the only real focus, the primary unit.

The question is whether or not there is not another way of thinking about life. The Pauline image of the body suggests an organic metaphor for looking at our relations to each other.

We use so much energy in part because we hold in principle the notion that the social or the economic realm is independent. Our doctrine of freedom as self-initiation has, I believe, led to the development of tremendous economic forces which in the name of initiation of whatever pleases them, developed control over huge segments of life, if not over most of the opportunities in life. I have already indicated what this means in describing the interrelated character of those who are interested in energy. By emphasizing self-initiation, we, in fact, allow for all kinds of limitations to be developed. Institutions with tremendous power develop without responsibility to the community as a whole. It is assumed that the interaction of self-initiations will lead to what is good for everyone or to what is the best that is possible for everyone.

We also live under the tyranny of technology. We do what we can do. Almost without exception if we have the technology we use it. We go to the moon if we can go to the moon. Here as in every other situation the problems lie in the one-sidedness with which we allow a principle to direct our living. Technology, some claim is a way of being. It is not neutral. It involves a way of thinking and acting in which we attempt to order things in such a way that they are at our disposal.

It is only a step from controlling things in order to use them to a way of thinking and acting in which everything is considered instrumentally. Human relations become a matter of calculation and manipulation. The present is always viewed as a step toward the future, as an instrument which serves a goal that can only be realized in the future. Thus the instrumental orientation leads to a tyranny of the future. We are unable to be present for anyone because we always have one eye toward the future. It is very much like the minister shaking hands at the door of a church after the service. The minister is shaking your hand and already his eyes are shifting to the next person.

The domination of a science which provides the knowledge to develop the technology supports the tyranny of technology and of the future. In science, following Theodore Roszak in Where the Wasteland Ends, the real in the world is what is open for experiment. What is sought and what is the object for experiment is what leads to further research. Even in religion one finds the domination of science. The emphasis is upon learning about religion. The problems of deciding what one believes are so great that it is much easier to organize an educational system on the basis of learning about religion, involving what other people believe rather than what one believes personally.

Then we have the domination of the technocrats. Robert McNamara as the Secretary of Defense represented this development. David Halberstam's story of Vietnam illustrates the way in which "the best and the brightest" failed

to provide constructive leadership. Ivan Illich suggests that we move toward
a society in which tools and other institutions are small enough so that we
can know about them and affect what happens. What we have done is to build
a society which we cannot understand or control. We are forced to turn over
technical decisions to those who have some special competence. Jürgen
Habermas comes to the same conclusion.[6] If we have to intervene in the
society, in theory operating on the basis of the interaction of freely moving
parts, we have to turn over the actual government to those who have enough
knowledge to legitimize them or at least have the possibility of knowing and
predicting the results from different courses of action. Then we, the people,
become clients. We can understand this relationship by analogy to our relation with our doctors. We are in their hands. They tell us what is wrong
in words we cannot understand and tell us that they can take care of the
problem by surgery on such and such a date; and on that date we cannot
watch the operation, even if we are able. We put our lives in their hands.
Just as we turn our health over to a doctor or to doctors (the specialists)
and their gadgets, we turn our politics and economics over to the technocrats.

     One significant way to look at what is happening to us that seems
related to our use of so much energy is to use the familiar distinction between achievement and ascription. We get status in our culture by having
more and by having the new, by producing and by controlling the more and
the new. This is to be placed over against the status that is given to us because we are. It is status of achievement versus status by ascription. This
distinction is frequently said to represent a modern versus a primitive motivational pattern. The more I think about these problems the less I think of
status by ascription as primitive, and the more I think that the acceptance
of the given or of the ascribed represents a very real and meaningful part
of the human--at least as over against the almost complete movement in
the direction of status by achievement. In part we use primitive and modern
as evaluative terms because we think the new is better; we think that there
is an evolutionary development toward the better; we think that history moves
forward with progress.

     Theologically, ascription corresponds to creation or to grace, the
action of another, and achievement corresponds to works, to one's own action.
Grace implies reception, advent, the coming to one of something or someone.
Works imply shaping or making, the control of or over, the going out to something or someone. Grace implies a gift, works a task. Grace implies being,
works implies will and constructing.

     This situation produces a schizophrenia for us. On the one hand
our faith suggests that we participate in faith in something that has happened.
If we participate in that happening symbolically our other problems are
solved. On the other hand our culture involves a faith in which we find
meaning only by producing, consuming, and possessing.

In each case what is at issue involves an ambiguity. It is not a
matter of either/or. It is a matter of both/and, and since we have made
it a question of either/or we must come down now on what seems to be a
one-sided emphasis--that is, in order to help a balance come into existence.
Thus it is not a matter of grace alone or of works alone. But today it is
chiefly a matter of grace. Viewed from this perspective the issue of conservation is a religious issue. It involves the meaning structure of our
lives. We will conserve in a meaningful way only where we find anew the
way to hold grace and works together.

Technical, Economic, Political, Moral, and Religious Issues

On the basis of what has been developed thus far I will now first
lift out a number of different types of issues that have emerged and then
indicate how they are related and dealt with somewhat differently depending
on where the emphasis is placed. There are technical, economic, political,
moral, and religious issues involved in thinking about how to respond to the
energy situation.

Technical issues abound! Are nuclear fission reactors' safety
risks "very low compared to other natural and man-made risks" as is
claimed by the Rasmussen report to the nuclear Regulator Commission? [7]
How does one store nuclear reactor wastes with minimum risks? How are
sabotage and theft to be prevented? How can solar energy be harnessed
efficiently? How can the mining of coal be made less dangerous? How can
we use coal to produce oil and gas efficiently? How can uranium tailings
be prevented from polluting? How can we use heavy water in a nuclear
fusion process to produce energy? How do we harness the wind, the tides,
the waves, and the thermal gradients in the waters, to produce energy?
How do we use oil shale, tar sands, hot rocks, steam and hot water from
underground, organic wastes, and crops as energy sources? How do we
use uranium and thorium from ore and water for energy? How do we develop
a fission process that generates more fuel than it uses (the breeder reactor)?
How do we store and transport energy safely? Can we use liquid hydrogen
as the vehicle for storage and transmission? How do we prevent pollution
of water and air with gasses, particles, and heat?

These and many other questions involve technical answers, answers
that are for the most part independent in the first place of other types of
decisions. Whether or not we use our resources to attempt to answer these
technical questions, of course, depends on economic, political, moral, and
religious decisions. Thus those who claim that money should be spent for
the development of solar energy rather than for the Breeder Reactor claim
that there is a moral issue involved. [8] The risks, they claim, of nuclear
fission power, are unnecessary risks to the lives of many people. Those

who push for the development of the breeder reactor see the issue chiefly as economic and political. They see no other substitute for oil and gas. They view excessive use of coal as more dangerous than the use of nuclear power. How else then are we to keep the economy growing and remain relatively independent of OPEC country sources of oil?

The economic issues loom large, because much of the popular widsom links economic growth with the growth in energy use. The electrical power industry forecasts that it will need $650 billion in capital in the next fifteen years. That will be one-third of all capital being invested each year by 1985. Comparatively the electrical power industry does not use much labor. For every dollar of sales $4.18 must be invested in electric power, $2.13 in gas, $1.15 in oil, $0.86 in steel, and $0.57 in automobiles. The economic meaning of such investment in an industry of such low demand for labor is something to be considered. The balance of payments deficit in foreign trade that is caused by the change in the cost of oil from $3.50 a barrel to $13.50/bbl. creates an economic problem. In August, 1975, we imported 4.6 million barrels of oil each day. The increased cost was thus about 46 million dollars per day, or about 16.8 billion dollars per year. The effect of the OPEC (Organization of Petroleum Exporting Countries) control of prices and production plays havoc with any conception of a free market. Many claim that the artificial price in the world market makes it impossible to operate on a free market system here. Hence they advocate a continuance of price controls on oil from oil wells that had been producing profitably before the OPEC policies caused the price to rise so drastically. It is also claimed that the oil companies are so interlocked with joint ventures in exploratory drilling and in pipe line operations that there is no way to secure real competition. The debate in Congress over conservation measures centers on the same issue; are market mechanisms or governmental controls the best means to secure more efficient utilization of energy and reduced utilization of energy?

A variety of economic issues are involved, some of which soon include political and moral issues. The dependence economically upon Arab oil has led to a weakening of the political power of the United States in the Mid-East. Hence any policy proposed to lessen that dependence or any policy advocated that continues that dependence economically has important political implications. If, in one way or another the economic must be subordinated to the political, the size and power of the energy industry, as I have already indicated, makes this a difficult task.

There are many political issues involved in the energy situation. The sale of nuclear know-how to other nations is in part a political decision. The leasing of public lands for development is a political issue. How much should be charged? To whom do the resources belong? Some would claim a moral issue is involved. How are the societal costs of development to be met? Who decides to tear up a countryside and to introduce into an area the

changes accompanying rapid economic development? What rights do the
people living there have? How is a decision made to turn over to a particular corporation technological processes for which the people through their
government have spent billions of dollars? A recent article points to the
turn-over of uranium processing technology to a group headed by former
aids of President Nixon. Who decides how much money is spent for what
in research and development? For what seem like obvious reasons private
industry has not chosen to develop many of the crucial resources in the
energy field. How much of the costs of development should those who in the
end profit from the development bear? And who decides who profits in
legitimate ways?

Many of these political issues become moral issues. They also
involve economic and technical matters. We have frequently referred to the
morality of producing energy in ways that destroy the economic and aesthetic
utility of millions of acres of land and result in pollution. These costs could
be passed on to the producers and the users of energy instead of being born
by the federal or state governments or not being taken care of at all. We
have also seen that the morality of energy consumption that pollutes and
threatens life now or in the future is questioned at many points. The use
of scarce resources, the wasteful use of scarce resources, the dispropor-
tionate share of resources used by the United States--all present moral
issues.

The moral issue, of course, immediately becomes related to the
political and the economic. How, without considerable political intervention,
will the moral issues be taken seriously? How does the political intervention protect the small people whose powers are very limited compared to
those of the economic forces interested primarily in growth? And how even
with political interventions do the future generations get a significant vote?
What interests guard the future?

And thus finally we come to the religious issue, an issue which
penetrates all the others. What is the meaning of our lives together which
sets the goals and determines the way in which we together meet challenges
whether they be of a technical, economic, political, or moral nature? I
have already developed the issue in connection with the discussion of different
approaches to energy conservation. There I suggested some fundamental
notions which provide the meaning structure of our lives. The overarching
issue involved the polarity of reception and making, or of grace and works.
Here I want to return to the same notions but to relate them to the American
faith and its central symbols.

A Reassessment of the American Faith

In conclusion, I will indicate the two major issues that have emerged from the immersion in energy affairs, issues that go beyond technical matters, issues that are rooted in the underlying American creed, in our faith, in our informing and directing symbols. The first issue stems from the fact that the free market, the mechanism which we have relied on to deal with economic matters, is less useful than we thought in handling energy problems. The symbol of freedom as self-initiation has shown itself to be inadequate, to need reconception, and to require more supplementation than we have considered.

Secondly, when we appeal to the other-symbols in the American creed, "equality, " "fraternity" or community and "nation under God, " we find the values that give these symbols content, "growth, " "nation, " technological development, G. N. P. and manifest destiny are inadequate.

First, then, the free market mechanism which appeals to the principle of freedom as self-initiation to bring about a fulfilling harmony, seems to be less useful than we have counted upon it to be. Freedom as self-initiation is the basic informing symbol of the American way of life. Individuals and corporate entities regulate each other. If no one has too much power to initiate, or if everyone has a more or less equal chance to initiate, what is generally best for everyone emerges. We have counted upon the market to bring about the goods without our having to plan and to control and to make hard decisions about the good for all.

How, it is being asked, do we protect the atmosphere, the rivers and lakes, and the oceans from pollution since they belong to no one in particular and thus are not protected by the assertion of the interests of those for whom they represent an extension of themselves? How do we assign costs to consumers for the results of production which do not enter directly into the exchange process? How do future generations make their demands effective in determining prices, and hence production and consumption levels? What kinds of interventions of governments in systems of freedom are allowable or practical without so affecting the market mechanism that the appeal to the market mechanism is questionable? For example, how does a natural free-market mechanism operate in the face of a world system in which more and more of supply and of the prices are controlled by nations or by organizations of nations, a system in which prices are artificially determined and supplies controlled by non-market mechanisms? How are national interests to be protected when huge multi-national corporations make economic decisions without being responsible for the political ramifications (e. g., the Arab's program of securing support from U. S. corporations for anti-Israeli policies in return for economic benefits)? How is it possible to use the market mechanism to secure conservation of energy without causing severe hardships for the poorer people? In a society that

has developed its patterns of life on the basis of cheap energy, how can we
rapidly increase the price of energy in order to affect its use and protect
national interests without seriously affecting the standard of living of those
who spend a fairly high percentage of their incomes for energy? By proposing taxes on energy in order to reduce its use, existing inequalities in
the standard of living are increased. The fact that those who are sensitive
to this issue insist that the government impose a tax and use the tax money
to offset the resulting hardships reflects the failure of the market mechanism to deal fairly with the rapid shift in allocations required by the situation.

The underlying issue is the conception of freedom to which appeal
is made to support the institution of the free market. Freedom as self-
initiation emphasizes the right of the individual to initiate action, to do what
he pleases within the context of a broad framework of general limitations.
These limitations are not meant to direct choices, they are meant only to
restrict choices which directly infringe on the self-initiation rights of others.
Government in this way of thinking is minimal. It is not responsible for the
content or direction of life either by rewarding some and punishing others
or by educating or socializing persons. Both government and education are
in theory neutral. They provide the conditions for individuals to direct or
to express themselves. What is excluded from this view of freedom is a
conception of freedom as an internal ordering of one's personality and the
opportunity to participate in a meaningful way of life. Such a way of life
involves freedom from internal compulsions and freedom for participations
that are given by the common life.

Where freedom is self-initiation, rights are emphasized and freedom
is understood as freedom from interference, or as external freedom. This
kind of freedom for the individual is limited by appeal to the principle of
equality. In the beginning equality meant equality of opportunity. Each
person was to have a roughly equal opportunity to initiate activity. One city-
planner in Chicago stated that the only principle city planners could use was
the "maximization of self-initiations." How one person's initiation is to be
equated with another person's initiation in order to judge maximization is
not clear, but what is clear is that one can make some assessments about
whether or not persons are given an equal opportunity to take advantage of
or to initiate in relation to a range of activities including education, transportation, the courts, housing, employment, entrepreneurship, marriage,
and other such opportunities or services. It is clear from the history of the
United States that freedom for such initiations was often very limited and
that much progress has been made in extending freedom as self-initiation,
at least formally. I use the term formally to indicate that real questions
have been raised about the meaning of equality as opportunity. What does
it mean to invoke the principle of equality of opportunity for black persons
who have been denied equal opportunities in the past? What does it mean to
appeal to equality of opportunity in education, for example, when some persons

are raised in situations of economic and cultural privilege and others are
raised in deprivation?

    The principle of equality of results has been invoked to establish
another starting place, another way to think about what justice involves.
From this point of view equality means looking at what has happened and
calculating what would be necessary to equalize results, to offset inequalities
of opportunities in the past. The appeal to freedom as self-initiation is supplemented by an appeal to freedom from internal forces that restrict and to
freedom for participation.

    Intertwined with the principle of equality is frequently the principle
of fraternity or of sorority or of community. The appeal to equality of self-
initiation may be based upon the notion that the interaction of self-initiations
results in a kind of harmony. But the appeal may also be based upon an
identification with those who are included in the community of equality.
Thus those who advocate price controls and allocation systems in the face
of rising prices and shortages and the need for conservation appeal to something beyond equality of opportunity or equal access. They think of the
result of the higher prices on families and wish to equalize hardships.

    The principle of equality in one way or another raises a question
about the limits of the community to be included, both in space and time.
Which persons in which countries of which generations are to be considered
in thinking about equality of results? What responsibility do we or the Arabs
have for preserving for future generations some access to oil? What responsibilities does one nation have for the billions of people other nations may
have in some not-too-distant future? What happens to our energy policy and
practice if we begin to doubt that the interaction of self-initiation will lead
toward harmony and toward a rough equality?

    When we begin to think about the meaning of equality of results in
the present human community, we draw back from the principles. If we,
in the United States use 6 billion barrels of oil per year for 6 per cent of
the world's population, world consumption equalized on our consumption
rate would be one hundred billion barrels per year. We know that it is not
very realistic to place this hypothetical 100 billion barrel consumption
figure in the context of estimated world reserves of 700-1000 billion barrels.
The possibility of economic development that would result in such high consumption is said to be problematic; and yet in some countries rapid economic
development has taken place. The possibility of the discovery of new resources creates a problematic in the area of production. Some predict that
China will discover resources that will rival those of the Middle East.
Nevertheless, conjectures about the meaning of equality in oil consumption
in the light of proven resources disclose a situation in which the principle
of equality appears to have a very limited meaning. We are not really
serious in our advocacy of equality as a guiding principle. We limit the
community in which the principle is to be a guide.

What is brought into question by our notion of equality is related to the notion of "this nation under God, " the notion of our manifest destiny, and the notion that by pursuing our own goals in a new setting free from relations to the rest of the world, in principle, we were setting the pattern for the rest of the world. It becomes clearer and clearer as we face issues like that of energy that we are bound to the rest of the world, that our pattern of life, especially as we consider energy use, is not a model for the rest of the world, and, therefore, that our vocation to be an example of freedom and humanity is empty or over. What we represent does not provide a viable pattern for humanity. If we take seriously our belonging to the community of mankind we are alienated from it. We can be what we are only if we try to isolate ourselves from any real equality and community, only if our God becomes very particular, a God of a particular people.

However, insofar as we do take seriously the imperative to make available to all persons what is available to us, whether as equality of opportunity or as equality of results, we find ourselves facing limits. Unlimited growth, when growth involves finite resources or finite capacities to absorb wastes, becomes a questionable principle. The more we press toward equality of results the more limits provided by nature, by the inorganic and organic dimensions of life, seem to be saying no to our way of life, to the use of undifferentiated growth as a standard. By implication our use of the human community (fraternity, sorority, community) as a principle is brought into question. New attitudes toward nature are called for, attitudes which suggest the need for something beyond an instrumental view of nature and a view of the human as having infinite capacities for change.

What this means broadly speaking is a recognition of the limits of freedom as self-initiation and a search for origins or givens which establish limits or foundations, which one disregards at peril of destruction and meaninglessness. Or to state it more positively, what is involved is the notion of creation as over against self-creation, of the integral as over against the instrumental, of the given as over against the demanded, of the unity of life as over against its isolated parts, of authority as over against rights, of ascription as over against achievement, of the transcendent as over against the immanent, of the enduring as over against the changeable, of receiving as over against shaping, of equality regarding what is significant as over against equality regarding whatever happens to be available, of freedom as self-perfection as over against freedom as self-initiation, and of being as over against becoming. But, of course, as has been evident all along, I am not suggesting an either/or regarding any of these polarities. However, in the face of what appears to be an overemphasis in one direction, I am suggesting a balancing emphasis. At the same time something more than balancing is involved. This something more is the more that expresses itself through or in the emerging structures, the emerging structures of given and demanded, of whole and part, of community of life and the individual, of reception and shaping, of self-perfection and self-initiation, of authority and rights, of the enduring and the changeable, and of creation and self-creation. This something more is what the symbol "under God" has meant in our national heritage. This something more is what is meant by the "holy" or the "sacred." It is what is designated by such symbolic concepts as "grace," "transcendence," "unconditional," "being," and "ultimate meaning." The foundation for a human future, then, lies in the recognition that the symbols that give meaning and direction to American life have to be reappropriated and reconceived. In this essay I have sought to examine energy issues in the light of some questions that I have about our dominant meaning structure and of what I consider the functioning meaning of symbols such as freedom, equality, fraternity, or community, and "under God." I have indicated some questions about the ability of the symbols as now understood to deal with the issues emerging in relation to energy. I have suggested some new meanings that might be emphasized over against the old, in the first place, and be related to the old meaning, in the second place.

What remains to be done, in order to indicate the full religious significance of what has been attempted, is to consider more carefully the emerging meanings and their relation to historic religious traditions, especially but not exclusively the religious traditions of the West.[9] It may well be that what has emerged in the West requires some supplementation by what has emerged in non-Western traditions. But we would travel far in the direction we need to go, I believe, by a serious effort to restore our relation to our origins in the Judeo-Christian tradition. This requires, I think, special attention to the roots of the Christian faith in Old Testament history and prophecy. It involves a reappropriation of the meaning of prophetic expectation in which the historical and the eschatological, the given and the demanded are bound together in a life-fulfilling unity. It is to act with decision and risk in the midst of a transcending action or movement in history.[10]

NOTES AND REFERENCES

[1] The annual consumption of oil in the United States in 1974 was about 6 billion barrels and about 25 billion cubic feet of gas. Estimates of the amount of oil that will be available vary from 150 to 600 billion barrels. If growth in the use of oil takes place at the past 6 per cent rate, we will be using 24 billion barrels a year in 1998 and 48 billion barrels by 2010; if the rate of growth slows to 4 per cent we would be using 24 billion barrels a year by 2010. Even 600 billion barrels does not seem like very much if we

are using 48 billion barrels each year. The annual consumption of gas in
the United States in 1972 was about 25 trillion cubic feet. At a 6 per cent
rate growth consumption in 1984 would be 50 trillion cubic feet, 100 trillion
cubic feet in 1998, and 200 trillion cubic feet by 2010. At a 4 per cent
rate of growth in use consumption would be 100 trillion cubic feet by 2010.
The estimates of reserves proven and recoverable eventually vary from
about 400 to 2500 trillion cubic feet. If we think of consumption growing at
the rate of 6 per cent and consider the outside estimates of resources we
are thinking about, we do not have many years of supply. From 1975-1986
we would use 750 trillion cubic feet, from 1987-1998 we would need 1800
trillion cubic feet. At a growth rate of 4 per cent we would use 2250 trillion
cubic feet in 36 years; at 2 per cent growth we would use about 510 trillion
cubic feet in 17 years. That represents almost all of the reserves that are
proven.

[2]See S.S. Penner and L. Icerman, Energy, Vol. I., pp. 313ff.
Addison-Wesley, Reading, Mass. 1974. Some indication of the extent of
the societal costs can be obtained from the Penner and Icerman estimates:
For the 8 million acres of undermined land in the Appalachian region about
395 million dollars had been spent by mid-1970; estimates vary from five
cents to two dollars a ton to neutralize the acid and to seal off the mines.
Costs of drainage channels are estimated from $300 to $3000 per acre.
Pennsylvania spent 60 million dollars in 1960 for mine-fire control. Costs
for reclamation of strip-mined lands run as high as $1500 an acre. The
total damage to Appalachia has been placed at 2.8 billion dollars; from
state and federal governments about 1 billion dollars per year will be required for death and disability benefits for 600,000 miners.

[3]David Comey, "The Legacy of Uranium Tailings, " Bulletin of
Atomic Scientists, September, 1975, pp. 43-5.

[4]Fred H. Schmidt and David Bodansky, The Energy Controversy:
The Role of Nuclear Power, Seattle, University of Washington, 1975, pp.
69-70.

[5]Allen Hammond, William Metz, Thomas Maugh II, Energy and
the Future, American Association for the advancement of Science,
Washington, D.C., 1973, p. 48.

[6]Jürgen Habermas, "Technology and Science as Ideology" in Toward
a Rational Society, Boston: Beacon, 1970.

[7]See News Releases of U.S. Nuclear Regulatory Commission,
Vol. I, No. 39, November 4, 1975.

[8]In 1974 Research and Development Funds were $644.1 million for
nuclear fission and $45.2 million for "solar, geothermal and others." The
budget for 1975 is $761.8 million for fission and $102 million for "solar,
geothermal, and others."

[9]Joseph Sittler does this in Nature and Grace, Philadelphia:
Fortress, 1972.

[10]Cf. my essay, "Racism and the Creative Recovery of American Religious Tradition," Anglican Theological Review, in July, 1973, Supplementary Series No. 1.

Part Two

CHRISTIANITY AND AMERICAN VALUES

CHAPTER IV

VALUES, TECHNOLOGY AND THE AMERICAN FUTURE:
A Comparative Analysis of Robert Heilbroner and Daniel Bell

by
Robert Benne

Robert Heilbroner and Daniel Bell are both concerned with values, technology, and the American future. One can almost construct a formula that, in a highly simplistic manner, applies to both: values + technology = future. Each identifies certain values that are, according to his perspective, the predominant values that shape our society. These values are wedded to the magnifying powers unleashed by technology. (Both see technology as instrumental, having no substantive life or direction of its own.) The effects of the wedding of our specific values to our technology constitute the future in which we will all share. Of course, the dynamics of this formula do not take place in a vacuum. They take place within the context of a natural and social environment. This context provides the limits in which the formula is played out. Resource and atmospheric limitations are key variables which set the parameters to the kind of future our values and technology can produce. But, again, there is little agreement about the precise nature and extent of environmental limits or about when they will be reached.

When we look at the specific content put into the formula by the two authors, we begin to get interesting divergences. In Heilbroner's An Inquiry Into The Human Prospect, [1] the values of "the industrial ethos" combine with an accelerating technological development to push us ever closer to the absolute limits of the environment. When the limits are reached a radical foreclosure of the future will occur. That is, if we're lucky. If things go as well as possible under the circumstances, we will be given a "contingent life sentence" rather than an outright death sentence. [2] (Another commentator on the future, Victor Ferkiss, shares the same kind of analysis of the problem as Heilbroner, but believes we can positively transform the future if we adopt a new political philosophy. [3])

Eschewing forecasts of radical downturns or upturns, Daniel Bell presents a more complicated picture of values, technology, and the future. [4] We will examine the details of his argument later. For the moment, let it suffice to say that Bell's analysis places the values of "economizing" in tandem with a developing technology that is moving us beyond the industrial age to a post-industrial society based on services rather than manufactured

95

goods. The contours of the new society bring fresh problems to the political sphere and sharp challenges to the new society's culture, which is un-
prepared for the rigors ahead. Bell sees a future of turbulent struggle,
but one in which continuities will outweigh any radical discontinuities. The
future weal is certainly not guaranteed, but it will be possible to meet the
challenges of the economy and polity. In the long run, the more serious
crisis inheres in the cultural sphere.

     In the following pages we describe and analyze the main arguments
of the two selected authors, attending to the authors' own orientations and
presuppositions, and inquiring into why and how they shape their conclusions.

                                    I

     Robert Heilbroner, Professor of Economics at the New School for
Social Research, provoked widespread discussion of his short Inquiry when
it appeared. While it is one of many recent books anticipating impending
doom, it had greater impact not only because of the long-respected reputa-
tion of its author but also because it represented a radical shift in the
author's thinking. Up until the appearance of this short book Heilbroner
had been moderately optimistic about the human prospect. Basing his
opinion on solid research and wide knowledge, Heilbroner had consistently
held out at least modest hopes for the future of American capitalism and
indeed for the whole industrial world. But all of the sudden he turned about
to pronounce doom on the whole project. It is such a dramatic reversal that
it caught many readers' attention. Moreover, almost all his conclusions
about the future shape of world society go counter to his own preferences
and hopes. This conflict also lends more credibility to his dramatic reversal.

     Heilbroner begins his reflections with the question: "Is there hope
for man?"[5] He answers his question by reflecting on the growing pessimism
about the future. Assuming there indeed is a widespread "oppressive anticipation" of the future, Heilbroner lists some of the causes: "topical" --
widespread violence and barbarism erupting through the veneer of civilization,
the failure to pass on values to the next generation; "attitudinal" -- the loss
of assurance about our ability to shape and control history, the lowering of
the quality of life caused by environmental damage resulting from economic
growth; and "civilizational" -- "the inability of a civilization directed to
material improvement . . . to satisfy the human spirit."[6]

     If the foregoing are the internal causes of our malaise about the
future, each item has a correlate in the external challenges that confront us.
The external challenges are four. First, there is the threat of uncontrolled
population growth. While the industrialized world will grow modestly to
1.4 or at the most to 1.7 billion in the next century, the underdeveloped

world, which today totals around 2.5 billion, will have to support something like 40 billion if the present growth rates continue.[7] Even if those
rates are checked by intentional intervention or grinding Malthusian restraints, there is no way, Heilbroner argues, we can avoid widespread
famine, urban disorganization, and strong-arm military governments in
the underdeveloped world.[8]

A second external challenge is war, not the conventional world
war between superpowers, but more likely nuclear terrorism and blackmail by underdeveloped nations against the wealthy and developed. These
"wars of redistribution" will be waged to extract concessions from the great
nations and will thereby necessitate on their part a strong military posture.
Further, they will have to use "bully-boy" tactics to force necessary resources from recalcitrant producer countries.[10]

While these two external challenges will tend to create authoritarian political regimes everywhere and will increase the drift toward nationalism, they are not the most threatening. The third challenge -- the
environmental -- is the most crucial and will force the most radical changes
in the world's future. (This external crisis correlates with the internal
experience of diminution in quality of life.) Heilbroner sees the raw materials resource squeeze as serious, but he believes we can overcome that
by discovery of new sources as well as better utilization of older sources
that were heretofore not feasible for extraction.[11] Rather, the decisive
constraint will be the absolute limits of the ecosphere for the absorption
of heat.[12] Heat emission from industrial production will increase because
underdeveloped countries will try to push their industrial growth upward in
order to ward off poverty. This certain challenge leads the author to the
following conclusion:

> The industrial growth process, so central to the economic and
> social life of capitalism and Western socialism alike, will be
> forced to slow down, in all likelihood within a generation or two,
> and will probably have to give way to decline thereafter. . . .
> The long era of industrial expansion is now entering its final stages,
> and we must anticipate the commencement of a new era of stationary
> total output and . . . declining material output per head in the ad-
> vanced nations.[13]

Heilbroner's belief in this environmental constraint is the linchpin
of his whole argument. The internal malaise and the other external challenges could be coped with given our present political, economic, and cultural apparatus. But the environmental challenge throws into question our
values and our economic and political traditions. It will provoke convulsive
changes, which we will examine somewhat later.

A final challenge, very important to our considerations in this paper, is not so much an "independent threat as an unmentioned challenge that lies behind and within all of the particular dangers we have singled out for examination. This is the presence of science and technology as the driving forces of our age."[14] The first three external threats have arisen only because scientific technology has been developed in a lopsided manner. Scientific technology could be used to mitigate and avoid such threats, but in fact it has not been used for those purposes. In this civilization, science and technology have been so fused to the values of the industrial ethos that no facile separation of the two is possible. Science and technology, having been harnessed to the values of the industrial ethos, are indeed part of the problem instead of part of the solution.[15]

Having elaborated the contours of the crisis, Heilbroner moves to an analysis of the capacities of socioeconomic systems for response. The discussion revolves naturally around the comparative capacities of capitalism and industrial socialism. While neither Soviet Russia nor the USA are pure types of either socialism or capitalism, they are the major objects of his analysis. Neither system, Heilbroner asserts, has been as bad as its detractors have believed nor as good as its proponents had hoped. And now both are challenged to their core by the emerging external realities already discussed. The challenge is so deep precisely because both systems are based on the values of industrial civilization. It is these values that are on a direct collision course with environmental limits. Neither capitalism nor socialism can avoid the collision because their underlying values are the same.

> For industrial civilization achieves its economic success by imposing common values on both its capitalist and socialist variants. There is the value of self-evident importance of efficiency, with its tendency to subordinate optimum human scale of things to optimum technical scale. There is the value of the need to "tame" the environment, with its consequence of an unthinking pillage of nature. There is the value of the priority of production itself, visible in the care both systems lavish on technical virtuosity and the indifference with which both look upon the aesthetic aspects of life. All these values manifest themselves throughout bourgeois and "socialist" styles of life, both lived by the clock, organized by the factory or office, obsessed with material achievements, attuned to highly quantitative modes of thought--in a word, by styles of life that, in contrast with non-industrial civilizations, seem dazzlingly rich in every dimension except that of the cultivation of the human person.[16]

In short, the values held commonly by both systems and given muscle by an expanding scientific technology are in the process of precipitating a crisis of worldwide proportions. When environmental limits are reached, drastic revisions will occur. Industrial socialism may have some short run advantages over capitalism as the no-growth point is reached. Its already centralized political power will be able to keep order and distribute declining goods more decisively and firmly. But the necessities of dismantling the whole apparatus of production and changing the expectations of the people will produce just as much shock and despair in industrial socialist countries as in capitalist.[17]

Capitalism will move gradually toward a managed state capitalism so that a stationary economy can be achieved. It will have to force income redistribution or use strong measures to squelch civil unrest. Economically, it will pump more money and effort into the service sector. It will allocate shares of the market to private corporations who will then operate under traditional economic logic. In short, Heilbroner believes a stationary capitalism is a possibility. But it will look remarkably similar to industrial socialism.[18]

Politically, Heilbroner believes that representative democracy will not be able to handle the stringent necessities generated by the movement toward stationary capitalism. A stronger, more authoritarian political system will emerge, though it may be able to provide certain civil liberties.[19] In a following section on "human nature," the author argues that there are also internal tendencies within humankind that will reinforce the movement toward authoritarianism and nationalism. Following a basically Freudian argument, Heilbroner believes that in the face of extreme crisis people will turn to father-figures and will identify with traditional tribal loyalties, i.e., the nation. Crisis pushes people back to elemental responses they learned as dependent children in a family context. The crisis we will reach will assuredly press people toward these kinds of responses. Thus, the external pressures toward authoritarianism and nationalism are matched by internal tendencies in human nature toward the same responses.[20]

Cultural life on the other side of the great change will be sharply different. Intellectual dissent will be a luxury that authoritarian regimes will not tolerate; they will need all the unanimity they can amass as they tackle the hard economic and political tasks ahead. Science and technology -- identified as they have been with the problems of economic growth -- will wane in importance. The uncongenial life-styles of industrial civilization will be abandoned. Frugality will be a prized trait. Heat-generating production will be regarded as a necessary evil rather than a social triumph. The work ethic may disappear with the need for expanded production.

It is therefore possible that a post-industrial society would also turn in the direction of many pre-industrial societies--toward the exploration of inner states of experience rather than the outer world of fact and material accomplishment. Tradition and ritual, the pillars of life in virtually all societies other than those of an industrial character, would probably once again assert their ancient claims as the guide to and solace for life. The struggle for individual achievement, especially for material ends, is likely to give way to the acceptance of communally organized and ordained roles. [21]

But there will be quite a stretch of time between now and the future that Heilbroner has sketched for us. The imperative for us now is to encourage technical advances that will permit extraction of new resources, discover new resources, and find new techniques for the generation of energy that will minimize emission of heat. The responsible intelligentsia, meanwhile, will prepare their fellow citizens for the sacrifices that will be required of them, and to "redefine the legitimate boundaries of power and the permissible sanctuaries of freedom, for a future in which the exercise of power must inevitably increase and many areas of freedom, especially in economic life, be curtailed." [22]

Heilbroner's attitude toward his own conclusions is highly ambivalent. He is first of all ambivalent concerning the fact that it is <u>he</u> who is bringing the bad news. He believes he must describe the future situation as he sees it in order to prepare people for the struggle that lies ahead. There is indeed a deep moral earnestness about <u>An Inquiry</u>. He also feels he has to state his realistic views about the irrationality and darkness in human nature so that the coming response to crisis is not built on false beliefs. [23] For both these reasons he feels constrained to make his case.

On the other hand, however, he has a constant fear that his analysis may be used by the forces of darkness themselves.

I am all too aware that these conclusions may bring dismay to many whom I consider my friends and comfort to many whom I consider my foes. To suggest that political power and hierarchy serve a supportive function in society plays directly into the hands of those who applaud the "orderliness" of authoritarian or dictatorial governments. To find a reason for the appeal of nonrational political beliefs is to encourage those who advocate irresponsible political programs. To stress the psychological roots of peoplehood is to weaken the cause of those who seek to overcome the curse of racism and xenophobia. [24]

Heilbroner also has an ambivalent response to the future he describes, although it is certainly accurate to say that his negative feelings outweigh the positive. But he does have a deep antipathy for the industrial ethos that both

captivates and enslaves the masses of people. The capitalist version is
"ultimately unsatisfying for the individual and unstable for the community. "[25]
His distaste extends to the industrial ethos that underlies both capitalism and
socialism:

> The rhythms of industrial production are not those of nature nor
> are its necessary uniformities easily adapted to the varieties of
> human nature. . . . Industrial production confronts men with
> machines that embody "imperatives" if they are to be used at all,
> and these imperatives lead easily to the organization of work, of
> life, even of thought, in ways that accommodate men to machines
> rather than the much more difficult alternative. [26]

Moreover, he speaks of the values inherent in tradition, ritual,
religion, communalism with a kind of indefinite longing. A return to them
may not be all that bad, if we can "rediscover the self-renewing vitality of
primitive culture without reverting to its levels of ignorance and cruel
anxiety. "[27] His stoic admiration for the struggling Atlas is another case
in point.

But it is clear that Prometheus is more to Heilbroner's liking.
And he grieves that "the search for scientific knowledge, the delight in
intellectual heresy, the freedom to order one's life as one pleases, are
not likely to be easily contained within the tradition-oriented, static society I have depicted. "[28] Many of the attributes of the future society are
deeply repugnant to his liberal temper as well as incompatible with his
most treasured privileges.

Indeed, the Promethean spirit that blossomed in the Renaissance
and has developed up until now -- in which Heilbroner was nurtured --
seems to be one flash of brilliance in an otherwise dark history. And the
fruits of the great ascent, made possible by the rise of industrial production,
were savored only by a few, while the majority followed the unnatural rhythms
of the industrial mode of production. This short duration of freedom --
economic, political, cultural -- is bounded by a dark, cruel, and disorderly
past and a future that may be worse.[29] It is as though the dark waves of
internal and external necessity return to cover inexorably the islands of
freedom and reason that have only briefly appeared. Heilbroner counsels
no passive acceptance of this. We are to fight for every possible space for
freedom and reason against overwhelming odds. What's more, even as the
waves of necessity roll over us, the human project is yet worth saving.
Survival under the conditions of necessity is better than extinction.

The summons he issues is not a sentimental one, for the threats
are great; we are bounded by external and internal constraints that cannot
be underestimated. The external restraints are clear. Humans are placed
in a limited, neutral cosmos that automatically checks the overly ambitious

incursions into it. (Heilbroner uses the myth of Prometheus but omits any notion that he is struck down by the gods. Rather, Promethean man has brought tragedy unwittingly upon himself. [30]) We are alone in the cosmos; myths are simply human projections onto that neutral cosmic screen. [31]

The internal necessities that drive man must also be taken into account. Here, Heilbroner, backing off the more classical liberal notion of rational, enlightened self-interest, attests time and time again to the powerful, dark impulses that defy reason and restraint. Even though humans know about the coming crisis, "no substantial voluntary diminution of growth . . . is today even remotely imaginable."[32] There are many who sacrifice much for their children; fewer who would do so for their grandchildren."[33] "We face the horrendous possibility that humanity may react to the approach of environmental danger by indulging in a vast fling while it is still possible--a fling entirely justified by the estimation of present enjoyments over future ones."[34] Humans, confronted by crisis, turn to strong father-figures and narrow, national loyalties.

Thus, Heilbroner appears to be a chastened liberal rationalist. Notions of progress have been dashed. Reason, as a mover of men and nations, is constantly overcome by dumb necessity. There is nothing in the "heart of things" that is either for us or against us. So, out of sheer moral courage we must decide to hide our grief and to conform with the figure of Atlas, straining ourselves in absurd commitment to generations yet unborn. Not an attractive picture, indeed, but one worthy of attention and respect.

II

What makes a comparative analysis of Heilbroner and Bell particularly interesting is that they both come from similar intellectual orientations but reach such different conclusions. Both are members of America's liberal intellectual establishment. Both have a distrust for tightly-knit ideologies that befits the American pragmatic tradition. Both are secularized Jews more comfortable with Enlightenment rationalism than with religious tradition. Both have encyclopedic competence and interest in a number of the social sciences. Both have been favorably disposed toward the development of liberal capitalism as a viable sociopolitical option.

But the conclusions they reach about the future are vastly different. Heilbroner, as we have seen, sees a radical downturn in human history -- a foreclosure on many of the values and possibilities that liberal societies have held dear. Bell, while he sees no Utopia ahead, believes we will have a whole new set of struggles brought on by the coming of post-industrial society, but we are by no means doomed to failure in meeting these challenges. There is little sense that the curtain is being rolled down on

the hopes and dreams of the liberal societies of the past and present. In
fact, where Heilbroner sees doom in the socioeconomic sphere, Bell anticipates the future hopefully. Where Heilbroner envisages dire political consequences following the arrival of stationary capitalism, Bell sees continued political turbulence but certainly not the onslaught of militaristic
authoritarianism. However, where Heilbroner sees some possibilities in
the new culture's life style, Bell fears a cultural decline into antinomianism
and license.

What are the sources of such divergent views of the future? We
will be asking that question as we proceed through our analysis. Before we
begin, we should deal with one relevant question: What is the time frame
projected when each writer talks about the future? Both are dealing with
the future of advanced industrial societies. How far away is the future they
are talking about? Heilbroner tends to speak from a longer perspective.
He believes the industrial machine will slow down in one or two generations
(30 - 60 years). If it does not, but rather out of some sort of last fling
mentality proceeds at its present rate, catastrophic climatic changes will
take place in three or four generations (90 - 120 years). [35] Thus, the downturn in human history he anticipates will take place within 30 to 120 years.
Bell speaks in a more detailed fashion about a shorter time span. The thesis
advanced in his book is that in the next 30 to 50 years we will see the emergence of post-industrial society. [36] So both authors are speaking of future
happenings during a time frame that overlaps. The difference in expectations, then, can be compared appropriately and fairly; they are not pro-
jecting events into completely disparate periods.

Bell breaks his study into three analytical categories -- society,
polity, and culture. The Coming of Post-Industrial Society is a detailed
examination of the first category. Bell projects two more books covering
the latter two categories. The present book focuses primarily on what is
happening in society -- the structure comprised by the economy, the technology, and the occupational system. However, Bell definitely takes ex-
cursions into the polity -- which regulates the distribution of power and
adjudicates the conflicting claims of individuals and groups; and the culture
-- the realm of expressive symbolism and meanings. [37]

Methodologically, Bell attempts to identify the axial structures and
principles operative in each of the three categories:

> The idea of axial principles and structures is an effort to specify
> not causation (this can only be done in a theory of empirical re-
> lationships) but centrality. Looking for the answer to the question
> how a society hangs together, it seeks to specify, within a con-
> ceptual schema, the organizing frame around which the other
> institutions are draped, or the energizing principle that is a
> primary logic for all the others. [38]

While the use of axial principles and structures is helpful in ar-
ranging clear schema, there is some confusion when we begin assembling
them from their scattered loci in the book. It is clear in Bell's thinking
that all industrial and post-industrial societies are economizing societies,
that is, "they are organized around a principle of functional efficiency
whose desideratum is to get 'more for less' and to choose the more rational' course of action."[39] Economizing is a way of allocating resources
according to principles of least cost, substitutability, optimization, maximization and the like. Such economic principles operate similarly in both
"bourgeois" and "socialist" approaches.[40]

However, in capitalist industrial societies, the mechanism of
market competition has insured the operation of these principles, and there
has been little government intervention concerning decisions of what should
be produced -- except of course for the production of goods in the public
sector. In industrial societies, the specific axial principle -- the energizing principle that is a primary logic for the whole society -- has taken
shape concretely in the production of goods, especially manufactured goods.

> Industrial societies--principally those around the North Atlantic
> littoral plus the Soviet Union and Japan--are goods-producing
> societies. Life is a game against fabricated nature. The world
> has become technical and rationalized. The machine predomi-
> nates, and the rhythms of life are mechanically paced. . . .
> Energy has replaced raw muscle and provides the power that is
> the basis of productivity--the art of making more with less--and
> is responsible for the mass output of goods which characterizes
> industrial society.[41]

The index of their strength is industrial capacity measured by the
production of steel. Their axial structure is the private manufacturing
concern. Their occupational concentrations are among semi-skilled workers
and engineers. Their specific axial principle is economic growth in manufactured goods with state or private control of investment decisions. Their
time perspective is based on ad hoc adaptiveness and their methodology is
based on empiricism and experimentation.[42]

The United States is in the process of moving out of such an industrial society into a post-industrial society. It is the character and implications of such a society that Bell's book is primarily about. (Incidentally,
Heilbroner calls the foreclosed society of the future a "post-industrial"
society.[43] The differences in content given to post-industrial society is a
measure of their disagreement about the future.) Bell spends the major
portion of his work detailing the contours of the emerging new society.

As we mentioned, the simplest and clearest characteristic of
post-industrial society is that it is based upon services as distinguished

from manufactured goods. Already the United States has 60 percent of its
population involved in service occupations; by 1980 the figure will have
risen to 70 percent. [44] The term "services" can be deceptive in this regard.
Bell believes that certain kinds of services are key in the emergence of
post-industrial society. Many agrarian societies have a high proportion of
persons engaged in services, but they are services of a personal sort, e.g.,
household servants, because labor is cheap and usually underemployed. In
an industrial society different services tend to predominate because of the
need for auxiliary help for production, e.g., transportation and distribution.
But in a post-industrial society service is of a particular kind.

> If we group services as personal (retail stores, laundries,
> garages, beauty shops); business (banking and finance, real
> estate, insurance); transportation, communication and utilities;
> and health, education, research, and government; then it is the
> growth of the last category which is decisive for post-industrial
> society. And this is the category that represents the expansion
> of a new intelligentsia--in the universities, research organiza-
> tions, professions, and government. [45]

The shift in our society toward this kind of service occupation
leads to the preeminence of the professional and technical class. According to Bell, the most startling change in the last decades has been the
growth of professional and technical employment -- jobs that usually take
some college education -- at a rate twice that of the average. A sub-group
within the professional and technical class -- scientists and engineers --
has actually grown at triple the rate of the working population. [46]
    The growth of services and the emergence of a new elite imply
and are a result of the new primacy of theoretical knowledge. Industrial
society is the coordination of machines and men for the production of goods.
Post-industrial society is organized around knowledge -- particularly
theoretical knowledge. This is a most important point for Bell; he identifies the centrality of theoretical knowledge as the axial principle of the
post-industrial society. It is the energizing principle that drives the
society in its economizing. It is incarnated most clearly in research
organizations -- private and governmental -- and universities. These are
the axial structures of the new society. Thus, money and effort spent in
research facilities that increase the amount and quality of codified theoretical knowledge provide the index of economic health in the post-industrial
society, not the amount of steel tonnage produced as in industrial society.
What is true of technology and economics is true, albeit differentially, of
all modes of knowledge: the advances in a field become increasingly dependent on the primacy of theoretical work. Bell lists many examples of how

fields of codified knowledge are built up and make possible further development. This stands in contrast to an industrial society dependent upon in-
ventors and uncodified, pragmatic knowledge. [47]

The expansion of codified theoretical knowledge, enabled by computer development, will make possible new modes of technological forecasting. Post-industrial societies may be able to reach a new dimension
of societal change, the planning and control of technological growth. We
are increasingly able to predict the deleterious side effects of uncontrolled
technological innovation. Bell believes that we will be able to "assess" our
technology so that we can find alternative strategies to harmful technological
intervention. [48]

The final mark of a post-industrial society -- inter-related with
all the foregoing characteristics -- is the growth of an intellectual technology. An intellectual technology is the substitution of problem-solving rules
and methods for intuitive judgments. The rules and methods are articulated
and codified; persons can learn them.

> In the same spirit, one can say that the methodological promise
> of the second half of the twentieth century is the management of
> organized complexity (the complexity of large organizations and
> systems, the complexity of theory with a large number of vari-
> ables), the identification and implementation of strategies for
> rational choice in games against nature and games between
> persons, and the development of a new intellectual technology
> which, by the end of the century, may be as salient in human
> affairs as machine technology has been for the past century and a
> half. [49]

All of the foregoing give post-industrial society vast potential for
dealing with problems that we have had with us a long time -- scarcity,
pollution, unintended social effects of technological intervention, economic
ups and downs, etc. -- as well as with problems brought about by the movement into the post-industrial society itself -- the conflict between equality
of opportunity and equality of results, the loss of mobility for unskilled
and semi-skilled laborers, the imperialistic tendencies of "intellectual
technology." But they guarantee a constructive effect on neither set of
problems. In fact, they seem to throw more and more weight on the political realm. This is one of the theses of Bell's study. There has been a
long-run historical tendency in Western society toward governance by
political philosophy and away from political economy where varied ends
desired by individuals are maximized by free exchange. [50]

The political realm of the future will be a cockpit of turbulence
and conflict. And, contrary to the dreams of the technocrats, the possibilities of post-industrial society hold no ready-made solutions to difficult

decisions. Bell believes that even though the technical and professional classes will constitute a new elite in post-industrial society, they will not ipso facto have more political power. They will be needed in the political decisions that are made -- for data, research, etc. -- but the political elite will still rise from different bases of power than the technical and professional intelligentsia. Political groups and parties overlap insignificantly with the new elite. [50]

So, the realm of politics will remain one of haggling, of bargaining, of passion rather than "rationality." And there will be much to haggle about. For one thing, the concerns of "sociologizing" sometimes conflict with the interest of "economizing." "Sociologizing" is sociologese for the public interest. Concerns such as national defense, police and fire protection, public parks, water resources, beauty and quality of life, a more differentiated and intellectual educational system, become ends that do not emerge from the free market mechanism. These social goods are expanding in importance and will have to be taken into account by the polity. [51]

These social goods will have interest groups demanding they be taken account of, and they will put pressure on the polity. As more and more matters of social concern are dealt with "publicly" through the government rather than privately through the market, social conflict will increase because public decisionmaking localizes and personalizes responsibility in contrast to the market which disperses it. [52]

One of the most powerful and demanding interest groups will be the unskilled and semi-skilled laborers left behind by the new requirements of educated skill and expertise. Even more threatened by the shift toward meritocracy will be minorities plagued by unemployment and underemployment. In an era of mass communication, they will be aware of and demand their "rights" to the goodies of the service economy. A large segment of the population will resist an ethic of distribution based on merit (equality of opportunity) and press for one based on equality of results. Bell is extremely concerned about what this latter demand might mean in the long run. [53]

The rise of an intellectual technology or the expansion of codified knowledge will not be of substantial help to political figures as they find themselves in a maelstrom of competing interests. Values cannot be ordered by the hardware of the post-industrial society. What is needed is a social ethic appropriate to the problems of the new society -- a social ethic that can undergird the action of political figures, help to give priority to competing values, sort out the sticky problems involved in meritocracy and equality. [54] But neither the society nor the polity can provide such an ethic. That is the prerogative of the culture -- the realm of expressive symbolism and meanings.

It is precisely here that Bell becomes wary, even pessimistic. And the pessimism is tinged with outright anger. For he has a very negative interpretation of the culture of post-industrial society, with little hope for renewal.

First, Bell believes that in post-industrial society, culture has achieved autonomy in relation to the society and polity. In fact, not only has it achieved autonomy but it is moving in disjunction with the needs of both the society and the polity. Each is in the process of being grasped by a different axial principle. The social structure is rooted in functional rationality and efficiency while the culture is rooted in "the antinomian justification of the enhancement of self."[55]

Bell locates the sources of this disjunction in two continuing tendencies. One is the tendency of capitalism itself to undermine the ethic of rational discipline and restraint by zealously promoting a hedonistic way of life.

> By the middle of the twentieth century capitalism sought to justify itself not by work or property, but by the status badges of material possessions and by the promotion of pleasure. The rising standard of living and the relaxation of morals became ends in themselves as the definition of personal freedom.[56]

The other tendency is a little more complex. An antinomian, Dionysian element has been a recurrent feature in human society. It is generally played out in subterranean impulses that are borne by minority groups or are accounted for by the general culture by a dialectic of restraint and release in either religion or the secular moral order. In recent times these minority groups have been designated "modernists" or "bohemians." They have been rabidly anti-bourgeoisie. Liberal culture has been titillated and entertained by the modernist impulses and has protected them by legal means in the realms of art and imagination.

However, both tendencies -- the hedonistic ethos of capitalism and the antinomian thrust of modernism -- have now been merged into a counter-culture, an adversary culture. Its axial principle is "self-enhancement." Bell believes that a new class has emerged that sustains the adversary ideology and that has gained domination in the media and the culture.[58] Liberal culture now has a difficult time dealing with the adversary culture, which uses the liberal rhetoric of "personal freedom" and "right to expression."

> (The adversary culture) seeks to take the creed of personal freedom, extreme experience, and sexual experimentation into areas where the liberal culture -- which would accept such ideas in art and imagination -- is not prepared to go. Yet the liberal culture finds itself at a loss to explain its reticence. It approves a basic permissiveness, but cannot with any certainty define the

bounds. And it leaves the moral order in a state of confusion and disarray. For this reason liberalism may yet suffer a reaction. [59]

What we have in the adversary culture is, according to Bell, a veritable nightmare. The transformation in cultural consciousness has brought a polymorph sensuality, the lifting of repression, the permeability of madness and normality, a new psychedelic awareness, the boundless exploration of pleasure. Its persistent attempts to attain some form of ecstasy are self-infinitizing and radically present-oriented. Its attitudes of carpe diem, prodigality and display, and the compulsive search for play "plunges one into a radical autism which, in the end, dirempts the cords of community and the sharing with others. "[60]

The adversary culture pretends to be involved in a heroic struggle against the Protestant Ethic and its religious and moral underpinnings. But the integrated whole of the nineteenth century in which culture, character structure, and economy were infused by a single religiously based value system has vanished long ago. What is left is a society (economic and social structure) with a lot of possibility for human betterment going on its own unguided way. Fortunately, it has not strayed too badly from human sanity. But it has no inner justification given to it by a social ethic; neither does it have the proper guidance from a polity shaped by that ethic. Unfortunately, the culture -- the area from whence we should expect new value formation -- has not only abrogated its proper task but has set our lifestyles upon a dissipating nihilistic course.

And there is little hope for a renewal that might avert a further disjunction. The system is completely mundane, for any transcendent ethic has vanished.

In a post-industrial society, the disjunction of culture and social structure is bound to widen. The historic justifications of bourgeois society--in the realms of religion and character--are gone. The traditional legitimacies of property and work become subordinated to bureaucratic enterprises that can justify privilege because they can turn out material goods more efficiently than other modes of production. But a technocratic society is not ennobling. Material goods provide only transient satisfaction or an invidious superiority over those with less. Yet one of the deepest human impulses is to sanctify their institutions and beliefs in order to find a meaningful purpose in their lives and deny the meaninglessness of death. A post-industrial society cannot provide a transcendent ethic--except for a few who devote themselves to the temple of science. . . . The lack of a rooted moral belief system is the cultural contradiction of the society, the deepest challenge to its survival. [61]

III

In beginning our comparative analysis and assessment of the works of Heilbroner and Bell, it might be well to start with several salient points of convergence. As we compare and contrast the two authors, we shall critically assess them where that seems appropriate.

A major point of agreement in the two studies is their common belief that the economic sphere will increasingly be shaped and controlled by the political. Both see a long-term trend toward political intervention in the "free market." And there is little in any modern analysis that would give us much evidence that such an observation is untrue. Future developed societies, whether capitalist or socialist, will look more similar economically that dissimilar.

But the reasons why such a trend will tend to increase are quite different. Bell argues that the growing possibilities and problems of post-industrial society will necessitate more political intervention. As the need for sociologizing increases, as social forecasting projects the problems of the future, as growth in the service economy presses toward meritocracy, as an increasing abundance leads to cries for fair distribution, the political apparatus will be called upon to adjudicate between more and more competing claims and to order the priorities of society. Heilbroner sees the closing in of ecological limits as the reality that will force a political solution of the crises touched off by the end of growth. Clearly, these external pressures will find an internal resonance in the tendency of humans to look to authoritarian father figures in times of crisis. So, in Bell the changes are wrought by the internal dynamics of post-industrial society; in Heilbroner by the external limits on growth. The former sources of movement toward political centralization are more benign and are compatible with representative democracy; the latter are extremely stringent and surpass the capability of democracy to deal with them.

Another -- and more authentic -- convergence of opinion concerns short-term strategy. Heilbroner believes that the next decade or so should be spent in developing our scientific technology so that we can find new sources of energy and conserve the ones we have. Bell asserts that we not only ought to do that, but in fact we are far along that path already. Heilbroner concedes that a movement toward a service economy and increased technical sophistication may indeed buy time. This may avert panic and a last fling mentality that could only bring about a sharper foreclosure.

As was mentioned earlier, both authors share a similar philosophical orientation -- the classical Enlightenment tradition of autonomous,
critical reason.   They enjoy the free play of reason, particularly scientific
reason.   Heilbroner prizes the "search for scientific knowledge, the delight
in intellectual heresy, and the freedom to order one's life as one pleases."[62]
Bell is more effusive in his accolades to the ethos of scientific reason: "As
an imago, it comes closest to the ideal of the Greek polis, a republic of
free men and women united by a common quest for truth.[63] Only the few
who devote themselves to the "temple of science" have any chance of being
grasped by a transcendent ethic.[64]

Recognizing as they do that economic, political, and cultural freedom do in some sense correlate historically, Heilbroner and Bell share a
preference for the freedoms of liberal society.   Heilbroner grieves over its
inevitable demise.   Bell is indignantly angry that the autonomous culture of
liberal society has opted for irrational license instead of responsible rationality, although he sees no necessary end to the characteristics he prizes.

Both writers also possess the prejudices and limitations of their
common philosophical orientation.   They tend to share a Newtonian view of
the world.   Nature seems mechanistically neutral.   There is no possibility
for a disclosure of meaning in the responsive relations of self and world.
This truncated view of reality leads in turn to epistemological closure.
Ways of knowing that rely upon myth, imagination, intuition, or revelation
seem futile to them.   At best these ways are primitive modes of expressing
meaning that can be exhaustively and more adequately understood by reason.
(It is significant that Heilbroner must reduce the myths of Atlas and
Prometheus to simple human projection, closing off any notion that they
may have deeper and broader meaning.[65]) Indeed, the definition of rationality itself appears to be narrowed.   Divorcing themselves from traditions
that attempt to speak of Reason or Logos, they tend to make reason merely
procedural (as in rational, objective rules of evidence) or critical (in a
questioning, qualifying, relativizing way).   They distance themselves in this
manner from perspectives that affirm the capacity of reason to identify and
propose substantive values.

Finally, in our catalog of convergences, both commentators share
a strong sense of the exhaustion of modern culture.   Bell's pessimism is
deeper and more pervasive on this score than Heilbroner's, but evidence of
perception of malaise is present in both.   Heilbroner laments the barbarity
lurking below the veneer of civilization, the moral chaos, the failure to
pass cherished values to new generations.   Bell, however, as we have seen
above, pours forth an impassioned jeremiad concerning modern culture.
We will no doubt see more of his pessimism in his forthcoming book, The
Cultural Contradictions of Capitalism.

This pessimistic perception of culture has, I believe, a significant
relation to their philosophical orientation.   There seems to be an awareness

in each of them that the values of Western culture have come, at least in part, from living religious traditions. But they have no hope that those traditions can still generate and communicate values, or that new out- breakings of religious meaning and power can serve that purpose. Nor do they have a concept of Reason that strives to grasp the logos in reality. Thus, reason -- in the narrow definition they have given it -- can only question and qualify; it provides no basis for the reconstruction of meaning and value. The old world of value has vanished and there seem to be no wellsprings for renewal. We see here, perhaps, not the exhaustion of culture but the ex- haustion of a variety of philosophical liberalism. (In this regard, Victor Ferkiss, coming from a non-liberal Thomistic tradition, demonstrates far more zest and hope in the task of value reformation and regeneration. 66)

If the foregoing constitute the convergences in the thought of Bell and Heilbroner, and some of the reasons for the convergences, it would be helpful at this point to examine the dissimilarities. The sharpest division of opinion surrounds their interpretation of what the crisis really is. And interpretation, of course, drastically affects the view of the future.

The crisis according to Heilbroner arises from the collision of Promethean industrial civilization with absolute environmental limits. Current cultural and political malaise recedes in importance in comparison to this central problem. The belief that clean cool air is fast disappearing provides the linchpin of Heilbroner's argument. The environment can tolerate only so much emission of heat. When those limits begin to be reached, there is a chain reaction. Environmental limits lead to a cessation of in- dustrial growth, which leads to civil unrest and international strife, which lead to strong, authoritarian governments, which lead to the limitations of cultural freedom; all combined lead to a "post-industrial" world which re- sembles the primitive past more than the present. Science and technology wane in importance because they have become inseparably linked to the in- dustrial ethos.

Whatever else might be argued, Bell does not locate the crisis in environmental limits. He specifically rejects the contentions of the crisis environmentalists.

> Paradoxically, the vision of Utopia was suddenly replaced by the spectre of Doomsday. In place of the early-sixties theme of end- less plenty, the picture by the end of the decade was one of a fragile planet of limited resources whose finite stocks were being rapidly depleted, and whose wastes from soaring industrial pro- duction were polluting the air and waters. Now the only way of saving the world was zero growth. 67

He flatly states that such an apocalyptic vision is wrong. 68 Later he lists his arguments against such a vision:

The difficulty with the Forrester model (upon which many grim predictions are based) is its simplified quantitative metric. The exponential growth of any factor in a closed system inevitably reaches a ceiling and collapses. . . . It assumes that no qualitative change in the behavior of the system takes place, or is even possible. But this is clearly not so. Materials can be recycled. New sources of energy can be tapped. . . . And technology makes possible the transmutation of resources. . . . The ecological models take the physical finiteness of the earth as the ultimate bound, but this is fundamentally misleading. Resources are properly measured in economic, not physical terms, and on the basis of relative costs new investments are made which can irrigate arid land, drain swampy land, clear forests, explore for new resources, or stimulate the process of extraction and transmutation. These methods of adding to the supplies of "fixed resources," as Carl Kaysen has pointed out, have been going on steadily throughout human history. [69]

Significantly -- and certainly Heilbroner would point this out -- Bell does not list cool air as a resource for which something else can become a substitute. No doubt Bell would argue that cool air is one of the resources that is not absolutely limited. Perhaps he would argue that technology may be able to reverse the process by radically reducing the emission of heat and by finding ways to collect and absorb it into some sort of receptacle, instead of into the open air. At any rate, he believes the post-industrial society is a "game among people," not a game against nature or fabricated nature. Neither the limits nor powers of nature can do us in:

If in the foreseeable future--say for the next hundred years--there will be neither Utopia nor Doomsday but the same state that has existed for the last hundred years--namely, the fairly steady advance of "compound interest"--the banality of this fact (how jaded we soon become of the routinization of the spectacular!) should not obscure the extraordinary achievement Keynes called attention to. For the first time in human history, he reminded us, the problem of survival in the bare sense of the word--freedom from hunger and disease--need no longer exist. The question before the human race is not subsistence but standard of living, not biology but sociology. Basic needs are satiable, and the possibility of abundance is real. To that extent, the Marx-Keynes vision of the economic meaning of industrial society is certainly true. [70]

The crisis for Bell is clearly not the result of ecological limits. Science and technology in the post-industrial world can bring us through the

threats and limits of the natural world. Rather, the crisis is located in the
culture -- the realm of expressive meanings and values. Post-industrial
society has given us openings to human opportunity that have not existed
before, but we have a culture lacking in the resolve and purpose needed to
grasp those new possibilities. Bell sees the cultural trends as perverse.
And these trends have been chosen by modern people; they no longer follow
necessarily from the socioeconomic substratum. That is the source of his
angry indignation. We could follow different paths but do not. Sadly, Bell
has few ideas about the source or ground of those new paths. From whence
cometh the rooted moral belief system he so genuinely seeks?

IV

        Whatever one might say in response to the efforts of Heilbroner
and Bell, either in agreement or disagreement, it is indisputable that they
have raised issues that are unavoidable for any responsible discussion of
the future. Both have tried to delineate long-term trends that set the
contours of the problems of the present and the future. Heilbroner sees a
coming collision between the industrial ethos, empowered by scientific
technology, and ecological limits that are now beginning to exercise their
constraints. That coming collision raises all sorts of crucial issues.
Bell forecasts an emerging post-industrial society that will be able to deal
with ecological limits, but will find its challenge in shaping a culture and a
social ethic to guide and ennoble its vast technological potentialities. Bell's
scenario of the future raises many of the same issues as that of Heilbroner.
        Thus, it is the task of this concluding section to attempt to focus
the issues. This will not only distill the questions posed by Heilbroner and
Bell into a clearer schema; it will also provide a framework for the concerns that our seminar has dealt with over the years. It may also, in a
preliminary way, sketch some of the viable options in the key issues of the
future. Part of the task of focusing the issues necessarily includes some
reflection on the issues that Heilbroner and Bell have not raised clearly and
adequately, but which are crucially important in the struggle for a human
future.
        It would seem that there are five key issues raised jointly by
Heilbroner and Bell that have at the same time been focal points for our
seminar's ongoing debate.

        1. The Location and Intensity of the Challenge. --While this may
properly be broken into two separate issues, it is helpful to keep them together because of their close interrelation. The first part of the issue --
the location of the challenge -- opens up many avenues of discussion. Is the
challenge provided by a set of inappropriate values? Heilbroner tends to

argue that the values of the industrial ethos are no longer viable in a world
of sharp ecological constraints. Victor Ferkiss asserts even more clearly
the utter bankruptcy of "liberal" values. Bell questions the cultural values
of "self-enhancement" but does not reject the socioeconomic values of
growth and efficiency.

Or, is the challenge provided by a fundamental defect in human
nature? Again, Heilbroner, when pushed more severely, locates man's
lack of an altruism in behalf of future generations as the hindrance to
reshaping inappropriate values. Bell talks of a persisting duplicity in man.

Can the challenge be located in a failure to distribute power? Is
the fundamental problem that of empowering the oppressed, be they the
third world abroad or the third world in our midst? In this interpretation,
the key problem is neither values nor human nature, though they are
certainly present. Here the key obstacle to empowerment tends to be seen
as demonic economic, social, and political systems which have to be over-
turned by revolution.

Or, perhaps we have not brought to fruition the promise within our
present system. The challenge is simply to do better and more consistently
what we have done in the past. No fundamental changes in values, humans,
or systems are called for; better performance is the imperative.

Finally, the challenge may be located completely outside ourselves.
There may be "principalities and powers" at work in the world that we have
no real control over. Their reign of death is inevitable. They may be seen
in the corruptions of social systems; or they may be seen in the grinding
Malthusian realities of famine, pestilence and war.

This final interpretation can be closely identified with an apocalyptic view of the intensity of the challenge. The time is short; collapse
is near. Not much can be done except to live in integrity in the midst of
the fall.

Heilbroner possesses a modified apocalyptic viewpoint. The intensity of the challenge is clear. Because of the sharp proximity of limits and
the inability of man to respond quickly enough to avoid them, history is
sentenced to a radical downswing. Irreconcilable conflicts and contradictions are indeed upon us, but we can live humanly within them.
Promethean man must learn the lesson of limits. If he does not teach
himself that lesson, history will.

Bell cannot be regarded in the same fashion. The intensity of the
challenge is not as great. Indeed, he rarely uses even the language of
"crisis." As mentioned above, the only place such language is used relates
to the challenge of developing a social ethic for post-industrial society. We
have time, particularly in the social and political realms. The future will
be relatively continuous with the past in those areas. The discontinuities
emerge in the realm of culture, and that is where the crisis is.

Others do not wish even to use the term "crisis" as a way of describing the intensity of the challenge. There are "problems" that must be struggled with but it is not helpful to deem them crises. Bell certainly takes this position with regard to energy, ecology, and the world economy. Several persons in our seminar have felt that historical continuities will be much more persistent than the "crisis" mentality permits. The force of the challenge may be great, but the resiliency of present vitalities prevents any notion of imminent collapse.

2. The Ability of Representative Democracy to Handle the Challenge. --This issue is raised powerfully by both Heilbroner and Bell. They share the belief that modern history has witnessed the gradual advancement of political control over economic decisions. The "free market" is less and less able to handle the challenge presented by the proximity of ecological limits or the coming of post-industrial society. In the former case, the stringencies of a no-growth economy will force a political trend toward centralized authority over economic matters. In the latter, "sociologizing" concerns will press for political hegemony over the market.

The "how" of political control is the key issue. Heilbroner believes that representative democracy, shaped as it is by the materialistic and individualistic promptings of the industrial ethos, is inadequate to the task. Strong leadership will have to emerge that can alter the basic shape of our values and style of life. If that leadership is intellectually far-sighted, there is the possibility that certain private and public freedoms can be maintained. But authoritarian rule can only be minimized, not avoided. [71]

Bell has more hope for representative democracy. The polity of post-industrial society will be more turbulent because tasks formerly dispersed by the market system will be joined in the political arena. More interest groups representing both private and public concerns will put the pressure on. But, basically, representative democracy will be able to handle the increased pressure. Its chances of succeeding will improve if it is able to come up with a social ethic that will define more clearly the priorities of justice in a novel situation.

This call for a re-shaped political ethic is echoed by Victor Ferkiss. If the political philosophy of "ecological humanism" really does catch hold among a significant number of elites, the framework of democracy will not only work, it will be able to lead us toward a future beyond our expectations. If values change in the proper direction, our present political institutions will be adequate to the challenge before us. [72]

Another option calls for decreasing the centralized functions of government and fostering more grass-roots voluntarism. In the area of economics, this viewpoint is held by Milton Friedman. The free play of the market can indeed handle problems of scarcity and distribution. Representative democracy can handle a decreased number of items not dealt with by the market. Politically, proponents of voluntarism suggest decentralization, reduction to the human scale, and increased citizen participation. If democracy is really made representative of all, it may succeed in democratizing the economic world as well, thus arriving at a new way of meeting the dilemma of freedom and control. This perspective generally interprets the challenges before us as less intense than the perspectives mentioned above.

If the relation of the polity to the economy is one of the main issues raised by the two authors, there are related issues that need to be mentioned in passing. One such issue concerns the relation of the cultural to the sociopolitical realm. Bell, for instance, sees a growing disjunction between the two that leads to schizophrenic individual and corporate existence. Worse, the emerging new culture not only fails to provide ethical norms for the polity and the society; it is downright contemptuous toward the task. Others, including Heilbroner, assert the interconnection of polity, society, and culture. From their perspective one must deal with the whole complex. This is why the approach of ecological limits will be so traumatic. It will, by the force of historical necessity, alter the whole complex; there will be convulsive change across the boards.

Another related issue concerns the role of the new informational elite (those in society who possess the intellectual technology) with regard to the polity. Bell is rather sanguine about the possibilities of expanded theoretical knowledge to enable social planning. Unfortunately, these useful data are funneled to political actors who are driven this way and that by interest, not knowledge. This fact, Bell believes, will be one of the ongoing frustrations of the post-industrial society.

Heilbroner has a similar lament. We know enough now about the impending ecological disaster, but we do not have enough wisdom, altruism, or courage to act upon that knowledge. The old inertias are too powerful. Others are not even so sure of the usefulness of expanded knowledge for making decisions. The data on a problem of any magnitude are so overwhelming in scope and complexity that they can be ordered to fit any argument, pro or con. It is very difficult to assemble convincing data on problems that are macrocosmic. Opposing theories held by experts concerning whether the atmosphere is heating up or cooling down illustrate the point. Experts on each side marshal rank upon rank of data for their own perspective. It may be that humankind is creating a new tower of Babel in its bid to assemble conclusive data. More data may simply make us more confused.

Be that as it may, reflection about future policy will have to take these problems into account. How can we use the expanding knowledge made available by computer technology? How can we winnow out the relevant data from the irrelevant so as to make decisions based upon a real situation? What is to be the political role of the informational elite? Can common, ordinary citizens be expected to have intelligent opinions on problems whose complexity baffles both the experts in the field and the political elite?

3. The Role of Science and Technology in Any Future Strategy. -- Heilbroner has broached this issue by arguing that science and technology have been so identified with the industrial ethos that they cannot be distinguished. As the industrial ethos is necessarily diminished, so science and technology will wane in importance. This does not mean that we should discontinue their use in the short run. Indeed, they are needed to buy time so that we can prepare for the convulsive changes ahead. But when the limits close in, the heyday of science and technology will be in the past.

Bell sees no such future in store for scientific technology. He believes they will and must increase in order to move us into the post-industrial society on a broader scale. Moreover, they are necessary to solve new problems posed by that society. Scientific technology cannot provide the values needed to guide itself, however, and that is where Bell sees the problem.

There is a broad range of positions on this issue. Some, like Ferkiss, believe science can discern the values that we need. Technology can empower those new values so that the earth can be shaped into a veritable utopia. [73] Thus, science and technology take on even greater importance than for Bell. Other commentators would probe the capacities for decentralization latent in technology. Others believe that science has developed a world view that itself provides a criticism of the industrial ethos, and therefore is an ally to those who want to reshape our values. The position one takes on this issue is crucial in constructing an adequate social philosophy.

4. The Relation of Nature and Culture. --Heilbroner calls attention to this issue by arguing that the culture shaped by the industrial ethos is destructive of the world of nature. Before the industrial revolution, man was perennially dominated by nature. For several centuries amid the flowering of the industrial revolution, man enjoyed a heady sense of triumph over nature. Finally he could begin to control some of the natural conditions of his existence. But now a vast super-structure, a "second nature" driven by the cultural values of industrial man, is rushing headlong toward a collision with natural limits. Nature will again dominate man. There is a sense of inevitable tragedy about all this for Heilbroner. Man constantly evades the harmony that he could have with nature; his restless spirit puts him into an adversary relationship with nature, to the detriment of both. So, we will be forced to live more harmoniously with nature if we are to survive at all.

Bell deals with this issue by placing post-industrial society above nature. Pre-industrial society was a game against nature; industrial society a game against fabricated nature. Post-industrial society has solved the problems involving natural scarcity. The domination of the natural world is assumed to be complete, or almost so. Post-industrial society is a game between persons and groups of persons, far above the level of nature. So Bell neither gains nor expects to gain helpful promptings or harsh limits from nature. The dichotomy between culture and nature is sharp and decisive.

     5. The Role of the Intellectual.--A final issue brought out by our two authors regards the role of the intellectual in society. Both of them view the intellectual as the one who gains a more expansive view of things by virtue of his learning and his capacities for critical reflection. In some sense the intellectual detaches himself from society in order to gain a more expansive perspective -- expansive in terms of both time and space. Both authors relish the position they have. It gives them opportunity to think, to engage in heresy from the conventional wisdom and to speculate about things to come.

     But both endure anguish because of their position. Bell knows that the political elite will continue to control the decisionmaking in our society. They may need the scientific and professional elite as a source of technical knowledge, but they, the politicians, still make the decisions, exercise the power. So, Bell is not sure what role the intellectual has. His critical and informational contributions may be ignored. Or worse, they may be used contrary to his own beliefs. (Bell includes a long excursus in his book on the dilemmas faced by atomic scientists when they were confronted with the political and military use of their discoveries.[74]) Moreover, the intellectual has no real role in shaping substantive cultural values. All he can do is to criticize those that emerge. So, while the intellectual is indispensable for the functioning of post-industrial society, he may be relegated to the periphery. The political and cultural elite may stand at more critical places

     Heilbroner has a sense of foreboding that the news he brings back from the intellectual mountaintop may serve only to comfort and reinforce the forces of reaction, and in that way produce the very effects he wants to avoid. Heilbroner is sounding the alarm in hopes that people will anticipate the crisis that is to come and therefore soften and minimize its deleterious effects. He fears that reactionaries will use his arguments to maximize the trends toward authoritarianism and restraint on private and public freedoms. Moreover, he is not at all sure anyone will heed his voice, even though he is convinced he is speaking the truth.

     Thus, the intellectual is both blessed and cursed by virtue of his detachment. He can see more; that is his blessing. But he is not sure that what he sees will be put to use. He stands outside the centers of power; that is his curse. Further, his critical detachment may distance him from the communal, traditional nexes of society that are more stable and cohesive than the circles in which he moves.

This observation leads us to the concluding part of this section. We have been lifting up the issues that Bell and Heilbroner make unavoidable for any responsible grappling with the future. Because of the nature of their projects and their intellectual orientations, however, there are issues that they have not raised adequately. This is not meant as a criticism, necessarily, even though the liabilities of the authors' perspectives were examined earlier. Rather, these remarks flow from the conviction that the constructive task of the future is dependent upon the careful address of certain issues that have not yet been satisfactorily probed.

An issue that needs further probing concerns the potentialities for renewal and change already present in American society. Bell and Heilbroner both lament the cultural chaos they observe in the life around them. But can it be that the disorder they see is only part of the story -- the part enacted by the "theory class" made up of the educated upper middle class and their children? The "adversary culture" that Bell fears so much seems to have its roots in that social segment. Bell may be over-estimating its power and pervasiveness.

One would do well to look more closely at what is happening in the middle and working class segments of American society. In the small towns, the stable elements of the middle classes, the persisting ethnic communities, and the institutional churches, there is a growing sense of identity that does not melt so easily into the morass of mass-media culture. Much of this is a reaffirmation of traditional values and mores that have been rejected by the avant-garde but which may be very appropriate to the challenges ahead. Commitments to values of self-sacrifice, discipline, fair play, familial belonging, harmony with nature, monogamy, church membership and support, and citizen responsibility have not disappeared. But people do need the moral leadership from political figures that can tap the strengths of their "civil religion." Concerning this, Heilbroner's call for far-sighted leadership is very appropriate.

In this regard, the continuing capacity of the historic church must not be underestimated. The spiritual renewal in the charismatic movement may be a sign of a new awakening. The consistent nurturing of sensitive moral leadership in the Roman Catholic church is impressive. The hunger of laypeople for continuing education in the faith among the Protestant communions must be taken seriously. In short, the cultural resilience of traditional American communities may be greater than either Bell or Heilbroner acknowledges. This cultural resilience, if skillfully tapped, may become the source of renewal and reform, not reaction. It is with this stratum of American life that our authors seem somewhat unacquainted.

The final issue concerns the task of what one could call "grounding." By this is meant the fundamental thinking that must be done to provide a deeper, clearer, and more profound way of envisioning man, the world and their interrelation. Out of this deeper vision will come the social ethic that

Bell calls for.[75] Out of it will also come the rationale for altruistic behavior that Heilbroner thinks is indispensable for the arduous challenges ahead.

The task of grounding means being receptive to the religious vitalities present in nature, in history, in man. It means the translation of the meaning of traditional religious symbols into the worldview provided by the most advanced and perceptive of scientists. It means searching for an adequate metaphysic that can undergird an ordering of priorities for the human future. In short, the task of grounding is the task of religious social ethics, and such a task is a needed complement to the perceptive analysis provided by Bell and Heilbroner.

NOTES AND REFERENCES

[1]Robert L. Heilbroner, An Inquiry Into The Human Prospect (New York: W.W. Norton & Co., 1974). (Hereafter designated as IHP.)

[2]Ibid., p. 138.

[3]Victor Ferkiss, The Future of Technological Civilization (New York: George Braziller, 1974). (Hereafter designated as FTC.)

[4]Daniel Bell, The Coming of Post-Industrial Society (New York: Basic Books, 1973). (Hereafter designated as CPS.)

[5]Heilbroner, IHP, p. 13.

[6]Ibid., p. 21.

[7]Ibid., p. 33.

[8]Ibid., pp. 35-40.

[9]Ibid., p. 43.

[10]Ibid., pp. 40-46.

[11]Ibid., p. 48.

[12]Ibid., p. 50.

[13]Ibid., p. 129.

[14]Ibid., p. 56.

[15]Ibid., p. 57.

[16]Ibid., p. 77.

[17]Ibid., p. 92.

[18]Ibid., pp. 82-88.

[19]Ibid., p. 90.

[20]Ibid., pp. 99-124.

[21]Ibid., p. 140.

[22]Ibid., pp. 137-8.

[23]Ibid., pp. 123-24.

[24]Ibid., pp. 122-23.

[25]Ibid., p. 70.

[26]Ibid., p. 78.

[27]Ibid., p. 141.
[28]Ibid., p. 140.
[29]Ibid., p. 22.
[30]Ibid., p. 142.
[31]Ibid., p. 144.
[32]Ibid., p. 133.
[33]Ibid., p. 115.
[34]Ibid.
[35]Ibid., pp. 128-29.
[36]Bell, CPS, p. x.
[37]Ibid., p. 12.
[38]Ibid., p. 10.
[39]Ibid., p. 76.
[40]Ibid.
[41]Ibid., p. 126.
[42]Ibid., p. 117.
[43]Heilbroner, IHP, p. 140.
[44]Bell, p. 15.
[45]Ibid.
[46]Ibid., p. 17.
[47]Ibid., p. 26.
[48]Ibid., p. 27.
[49]Ibid., p. 28.
[50]Ibid., p. 298.
[51]Ibid., p. 360ff.
[52]Ibid., p. 282ff.
[53]Ibid., p. 364.
[54]See Bell's long discussion of meritocracy and equality, pp. 408-455.
[55]Ibid., p. 483.
[56]Ibid., p. 477.
[57]Ibid.
[58]Ibid., p. 479.
[59]Ibid.
[60]Ibid., p. 480.
[61]Ibid.
[62]Heilbroner, IHP, p. 140.
[63]Bell, CPS, p. 380.
[64]Ibid., p. 480.
[65]Heilbroner, IHP, pp. 142-44.
[66]Ferkiss, FTC, p. 120ff.
[67]Bell, CPS, p. 463.
[68]Ibid., p. 38.
[69]Ibid., p. 464.
[70]Ibid., p. 465.

[71]Heilbroner, Challenge, May-June, 1975, p. 27.

[72]Ferkiss, FTC, p. 213ff.

[73]Ibid., p. 102ff.

[74]Bell, CPS, pp. 386-408.

[75]Bell's new book, The Cultural Contradiction of Capitalism
(New York: Basic Books, 1976.), which has already been mentioned on
page 111, contains a rather surprising reversal of his argument in The
Coming of Post-Industrial Society. In this new work Bell looks for a religious renewal to bring forth this deeper vision, which in turn will provide
a basis for a new social ethic. Up until the appearance of this latest book,
Bell has given little attention to religion as a contemporary source for the
regeneration of values. His new departure coincides with the concluding
point of this article.

CHAPTER V

RECLAIMING THE LIBERAL ARTS

by
John Fish and
John Kretzmann

Traditionally, higher education has functioned as a repository for and transmitter of civilization's basic wisdom and values, and also as the final step in the process of training and socializing successive leadership generations. The trend toward mass higher education and the increasing urgency with which larger social, political, economic, and cultural dislocations impinge on the academic world have led many to rethink these traditional functions in the light of changed conditions. From Robert Hutchins' The Higher Learning in America to the recent Kerr Commission studies we have had a fairly steady flow of studies, books, commissions, and reports analyzing the plight of higher education in America and indicating a variety of lamentable conditions: specialization, fragmentation, credentialism, vocationalism, professionalism, the credit system, the military-industrial-educational complex, the eclipse of liberal arts, etc.

Most of the very recent literature on the current status and problems of the liberal arts college in particular reflects an attempt to respond to current economic "hard times." The nature of these analyses and prescriptions provides us with a revealing lever by which to uncover some of the underlying issues we will move toward later in these reflections.

The Undergraduate College as a Socializing Agent

The dilemma of those faculty and administrators who face increasing demands for a vocationally relevant undergraduate curriculum is a hard one indeed. The demands originate from two different directions--from students and their families on the one hand, and from public and private sources of revenue on the other. What is to be the response of those holdouts who believe, as we do, that undergraduate education should be about much more than job or skills training?

In reality, recent proposals for reform follow two divergent lines: some educators call for the recovery of the liberal arts, while others press

125

on toward more adequate vocational-professional preparation. It is proving
very difficult, within the existing educational system and its assumptions,
to ply a course between the romanticism of the liberal arts purists and the
practicality of the vocational trainers.

Yet more than six years of experience with the Urban Studies Program of the Associated Colleges of the Midwest (ACM) has convinced us
that a pedagogically valid middle ground exists between these two extremes.
Undergraduate education is capable of taking the vocational-professional
pressure very seriously, and of using that narrow but deeply felt set of
interests to open up the broader areas of discipline and inquiry represented
by the liberal arts tradition at its best.

Before attempting to generalize about the ways in which these
currently polar tendencies might be made to dovetail in undergraduate
education, we ought first to sketch the experiences at ACM Urban Studies
which have affected our thinking.

Very briefly, the Chicago program brings 60 to 100 undergraduates
to the city for a 3-1/2 month semester-equivalent period. The students--
sophomores, juniors, and seniors from small liberal arts colleges--come
with a wide variety of majors and interests. Some have defined career goals,
most have not.

Once in Chicago, they move into program-rented apartments which
are located in some five different city neighborhoods. Apartments are clus-
tered so that approximately fifteen students live within easy walking distance
of one another and form a support-discussion group which meets two eve-
nings a week under the direction of a faculty member.

Mornings in the Urban Studies Program are given over to classes.
Seminars on special topics-- urban politics, health care, women in the work
force, changing neighborhoods, media, corporations, city literature, etc.
-- meet twice a week. A Core Course on the city and its institutions occupies
the other mornings. Both the seminars and the Core Course utilize encounters with persons active in the city as their chief pedagogic format.

In addition, each student in the Urban Studies Program takes on a
volunteer work placement in the afternoons. The placements cover a broad
range of urban institutions: hospitals, political offices, theaters, schools,
community organizations, unions, law offices, and settlement houses. Each
student is also expected to produce an Independent Study Project, a piece of
work which often grows out of the volunteer placement.

An independent faculty of from eight to twelve persons teaches and
coordinates the program, reporting directly to the ACM President (also
located in Chicago), who in turn reports to the Deans and Presidents of the
thirteen ACM colleges. The faculty strives to keep itself diversified in
terms of areas of competence, contacts, and experience in the metropolitan
region.

The program's basic pedagogy involves utilizing fully the vast resources of the city as catalysts to open up discussion of the fundamental issues facing modern society. The approach is inductive, beginning with the students' own experiences and encounters, sharpening the tools of observation and inquiry. These various experiences and encounters begin slowly to build upon one another, sometimes complementing and confirming earlier observations, sometimes contradicting them.

Gradually, the larger questions begin to open up--questions about polity and power, change and community, hope and happiness and meaning. But these are questions which, by now, carry with them an intensity and excitement that makes "teaching" an immensely rewarding experience. They are questions which are informed with an urgency born of personal contact with the so-called urban crisis. They are also questions which are based on a growing sense of realism about both the limitations and possibilities of individual and group activity. And probably most important, they are questions which arise out of a deep concern about the student's own life and direction. They are, in brief, anything but "merely academic."

But do not these fundamental questions also constitute the irreducible core of a liberal arts education? Is it not possible to speak of being faithful to the "spirit" of liberal arts inquiry as well as to the content of the tradition? Is it absolutely heretical to suggest that a lively interest in that tradition might be born of an urgent inquiry into the contemporary forms of "timeless" topics?

The spirit of the liberal arts aspires, above all, to a habit of mind--reaching and probing, questing and questioning, a kind of intellectual restlessness which, when combined with a trained moral sensitivity, still represents a compelling image of human possibility. Engendering, encouraging, and guiding that spirit ought to remain the most pressing challenge for teachers in this time.

Surely good teaching is partly good timing. And the moment when deeply felt questions about highly significant matters arise is precisely the moment when all the resources of learning and experience which inhere in the good teacher will find an eager and receptive audience. These times will continue to have a dialogic character, as the students involved have not only seen something of the world but they actually consider themselves a part of it. If the teacher imbued with the spirit and some of the discipline of the liberal arts cannot thrive in such a setting, where can he or she?

Clearly our experience in the Urban Studies Program has caused us to rethink many of our assumptions about the teaching-learning process. We enjoy a unique vantage point from which to evaluate particularly the performance of the liberal arts college. The kind of education we are now thinking about lies beyond the capabilities of a single semester program such as our own, so we would like to lay the groundwork for an interchange with other educators.

Any propositions for reform must be closely tied to an analysis of both the institutional and pedagogical assumptions which inform undergraduate education today. For what may be needed most are clear and realistic proposals which honor the ancient aims and spirit of a liberal arts education while reformulating the pedagogy to respond to our own complex technological age.

We have become convinced that this spirit is often honored more in rhetoric than in practice. For despite the liberal arts jargon which still adorns the opening pages of college catalogues, we are continually struck by the overwhelming pressure toward social, political, and economic accommodation which permeates the liberal arts college. This institutional tendency toward acceptability in the eyes of the larger society is hardly new. For some time now, in both private and public institutions, survival and growth has dictated an increasingly amorous and uncritical tie to both public and private centers of power. At the same time we have witnessed the steady erosion in practice of the college's isolationist stance. In both style and substance, the ivory tower and the board room have become indistinguishable.

Analysis of this marriage of convenience (and of survival?) should embrace not only the well-documented ties of colleges and universities with government bureaucracies, or of research oriented institutions with their myriad public and private sponsors, but it should include also what appears to us to be both a more subtle and perhaps more far-reaching aspect of the problem--namely, the growing role and shifting emphasis of the undergraduate college as a socializing agent.

That colleges have always performed socialization tasks is obvious. The status and power of an institution reflects the social and economic class of its constituents and graduates. Recent studies have tended to confirm what many have long suspected--that colleges, far from being a crucial factor in providing upward mobility for individuals in the society, function rather to replicate the social and economic classes which send their offspring to them.

The liberal arts college, though, has often been most reluctant to examine its role through this prism. When the college actually does talk about its "product," the language it uses comes close to a description of the "Renaissance Man" as an ideal type.

This is particularly disturbing, since it seems all too clear that the function of the liberal arts curriculum has become virtually indistinguishable from that of either the hard or soft sciences. All too often, ossified curricula and the ritualized classroom seem to signal the real message to the student: that acquisition of specialized knowledge and language, and of certain traditional sets of values and modes of behavior is what is required for a professional future. It is our experience that students of the mid-1970's are as

quick at perceiving the seductiveness of that message, albeit with a different
response, as were their counterparts in the "student movement" a few years
ago.

In addition, more and more liberal arts faculty are discovering that
the pursuit of knowledge "for its own sake" is no longer the persuasive
rationale it was before hard times descended on academe. For in a growth
economy begging for college graduates, both the stronger and weaker liberal
arts student could expect useful employment. Faculty could easily steer
their favorites into the booming field of higher education, while assuring the
remainder that some business or government agency would be perfectly
willing to train them for something useful after graduation. Thus assured
vocationally, students were in a position to accept readily a whole series of
rationales which persuaded them of the non-utilitarian value of a liberal arts
"background."

Today the substantive message of the liberal arts classroom has to
do with "making it." The "hustle" is on as the real world impinges on the
purity of the humanities with ever-mounting harshness. Stronger students
are forced into an increasingly competitive posture as they struggle for the
few slots at the top of the education pyramid, while weaker students accurately perceive the coolness with which hard-pressed employers view their
"wasteful" venture into "merely academic" subject areas.

The impact of these developments on the whole teaching-learning
process must be substantial. From conversations with hundreds of students
and faculty on liberal arts campuses, we can begin to outline certain elements
of that impact. It ought not to come as much of a shock to discover that developments in pedagogy mirror quite directly the tendencies we've already
observed at an institutional level.

In the broadest sense, classroom teaching in the liberal arts and
humanities is moving into its own period of severe retrenchment. The
critiques of curricula and of classroom teaching which were popularized
by the student movement in the late sixties, and which gave birth to a variety
of pedagogic experiments on liberal arts campuses, have now largely been
rejected. The common targets of those critiques--the authoritarian classroom, the tightness of boundaries separating academic disciplines, the
invulnerability of faculty, the absence of conflict and controversy from the
classroom scene, the separation of analytical methodologies from both
ideology and emotion, the lack of significant student input, the severely
competitive nature of the classroom experience, the isolation of the classroom from the "world outside"--all of these elements seem to have re-
emerged with a new vigor in the liberal arts classroom.

Clearly the reassertion of these factors embodies a partial response
on the part of well-meaning teachers to the pressures of "hard times." When
faced with a clear threat to the "knowledge-for-its-own-sake" rationale, the
rationale which gained such wide acceptance as long as the problems of jobs

and advancement took care of themselves, faculty have understandably
tightened the reins on both their disciplines and their classrooms.

We would suggest, however, that this approach might, for both
the middle and long run health of liberal arts teaching, be precisely the
opposite of what is required. For it is becoming more and more clear that
most students have ceased to share their faculty's belief in those elements
of the liberal arts rationale which focus exclusively on analytical detachment,
and on the pleasures of discovery which arise solely out of contact with the
artifacts of the liberal arts tradition. In brief, the increasingly typical
liberal arts classroom features a growing gap between faculty who believe
in these verities and students who have "making it" on their minds.

Certainly a classroom based on such widely divergent assumptions
about why it is important to be there can only impede, or at least retard,
the entire teaching-learning process. And surely it is unrealistic to ask
that students shelve temporarily their vocationalist bent. Only the teaching
faculty retain the potential for role flexibility which could begin to reinvig-
orate the liberal arts classroom in this period of hard times.

Critics of Society, Critics of the Campus

It may well be that the constructive reassessment of liberal arts
traditions and institutions will find its strongest adherents among those who
share one or another fundamental critique of the direction of American
society. For the basis of these ruminations is partly the assumption that
the socializing function of the liberal arts institution is, in the broadest
sense of the term, a political function. Clearly educational institutions
reflect the dominant values of the society. They all respond to certain
social and economic demands. They help to sort out the labor force. Most
reinforce the barriers of race and class. And at the level of the liberal
arts college, they tend to inculcate the skills and values appropriate to the
professional-managerial strata.

For those working within the liberal arts institution who find themselves at peace with the overall direction of American society in the last
quarter of the twentieth century, these latent social functions may pose no
significant problem. For those, on the other hand, who find cause to pose
fundamentally critical questions about the society, the politically integral
role of the liberal arts college may well raise serious doubts about the
form and content of higher education.

We do not propose at this point to defend one set of systemic criticisms over against others. But we would like to point to some of the ramifications for liberal arts education which flow from three distinct, though
interconnected, systemic critiques. In shorthand, we will label these the

Power and Justice perspective, the Mass and Techno-Society perspective, and the Limits of Growth perspective.

Each of these basic critiques raises questions of meaning and purpose and polity and community and citizenship--questions which go to the heart of the form and function of a liberal arts education. Though they intersect and overlap at many points, (and though none may exist in pure form), each of these critiques could provide a framework out of which one might both judge and begin to reform one's own institution.

By the Power and Justice perspective, we mean that set of analytical and critical categories which take seriously some variant of a Marxian framework, from C. Wright Mills to Marcuse. The analytical focus is on the continuing function of economic class as the basic determinant of power and upon class conflict as the necessary harbinger of justice. The concentration of political and economic power in the hands of the few provides the key to understanding not only the broad strokes of domestic and international developments, but also the value orientation and community structure adhered to by individuals in the society. In this view, of course, the economic function of the liberal arts college becomes both clear and unacceptable. The top strata of these schools simply reproduce some variant of a national or regional ruling class, while the rest train the professionals and managers who make up the top portion of the white collar work force.

In the Mass and Techno-Society perspective, we mean to include a whole range of social critics from Ortega to Gibson Winter who highlight the increasingly homogenizing effects of huge bureaucratic organizations and the spread of a narrowly instrumental technological ethos in our culture. Most of the variations on this theme tend to locate their critiques in the cultural sphere and to focus on the difficulty of authentic freedom and community in the face of what Winter calls the "totalization" process. The basic problem with the liberal arts college, in this view, must include not only the increasingly restricted yet standardized nature of the curriculum and training, but also the almost total surrender to technical rationalism--to "problem-solution" or "how-to" modes of thought.

The Limits of Growth perspective refers, of course, to the entire series of ecologically-based critiques of growth-oriented societies. From Paul Ehrlich to Robert Heilbroner to Alvin Pitcher, these critics tend to locate basic dilemmas in our destruction of the natural order. The drive to dominate nature and the attachment to long-standing notions of material progress can only lead us down the self-destructive path toward collision with the immutable limits of the ecosystem. A liberal arts education which serves as the accrediting agent for upward mobility and which fosters a view of culture as simply another consumer item, clearly demands fundamental questioning.

Again, it is not our purpose here to explore these three critical perspectives in any detail. Though each represents a potentially total critique

of society, none is inevitably holistic in its impact. Reformers from different
political orientations will adopt parts of each perspective in the belief that
major or even minor adjustments in the system will suffice. Nevertheless,
we are convinced that these three critiques encompass all of the important
questions which need to be asked about our kind of society. In addition, each
of them, or any combination of them, provides a constellation of values from
which one might begin to rethink liberal arts education.

It seems quite clear that educational institutions need not always
serve the established society. Ample precedent for a more critical role
exists in the now largely mythical notion of the liberal arts college as a place
apart, even an ivory tower. While this notion in itself has obviously proved
too insubstantial to serve as a base for critical examination, the three more
politically substantive perspectives outlined above hold rather more promise.

What we are proposing, in brief, is a reconstruction of educational
philosophy which takes seriously fundamental critiques of the society and
which in a more positive vein concerns itself with alternative versions of
our future. This is a task which blends politics, again broadly conceived,
and education. This is also a task which may well lead us into uncharted
waters, for such a reconstitution may involve us less in work with different
content than in work with different processes.

An Alternative Pedagogy

In advancing the following argument as an approach to higher education, more particularly an approach for the recovery of some of the aims
of liberal arts, we suggest that we as college faculty key our teaching and
our thinking about curricula to this disarmingly simple question: "What is
it that young Americans most need to know about themselves and their society?" The question is an obvious Pandora's box; much of its varied con-
tents have been clarified for us by our experience in using the city as our
primary resource over the past six years.

We are discovering that one of the keys to answering this question
lies in an examination of the paradox of social relationships -- that is, in the
individual's recognition of, on the one hand, his or her relatedness with
larger groups and, on the other hand, his or her difference from others.

In an increasingly complex and interrelated culture and world,
many critics have already perceived the need to greatly extend our refer-
ents for choosing and acting. If what we do and how we live affects people
in all corners of the globe, then we must begin to identify with people in all
corners of the globe.

But this new awareness of an expanded social identity must be
balanced with a recognition of differences among peoples and among classes
of peoples. For while it is true that all of our fates are interrelated in the

modern world, it is emphatically not true that those fates are all the same.
Widely variant cultures and conditions have produced widely divergent worldviews. Understanding and tolerance of these positions, and respect for these
differences are crucial qualities, especially for those who mature in the most
powerful and wealthy nation on earth.

Unfortunately, these paradoxical elements of social relationships,
relatedness and difference, are precisely the elements which growing up in
America today tend to distort in a devastating way. We are led to deny
relatedness in the first instance, clinging instead to mythologies about
individualism and autonomy, and in the second instance, we are led to deny
difference, seeking instead to universalize the anxieties and (manufactured)
needs of the affluent Westerner.

From childhood onward in modern America, we nurture the myth
of autonomy. We develop a notion of identity which is almost exclusively
self-centered. That many of our young develop nebulous self-definitions
which are asocial, ahistorical and apolitical should come as no surprise to
us. For in this process, the denial of interrelatedness with nature and with
others destroys caring. The individual's horizon of responsibility extends
at most to the limits of his or her nuclear family, perhaps including a few
friends. Effective activity too is limited to the interpersonal realm. The
privatization of religious belief insures the trivialization of religious organizations. The "autonomous man" rationalizes inequity and exploitation in
terms of the market or a hidden hand that somehow regulates all the autonomous parts.

The denial of difference, on the other hand, is equally serious.
Children who are raised in class and racial and cultural isolation have little
opportunity to come into contact with--let alone to inspect and analyze --
different perspectives which arise out of different conditions. As one result,
real differences in culture, values, and aspiration tend to be perceived as
aberrations. They are not normatively divergent, they are deviations from
the one and only norm.

Obviously, when this denial of difference comes from the wealthy
Westerner, it leads inevitably to an imperialistic posture, to problem-solving
rather than to problem-discovery. What is good for the professional is good
for the client. The maximization of private consumption, however unsatisfying culturally and impossible economically, remains the unexamined touch-
stone of both private life and public policy.

But the dawning recognition of interrelatedness on the one hand and
difference on the other, tends to be radically immobilizing. For in relationship to practice, the discovery of both the human and natural connections
broadens infinitely the context of moral choosing. And the recognition of
difference tends to constrict both the efficacy of acting and the possibility
of universalizing action.

Return to the simple question: "What is it that young Americans most need to know about themselves and their society?" An answer to this question, in the light of what we have just said, would imply a number of things about teaching and curricula.

In the first place, the question implies at least a suspended judgment, and quite possibly a negative one, on the inevitable value and ascendancy of the academic disciplines as presently ordered. Not only have we found that the web of a modern metropolis refuses to conform to traditional disciplinary boundaries, we have also discovered that the undergraduate mind--and our own as well--once freed from the necessity of continually defining conceptual limits and boundaries, tends to roam freely and often creatively over and between previously circumscribed "fields."

Secondly, the question implies a rather stringent historicity. That is, what young Americans need most to know about themselves and their society today, may not be precisely what their grandparents needed to know, or even what their contemporaries in Europe, Japan, or Latin America need to know. Time, place, and circumstance infuse certain questions with a new urgency, while at the same time relegating others to a lesser magnitude. The "eternal topics," therefore, which ought to lie at the core of every liberal arts education, must be constantly reexamined so that newly fruitful avenues of approach to them can be discovered. Curriculum development, in this sense, becomes the central activity of the critical education institution. This process implies not the death of the liberal arts curriculum, but quite the opposite--its continuing reinvigoration.

Thirdly, of course, our basic question imposes the imperative that students themselves must be active participants in their own learning process. This is such a fundamental ingredient in any process which addresses our basic question that even when the impulse for active participation does not emerge from the students themselves, as it did sporadically during the sixties, pedagogies must be devised which spark that impulse.

Finally, it follows that our basic question places a different and awesome responsibility on both administrators and faculty. It demands, quite simply, that the faculty member in particular be prepared to make social judgments, and that these social judgments be incorporated into the job of teaching. That is, faculty must take far more seriously than they now do--and at least as seriously as their students do--the socializing aspects of their work. Both the form and content of their educational practice depend upon the results of this assessment. For the most part, such an assessment involves a careful examination of the social role assigned to educators, and a decision to take that role as rather more fundamental than most do now. No longer is it sufficient that faculty members qualify simply by absorbing the scholarship and traditions of their field. They must also relate their expertise to an analysis of the directions and needs of the larger society. It is only too clear that the larger society will continue to make such demands on the academic world. The point here is that the defense against such intrusion is not a retreat into some largely mythical notion of academic neutrality of "objective" and "value-free" scholarship, but rather the adoption of a critical, independent, and value-laden stance toward the larger society.

If an educator consciously fails to make such an assessment, (develop a "politics," broadly conceived), or if his conclusion basically reaffirms the extant social order or baptizes it as beneficent, his teaching task becomes clear and relatively uncomplicated. He simply slides into the mainstream of current educational practice, and adopts the values of his profession as his own. What is taught as a result of this decision clearly has less to do with the particular subject matter or discipline than it does with the value for students of making a similar choice.

What we are asserting is that if we keep foremost in our minds the question about what young Americans most need to know about themselves we soon realize that education involves fundamentally a moral dimension. Education is not primarily the passing on of information. It is not the mastering of a body of knowledge which has been parcelled out in pre-cast catagories called disciplines. It is not simply the appropriation of eternal verities. In general, it is not the answering of questions that have not been asked.

It is our contention that education essentially is helping young people decide what is worth being and doing. Most of us and most of our students exist in the contemporary scene as "pre-moral" beings. "Ethics no longer matters," or more accurately does not yet matter, for those whose basic choices have all been made by circumstance. Thus the moral dimension is found not in the passing on of values or in providing "right" or "good" solutions, but rather in challenging prevailing solutions and in raising new questions.

As a prelude to active citizenship in the contemporary scene, the moral dimension is found in responding to the specific pathologies of technological society, passivity and non-thinking. Eric Fromm summarizes the effects on men of a technologically-centered society where "how to" questions rule and expertise is king.

> The passiveness of man in industrial society today is one of his most characteristic and pathological features. He takes in, he wants to be fed, but does not move, initiate, he does not digest his food, as it were. . . .Man's passiveness is only one symptom among a total syndrome which one may call the "syndrome of alienation." Being passive, he does not relate himself to the world actively and is forced to submit to his idols and their demands. Hence, he feels powerless, lonely, and anxious. He has little sense of integrity or self-identity. [1]

More penetrating is Hannah Arendt's analysis which identifies passivity's twin, non-thinking.

> However, non-thinking, which seems so recommendable a state for political and moral affairs, also has its dangers. By shielding people against the dangers of examination, it teaches them to hold fast to whatever the prescribed rules of conduct may be at a given time in a given society. What people then get used to is not so much the content of the rules, a close examination of which would always lead them into perplexity, as the possession of rules under which to subsume particulars. In other words, they get used to never making up their minds. [2]

"Making up their minds" is precisely what education is about. Minds have to be "made up" and this making is an active process which involves commitment and contention. It is not simply a filling up of minds and a periodic assessment of the content.

For Arendt the moral dimension in education is clearly tied to this active process of making up minds which she calls "thinking." And

> thinking accompanies living when it concerns itself with such concepts as justice, happiness, temperance, pleasure, with words for invisible things which language has offered us to express the meaning of whatever happens in life and occurs to us while we are alive. [3]

As we broaden the context of ethical thinking to the global level, this recognition of relatedness and difference which we have referred to earlier presents a profoundly new set of challenges for every "thinking" person. But for students especially, this recognition often leads to inarticulateness (distinct and distinguishable from the silence of passivity). Arendt speaks of this moment when thinking is born:

> It is in its (thinking's) nature to undo, unfreeze as it were, what language, the medium of thinking, has frozen into thought. . .These frozen thoughts, Socrates seems to say, come so handy you can use them in your sleep; but if the wind of thinking, which I shall now arouse in you, has roused you from your sleep and made you fully awake and alive, then you will see that you have nothing in your hand but perplexities, and the most we can do with them is share them with each other. [4]

Insofar as this inarticulateness is engendered by a dawning recognition of human relatedness and human difference it is not to be discouraged. The discovery of the inadequacy of "frozen thoughts," be they the academic categories, class-conditioned styles of speech, or sophisticated "problem-solving" techniques, this discovery is the precondition of what Gibson Winter refers to as the "receptive moment, " the moment when "technique talk, " however tempting, becomes inappropriate and "moral talk" or problem discovery becomes possible.

In education, encounter and experience must play a central role in such an awakening. For as we have argued, the basic content of any class-room encounter with a great text must be the acquisition by the student of the "correct" (or at least acceptable) reading of that text. Professional socialization remains stubbornly at the top of the schooling agenda. In the schooling agenda, students are clients, curricula are hurdles to leap over, and degrees are the certificates of "accomplishment. " Articulateness, problem-solving, and technique mastery are rewarded. The inarticulateness of the listening, hearing, seeing, sensing receptive moment is discouraged.

But when the self confronts the other, questions of relatedness and difference emerge. It is for this reason that, at least when dealing with the education of middle class students, the geographically defined city becomes an appropriate (perhaps the only appropriate) educational setting. Part of the necessary process involves simple observation and awareness. For example, the interrelatedness--the social, cultural, political, and economic bonds--which still hangs on in the city's traditional ethnic communities, presents the highly mobile, pre-professional, suburban oriented college student with a set of realities totally foreign to his experience. On the other hand, the cosmopolitan tolerance for difference and eccentricity pushes this same student toward a more limited and even humble self-definition.

The student tutoring inmates at the Cook County jail finds himself or herself both more personally involved in the lives of the inmates and more aware of the distance between himself and them that he had imagined. Both the academic categories and the traditional presuppositions which "explain" criminal behavior and the inmate situation prove inadequate. For the student this situation becomes a receptive moment precisely because he or she is on the one hand unable to relate through customary modes of language and experience and on the other hand unable to remain detached. New questions and problems emerge and these become the curricula for pre-moral development. Who are they? Who am I? Who are we? And questions of deviant behavior and criminal justice then become raised in a new way.

But a crucial part of this pre-moral development involves some-thing beyond simple experience. A lengthy encounter with an ADC mother in her Robert Taylor Homes apartment, for instance, often involves the student with richly contradictory messages. The mother-teacher may exude love, warmth, and acceptance (relatedness); yet the very context of the en-counter, the stark sixth floor apartment reachable only by stair and only with the assistance of armed guards, drives home the depth of difference which separates the mother-teacher from the student. Most often, such an encounter is simply too rich and challenging to admit easy assimilation.

Similarly, a morning with a bank president in his fortieth floor office wreaks havoc with "frozen thoughts." Here the student often senses a relatedness in style and tone (class) with the president-teacher, but is often alienated on an emotional level by what he senses as an overwhelmingly rationalized and instrumental view of human connections. Again, this is the pre-moral moment when the teacher-teacher can begin to probe and bring back to the point of articulation that which the student finds profoundly troubling. If, in addition, the student must relate these encounters to his own activity and work in the city, the richness of the mix serves almost invariably to begin reconstituting fundamental and previously unquestioned assumptions.

The process we are discussing can be termed pre-"urban studies" because it facilitates what in various ways we have called recognition, awakening, or receptivity and it deals with the inarticulateness that these moments engender, the further questions they uncover, and the thinking or making up of minds that these occasions require. This is pre-"urban studies" because the city appears not as a set of problems to be solved or a constellation of manpower needs to be filled, but as a varied context for the disclosure of meaning and the discovery of new problems.

It is a process which opens up new questions. For example, in a seminar on Health Care, what begins as an examination of the medical system in Chicago and a consideration of proposals for reform, including health maintenance organizations, national health insurance, etc., proceeds to explore more fundamental questions of the meaning of health and the role of the medical system. More than the content of the written curriculum, the ongoing discussions with representatives of medicine-- doctors, administrators, the AMA, free clinic folks and others, along with the student's own work assignments at Cook County Hospital or neighborhood health centers, lead the student beyond "reform" and "problem-solving" questions toward questions about the "therapeutic ideology," professional dominance, and the relationship of scientific medicine and drugs to health. What is health? Who are the healers?

Or, in a seminar on Outcasts in Chicago, what begins as a course on "deviant behavior" moves to issues that are more personally problematic after students meet in small groups with members of the skid row, youth gang, and gay communities. The distancing mechanism of so-called "objective" categories is suspended and other more personal dynamics of identification and distancing arise.

The impact of the pedagogy we are describing is varied. For many students the fundamental questioning of prevailing institutions leads not to any systemic critique of American society but rather to fairly specific critiques and specific proposals. For some students such an approach opens up ways for them to move toward professional goals and to adjust to the realistic expectations of the world of work. But for others, this experience provides the occasion for a serious societal critique. And for those faculty who wish to tie their teaching practice to such a larger critique, this pedagogy may be of particular interest.

For instance, the process can be very useful for opening up the questions and concerns which rise out of a Marxian critique. Generally, the political perspectives most students bring to the city tend to reflect a combination of their parents' views and the vaguely liberal ethos of the campus. They are consensus-oriented, tending to think in terms of "social problems" and technically-oriented "solutions," often coated with a kind of missionary appetite for "good works" and person-to-person "service."

Most students have very little experience with or sense of such categories as power and powerlessness, class and racial divisions, conflict and controversy. Only through experiences and encounters with people and organizations that embody alternative perspectives can students begin to acknowledge and deal with these categories. At first, these encounters and experiences will tend to engender the inarticulateness and confusion we've discussed. Gradually, though, through prodding and questioning, the process of redefining both the political-economic order, and the student's own role in it, accelerates. Many who have gone through this process have turned to some variant of community or workplace organizing as an expression of their politics and commitment. Others have broadened their conception of their professional role to respond in a variety of ways to changed perceptions.

This same basic awakening process may also be interesting for teachers whose systemic critique falls into the mass and techno-society category. Coming out of the basically homogeneous campus setting, students are astounded by their encounters and experiences with all kinds of people who are very different from themselves. The remnants of urban pluralism, the varieties of ethnic, religious, racial and "life-style" options which are opened up for the student--all of these cause the process of self-redefinition to accelerate. In addition, these same encounters and experiences challenge radically the urban service version of the technical rationalist mindset, that "what is good for the professional is good for the client."

Finally, any faculty who are influenced by the limits of growth critique will want to see their students begin to think in macro-systemic categories. The rampant, (and in many ways self-delusive) individualism of the campus scene often makes this leap impossible for students, or at the very least keeps discussion at a totally abstract level. First-hand experience with huge (urban) institutions, with their own commitment to growth as an integral part of their basic mission, and with the effects of unbridled expansion as they are now felt in the city forms the necessary backdrop for further exploration into this particular set of issues.

For those educators whose considered judgment of American society leads them to question some of its major premises and current directions,

there can be only one goal in their role as educators, the continual enlarge-
ment of the questioning community. The moral dimension of such a community is most clear in problematic times. One further observation from
Arendt is to the point:

> For thinking as such does society little good, much less than the
> thirst for knowledge in which it is used as an instrument for other
> purposes. It does not create values, it will not find out, once and
> for all, what "the good" is, and it does not confirm but rather
> dissolves accepted rules of conduct. Its political and moral signif-
> icance comes out only in those rare moments in history when
> "Things fall apart; the centre cannot hold; / Mere anarchy is
> loosed upon the world," when "The best lack all conviction, while
> the worst/ Are full of passionate intensity."

> At these moments, thinking ceases to be a marginal affair in
> political matters. When everybody is swept away unthinkingly by
> what everybody else does and believes in, those who think are drawn
> out of hiding because their refusal to join is conspicuous and there-
> by becomes a kind of action. [5]

The questioning community thus becomes "political" without, however, advocating a single "politics." Entrance into it assumes a continuing
ability to entertain astonishment (the "receptive," or "dialogic" moment),
a healthy scepticism toward all that is merely instrumental and technique-
oriented, and an ongoing struggle for meaning in history.

The questioning community involves also a mode of acting and
thinking together which overcomes the divisions of subject matter, disciplines, institutional roles, vocational and professional specialties, and
student and teacher roles that have become frozen assumptions of the educational process. The questioning community treats with irreverence cre-
dentials, academic disciplines, and traditional forms of evaluation. Playing
what Lezek Kolakowski calls the jester's role, the questioning community
"exposes as doubtful what seems most unshakeable, reveals the contradictions
in what appears obvious and incontrovertible." [6] It is precisely in the imper-
tinent juxtapositions that thinking, in Arendt's sense, is possible. And because, as she put it, "thinking itself is dangerous," the questioning community becomes a community of mutual support and caring.

These then are the two attributes of the questioning community.
First, it is a setting where fundamental questioning is not only tolerated but
also encouraged. And secondly, it is a scene of caring and support.

These characteristics can be illustrated, in part at least, by the
Urban Studies Program. The students find themselves regularly in situations

where any set of approaches, presuppositions, definitions, and resolutions are challenged and contested. This happens at a fascinating mix of levels.

In their contact with the city the students are confronted with a variety of perspectives on any one issue. Speakers at Core Course provide this conflict in the student. An anti-Machine alderman speaks one night and is followed the next day by a regular organization precinct captain. Or, in a seminar, the perspective of the AMA staff is placed against the analysis of staff members of a people's health clinic. Guest speakers usually know who preceded or will follow them and do not hesitate to comment on or disagree with other speakers. Furthermore, students often come in contact with ongoing controversies in their work assignments, whether at Cook County hospital, community organizations, legal defense groups, or in government funded service programs. In work and through speakers, the students are faced with conflicting perspectives.

In addition, the students soon discover that the staff members have different perspectives and interpretations of the issues at hand. They find that the staff members argue not only among themselves but also as they evaluate perspectives raised by speakers and as they deal with the issues raised in Core Course and seminars. So the staff provides no ready resolution to the controversies of the city.

Students also find themselves increasingly aware of the differing perspectives and assumptions within the student group. As they respond to the impact of their work assignment and the various speakers and experiences the students begin to formulate their own perspectives in relations to other students and to the staff.

The dynamics of contention in these three levels get complex. Students argue with students about the staff's conflicting evaluations of a speaker. Or students see speakers challenging a staff member's assumption about a particular issue. Or a staff member argues with students about the conflicting perspectives of a Core Course speaker and a work assignment supervisor. In contrast to the classroom where there is subtle pressure to discourage questioning and where conflict is often present only through arranged "debates, " the urban experience provides a setting where contention is normal, where unchallenged answers are not found and where the likelihood of fundamental questioning of even the most assumed values and perspectives is considerable.

The educational approach we are increasingly committed to is one which not only stimulates questioning but also both allows and requires the nurturing of communities. It allows for such communities because it provides the setting and encouragement for new student and teacher roles. We have earlier referred to the various effects of the highly structured classroom and fragmented curricula on liberal arts education. We are further convinced that such a process has been destructive of questioning communities. They tend not only to separate experts (teachers) from clients (students) but also to place clients in a competitive struggle for favored positions on the educational/job seeking ladder.

With an alternative setting and pedagogy new kinds of roles and relationships can be encouraged. In the Urban Studies Program, for example, staff and students are joined in a variety of informal and formal learning situations, projects and small groups that are not saddled with some of the trappings that have accrued to academic institutions. Couple this frequency of staff-student interaction with the urgency and intensity of the issues explored together and you have a basic prerequisite of the questioning community. Student-student relationships also shift as they move from the competitive classroom to situations of cooperative learning. They find that it is both possible and enjoyable to teach each other (and the staff) and to learn from each other. In this situation the staff members also have the possibility of relating to each other in new ways, seeking new modes of decisionmaking, rotating the various program responsibilities, benefiting from each other's strengths and supporting weaknesses. These kinds of staff-student, student-student, and staff-staff relationships provide the necessary conditions for nurturing a questioning community.

We are convinced, further, that the short term bonds formed among most students in the Urban Studies Program, the longer term connections among alumni of the program, and the continuing work-community shared by the staff become not luxuries but necessities central to our task. It is necessary to maintain the kinds of relationships and the kinds of roles that help form those supportive communities which sustain and reward people who are asking tough questions and making tough decisions. It is important, for those who begin to develop a critical stance toward the prevailing cultural or societal drift, to participate in communities concerned with both the substance of these critiques and the decisions participants are making to pursue them. This, we feel, stands in contrast to the college process where the substantive issues are dealt with in structured classroom settings and where community-forming may be limited to the social areas of dorm life, fraternities, clubs, and athletics.

More could be said about this and other attempts to develop the questioning community: that it involves activity and reflection, that it involves both commitment and openness, that it struggles to sustain both local roots and global comprehension. But at the center of the community is always the continual unfreezing of all that is petrified and dead.

Such a conception might provide us not only with a new way of thinking about the liberal-liberating arts for our times, but might also return us to the traditional heart of the liberal arts community through the ages. For the "eternal topics"--life and death and meaning and communication and community--can meaningfully reoccupy center stage in the young American mind only if they arise out of meaningful activity and encounters. Then and only then will teachers be able to bring to bear the richness of the liberal arts tradition as a guide to analysis and choice. And then and only then will we have begun the enormously important task of reclaiming our socializing institutions for their real purpose--education.

NOTES AND REFERENCES

[1]Eric Fromm, The Revolution of Hope (New York: Harper and Row, 1970), p. 39.

[2]Hannah Arendt, "Thinking and Moral Considerations," Social Research, Vol. 38, No. 3, pp. 435-6.

[3]Ibid., 436-7.

[4]Ibid., 433-4.

[5]Ibid., 445-6.

[6]Leszek Kolakowski, Toward a Marxist Humanism (New York: Grove Press, Inc.), p. 34.

CHAPTER VI

CHRISTIAN THEOLOGY AND AMERICAN DEMOCRACY

by
Franklin Sherman

These final years of our second century as an independent nation
have not been placid ones for the citizens of the United States of America.
The succession of crises, including a bitterly divisive overseas war, racial
strife, economic turbulence, the upsurge of crime and violence, has been
such as to cause us to wonder at times, with Lincoln, whether American
democracy as we have known it "can long endure." Yet as the Bicentennial
approached, the citizens found, to their rejoicing, that the constitutional
framework had proved able to survive not only the challenges mentioned but
also the ultimate political crisis represented by the impeachment of a President.

At such times, we are driven back to a reexamination of our roots,
both for the sake of a due appreciation of the heritage that is ours, and in
order to ascertain the points at which this heritage needs to be criticized
and transformed if it is to be serviceable for the future. Of special importance is the question of the nature and sources of American democracy, including its religious sources. This is the question that we want to examine
here; and in order to make our inquiry as empirically relevant and concrete
as possible, we shall focus it on the understanding of the Christian faith
embodied in one particular tradition, namely, that of Lutheranism. Our
interest is both historical and contemporary. In what sense or to what extent, we want to ask, can this tradition be regarded as a source of modern
democracy; and secondly -- however that historical question be answered
-- in what way can it serve as a resource for the maintenance of a viable
democracy today?

The word "democracy" has a broad range of meanings, and if confusion is not to ensue, we shall have to specify rather closely what we mean
by it. Literally, of course, it means "rule by the people" (demos). Now
it is noteworthy that to the ancient Greeks, who invented the term, it had
a decidedly negative connotation -- at least if we can judge by the writings
of Plato and Aristotle. Both of them considered democracy one of the less
desirable forms of government, inferior to monarchy or aristocracy. They
seem to have been animated by an image of "the people" as an untutored and

unruly crowd (and this despite the fact that the lowest class, that of the
slaves, was excluded entirely from consideration). Democracy meant to
them, in fact, "mobocracy."

If we move ahead two millennia and consult the writings of such
American founding fathers as Hamilton, Madison, and Jay in The Federalist
Papers, we find that this tone of distrust of the common man has largely
(though not entirely) disappeared. However, for yet another reason they
were reluctant to use the word "democracy." Democracy signified direct
rule by the people, that is, all the people concerned. This, however, is
literally possible only in a local setting, for example, in the New England
town meeting. There the governed and the governors are one. In any larger
area, and especially an area as large as that of the thirteen colonies -- and
we must remember what a huge area that was, in view of the transportation
and communication facilities available then -- government could function
only by the delegation of power to chosen representatives. The system set
forth in the U.S. Constitution clearly is such a delegated system; hence the
authors of The Federalist Papers insist that the polity they are defending is
in no way a democracy, but rather a republic.

What has happened meanwhile is, obviously, that the word "democracy" has broadened its meaning to include also this system of rule by
elected representatives. Nowadays we use the terms "direct" and "indirect"
democracy, or "pure" and "representative" democracy, to indicate this difference.

The importance of this distinction lies in its reminding us that the
notion of democracy is not incompatible with the notion of leadership. Certainly, in the face of the urgent and complex problems confronting American
society today, vigorous leadership is called for. The energy crisis, the
whole problem of reshaping our relation to the natural environment, the need
for new systems of mass transportation, the problem of balancing food and
population (both at home and overseas), the redefinition of national purpose
and policy in a world of shrunken American power -- all these require hard
thinking and the making of difficult choices, and many are tempted to question whether or not democracy is adequate to the task.

If democracy consisted merely in head-counting, there might be
grounds for such uncertainty. But in fact, the representative democracy
that we have calls not only for the expression of the popular will, but also
for the exercise of intelligence, expertise, decisiveness, and imaginative
vision -- in short, leadership -- on the part of those who are elected to
positions of responsibility. There is no need, therefore, out of a hunger
for such leadership, to turn to authoritarian solutions as the German people,
for example, did in the 1930's. (Remember the title by which Adolph Hitler
was known: der Führer, "the Leader.") Rather, we have the right and the
duty to look for bold and creative leadership from those whom we elect to
public office, whether at the local level, in mayors and city council members,

or among our state legislators, governors, senators and representatives, and presidents. It is to this that they are called, and for this that they are to be held responsible. They are not to be robots or weather vanes, but leaders!

＊ ＊ ＊ ＊ ＊ ＊ ＊ ＊ ＊ ＊

In all that has been said thus far, however, we have been dealing with the realm of the political, in the sense of the mechanisms by which society is governed. But there are other meanings to the term "democracy." It can be used to refer not only to the process of decision-making, but also to the substance of human relationships within a society: the question of whether there is a structure of privilege or prejudice that gives some a greater access than others to wealth, power, educational opportunity, or whatever else is prized by the society. All of this constitutes what is known as "social democracy" as distinct from "political democracy," and it is important to bear this aspect of the question also in mind as we ask: "How democratic is our society?" Do we really believe that all men are created equal, and do we strive to embody this in our human relationships? Or do we accept the qualification, "But some are more equal than others"?

In summary, I should like to suggest that there are at least four basic aspects of the meaning of "democracy," all of which are of vital concern to Christian faith and ethics. I suggest that we call them "democratic structure," "democratic process," "democratic ethos," and "democratic substance."

Democratic structure. By this I mean the basic elements of polity as set forth in the U.S. Constitution (governance by elected representatives serving for limited terms; separation of powers among the three branches of government; lodging of ultimate power in the people; etc.).

Democratic process. This refers to the way in which governance is actually carried on and political decisions are made. Here we have the role of political parties (which were not foreseen by the makers of the Constitution), public opinion, etc., in the establishment of public policy and in the replacement of one set of representatives and governors by another.

Democratic ethos. This is the philosophical or ideological dimension, and it involves two complementary motifs: the strain toward liberty (individual freedom, protection of human rights), and the strain toward justice (understood as a corrective of inequities). Cf. the Pledge of Allegiance: "with liberty and justice for all." Both are important -- we would not want freedom without justice, or justice without freedom.

Democratic substance. This refers to the extent to which the democratic ethos is actually embodied in the life of the society, including social and economic as well as political dimensions: substantive
freedom and justice.

These distinctions enable us to formulate two crucial questions which
we can put to our American democracy:

(1) To what extent does the democratic structure serve the democratic process?

(2) To what extent is the democratic ethos embodied in democratic
substance?

Both of these are questions that need to be put not just once and for
all, but continually, for changes and corrections in the structure of our
political life (for example, reform of the method of financing political cam-
paigns), as well as fresh efforts to embody the democratic ethos in the substance of our social life and institutions, need to be made continually. We
can hardly begin to unfold the significance of these questions here; they are
proposed as tools that can be used repeatedly in the process of national self-
examination.

The distinction between democratic ethos and democratic substance
will enable us to deal with the charge that has been made by recent social
critics and revisionist historians, that amongst the founding fathers themselves, some of whom were slaveowners, the high ideals of the charter
documents (the Declaration of Independence, the Preamble to the Constitution,
the Bill of Rights) were scarcely realized. America, one critic has said,
was not so much "conceived in liberty" as "conceived in the rhetoric of
liberty."

I would acknowledge the considerable justice of this charge, but
with the following two comments. First -- what is reflected here is the
distinction we have made between political and social democracy. The Revolutionary period was concerned largely with the former; it is during the
following two centuries that the latter came increasingly onto the agenda.
This is not said to exculpate the founding fathers, but simply to locate them
in the history of ideas. Secondly, it should be pointed out that a meaningful
statement of the democratic ethos will, in any case, have somewhat of a
"transcendent" character. That is, it will state a set of ideals that do not
at any given historical moment have a perfect embodiment, but which serve
as a permanent challenge to ever greater realizations. In that sense, we
can say that these founding documents present us with an "eschatological"
ethos.

* * * * * * * * * * *

If all these are aspects of what we mean by "democracy," then the
question of the sources of American democracy is a complex one indeed.

Interpreters seem to divide themselves into those who stress the practical or experiential sources of democracy, and those who stress the ideological factors. Among the practical sources are, for example, the interest of American merchants in securing freedom from the restrictions laid upon them by the British crown, or -- as a pervasive, long-term factor--the egalitarian effects of life on the frontier. By the "ideological" factors, I mean the explicit statements of a democratic vision. Among these, emphasis can be laid on the secular or the religious components: on the philosophy of the Enlightenment as represented by a Benjamin Franklin or a Thomas Jefferson, or on the heritage of New England Puritanism. Such scholars as A.D. Lindsay, Ralph Barton Perry, and James Hastings Nichols have thoroughly explored the relation between Puritanism and democracy. Although this movement did have its authoritarian face, it seems indisputable that by virtue of its origins in protest against a monarchical regime, its stress on the equality of all believers under God, and, especially, its notion of the covenant, Puritanism made powerful contributions to democratic theory, ethos, and experience. It was easy to analogize from the believers' covenanting or compacting together to set up a form of ecclesiastical governance and hold it responsible, to a similar procedure and a similar structure of accountability in the civil realm. And exactly this is what had transpired in the New England colonies. The Mayflower Compact of 1620 is rightly regarded as a precursor of the United States Constitution adopted a century and a half later.

What is clear is that in making a list of the practical and ideological origins of American democracy, no one would think to include Lutheranism or Lutheran theology. The immediate reason for this is obvious: namely, the rather minor role that Lutheranism played in the affairs of colonial America as a whole. The colonies were, after all, primarily British settlements, and Lutheranism is not one of the British varieties of religion. The pardonable pride which Lutherans at this time of Bicentennial remembrance may take in the contributions of a John Peter Gabriel Muhlenberg, Revolutionary general, or a Frederick Augustus Muhlenberg, first Speaker of the House of Representatives, should not delude one into exaggerating the Lutheran role in the affairs of colonial or revolutionary America. Most Lutherans, after all, still worshipped in a foreign language until well into the nineteenth century or even the twentieth century. This is symbolic of their relative isolation from the cultural mainstream and from the centers of political power.

There is no reason for contemporary Lutherans to be apologetic about this; it is simply one of the facts of history. What is more serious is the charge that Lutheranism is in its very nature antipathetic to democracy -- that it has had to be dragged kicking and screaming, so to speak, into the modern democratic world. Lutheranism, it is said, is inherently authoritarian; it inculcates a social and political passivity, and encourages

an uncritical obedience to the powers that be. Its natural affinity is with
monarchical or even dictatorial regimes. This is the conclusion most likely
to be drawn by the reader of James Hastings Nichols' study Democracy and
the Churches, if he attends primarily to what Nichols says about German,
and especially Prussian, Lutherans. They were seldom on the side of the
angels, so far as the development of modern democracy is concerned. One's
impression will be otherwise, however, if one attends to the exceptions that
Nichols is forced to make with regard to Scandinavian and American Lutheranism.

  The Scandinavian example is particularly important, since Lutheranism has been predominant in that part of the world to a degree that is
probably at least equal to the predominance of Puritanism in colonial America,
and moreover, this predominance has continued (at least in terms of outward
ecclesiastical allegiance) down to the present day. Yet the Scandinavian
countries are widely regarded as models of both political and social democracy. We cannot, of course, attribute all these good things directly to
Lutheran influence; we know that there was a strong element of anticleri-
calism in the labor movement, for example, in Scandinavia. Yet even such
a movement can draw deeply, if disguisedly, on the religious ethos of the
culture in which it comes to birth.

  At the very least, the existence of this vast exception should cause
us to question whether the anti-democratic tendencies mentioned above are
truly integral to Lutheranism. My hypothesis is that they are not, and that
the Lutheran tradition can not only be cleared of its authoritarian characteristics in such a way as to be able to bed down happily with democracy -- this
the American experience has already shown -- but that Lutheran theology,
properly understood, can even make some contribution to democratic theory
and to the vitality of democratic life. If this is the case, it should be a
cause for rejoicing not only by Lutherans but also by all who care for
American democracy. Nichols himself encourages us to undertake such a
task of disentanglement and reconstruction when he comments, regarding
the Scandinavian situation, that it represents "possibly that normal development of Lutheran church life and political ethics which was stifled in the
cradle in Germany."[1]

* * * * * * * * * * * *

  In undertaking this task -- which is far too vast to be completed
within the confines of this essay -- we can find a beginning point in the work
of a theologian who is one of the sharpest critics of Luther and Lutheranism,
and yet who himself has drunk very deeply from the Lutheran tradition --
Reinhold Niebuhr. It was during the Second World War that he wrote his
book The Children of Light and the Children of Darkness (New York:

Scribner's, 1944), a volume devoted directly to our problem. Note carefully its subtitle: "A Vindication of Democracy and a Critique of Its Traditional Defense."

Niebuhr maintained that the traditional defenders of democracy
(the "children of light") had served it poorly by resting their arguments on
an overly optimistic doctrine of man. True, man does have the capacity to
respond to rational discourse, to act out of fellow-feeling, and even at times
to sacrifice his own interests for the sake of the whole, and these are important factors in the successful functioning of a democracy. But man also
has another and meaner side to his nature, and when this comes to the fore,
as it has in the pathology that has gripped Western civilization in the twentieth century, one is tempted to think democracy too weak to grapple with
these darker forces.

But in fact democracy, viewed from another standpoint, is designed
precisely to guard against the effects of corrupt human passions (greed,
mendacity, the love of power). For democracy, as we know it in the American
system, is built on the principle that one should trust no one -- and especially
no leaders -- to an unlimited extent or for an unlimited period of time. This
is not cynicism, it is realism -- indeed, it is what Niebuhr called "Christian
realism," founded on the Biblical doctrine of man. It is because this kind
of realism about human nature was assumed that we find built into the U.S.
Constitution a separation of powers, a complicated system of checks and
balances, and a scheme for a constant change of leadership (and this in over-
lapping two-, four-, and six-year cycles) that constitute a remarkable set
of safeguards against the misuse of power. And as we have recently redis-
covered, the mechanisms for a change of leadership can be brought into play,
if need be, at the presidential level even within the stated four-year terms.

Democracy teaches us -- it is worth repeating -- to trust no one to
an unlimited extent or for an unlimited period of time. And it provides a
means for regular replacement of those who are entrusted with the tasks of
leadership. It is difficult to exaggerate the significance of this point. Democracy would be "worth it," so to speak, if it were this alone: a peaceful means
for the replacement of regimes. For this is a problem for which, I dare say,
no other satisfactory solution has been found. Certainly the biological principle, which served as the principle of succession in monarchical regimes,
is inadequate in the modern world. We demand talent, not merely biological
relatedness to the former ruler. And the other great alternative -- a sheer
struggle for power, violent or otherwise, such as commonly ensues in the
Communist world when one generation of leaders is forced to give place to
another -- is equally unsatisfactory. A democratic system, providing for
free elections and a peaceful transfer of power, manages to combine most
remarkably the factors of continuity and change.

In this connection, we may add, parenthetically, that one of the
finest and most vivid symbols of democracy is the picture of an outgoing

president handing over the reins of office to another -- of President Eisenhower, the elder statesman, for example, standing beside the young John F. Kennedy as the latter takes the oath of office, administered by the Chief Justice of the Supreme Court.

* * * * * * * * * * *

Democracy, then, is founded on a peculiarly twofold or stereoptical view of man, which has never been better summarized than in Niebuhr's well-known aphorism: "Man's capacity for justice makes democracy possible; but man's inclination to injustice makes democracy necessary." Here is the briefest possible statement of the anthropological presuppositions underlying the formation of the American republic. On the one hand there is the qualified optimism of the Enlightenment; on the other hand, the qualified pessimism derived from the Puritan tradition. The people are capable of governing themselves: this is the basis of the democratic vision. Yet within the structures of self-rule, the potential for misrule is enormous: this is the basis for democratic realism. What is needed to provide both the "accelerator" and the "brakes" for the democratic process is a view of man that regards him in terms both of his essential goodness and of his existential tendencies towards evil (to use Tillich's categories). But this is the classical Christian view; it is the Biblical view; and it is the view of the Reformation, both Lutheran and Calvinistic. So to view man is to understand him in terms of Creation and Fall, of the perpetual dialectic between original righteousness and original sin -- neither of which refers merely to "once upon a time," but rather, to continuing factors in human life and history.

Niebuhr, however, does not see Lutheranism as a faithful conveyor of this balanced view. Rather, he believes that Lutheran theology is guilty of breaking the dialectic and emphasizing only one side of the story, namely, the dismal side. Man is not just or good enough to rule himself; hence he needs authorities appointed over him by God, and to these authorities he owes an unquestioning obedience. Niebuhr groups Luther with Thomas Hobbes as one of the chief sources of this view, and hence of anti-democratic theory in the West.

In this I believe that Niebuhr is partly right, but partly, and importantly, mistaken. He is right that Luther has many extremely critical things to say about human nature, as does Calvin. The Reformers here echo St. Paul's analysis of the corruption of the Roman society of his day (they are "foolish, faithless, heartless, ruthless" [Romans 1 : 31]). It is the natural language of prophetic denunciation, or of the preacher who wants to drive home a point. Niebuhr is mistaken, however, insofar as he overlooks the other side, the very positive side, of Luther's estimate of the capacities of the "natural man." He can appeal to human reason, not only on minor matters but at crucial points in his own career ("Unless I am persuaded by Scripture or by right reason, I will not recant"). He can praise the political sagacity of an Aristotle or a Cicero, even while he condemns the Aristotelian influence on the interpretation of Christian doctrine. The Lutheran Confessions likewise have a great deal to say in praise of "civil righteousness."

It is crucial to recognize that most of what Luther says in disparagement of human nature and human striving applies in loco justificationis, i.e., with reference to the question of eternal salvation, and not to the civil sphere. One of the most important functions of the Two Kingdoms doctrine is to make this distinction clear. With reference to "the things that are above him," man is to be passive and receptive of God's grace. But with reference to "the things that are below him" -- and this includes the whole realm of what we call social and political affairs -- man has the competence and the capacity to act, with a view to bringing the historical situation into closer conformity.with the will of God.

This is far from perfectionism, which Luther would always dismiss as a form of Schwärmerei, but it is not far, we submit, from the spirit of sober yet hopeful realism that underlay the formation of the U.S. Constitution. The more cynical spirit of which Niebuhr spoke might better be attributed to Pietism. It is Pietism that engaged in what Lutheran theologian Gustaf Aulen calls the "false blackening of the world," and that dismantled the structure of social ethical concern that always accompanied the classic theology of the Reformation. When such a blackening was attempted during the Reformation period itself, in the form of the Flacian heresy, it was decisively rejected. (I have tried to draw out the ethical consequences of this rejection elsewhere.)[2]

It is true that Luther, in his writings on the Peasants' War, refused to recognize any right of the lower estates to resist the higher authorities by force. The tone and character of his recommendations for the suppression of the revolt ("Smite, slay, and stab") are indefensible, though it must be recognized that he felt himself and all of Germany to be faced with a genuine threat of anarchy. What is far less known is that five years later, in the midst of another crisis, he did bring himself to endorse such a right to resist. Documentation for this is to be found in the treatise entitled "Dr. Martin Luther's Warning to His Dear German People" (1531), which appears in English translation in Volume 47 of Luther's Works (American Edition). In the face of anticipated efforts to wipe out the evangelical movement, Luther there counsels the leaders of the movement to resist even the Holy Roman Emperor, Charles V, if the latter tries to use military force to do so.

The treatise was widely read, both at the time and subsequently, yet these remarks of Luther somehow never achieved canonical status, as did Calvin's similar admonitions in the last chapter of the Institutes, wherein he speaks of the responsibility of the "magistrates of the people" to withstand the "fierce licentiousness of kings." That text of Calvin's is an important milestone in the evolution of democracy, for its import was conveyed throughout Western Europe by the spread of the Calvinist movement and was embodied, especially in Britain, in the struggle of the Puritan-parliamentary party against the monarchical establishment. So both Luther and Calvin deserve some credit. If Luther "said it first," Calvin gave this motif a place of greater prominence in his theology; and even more important, later Calvinists learned what it meant to institutionalize this "right to resist," that is, to create a structured and continuously available means to do so.

The institutionalization of the right to resist: this is not a bad definition of political democracy. Rather than having to resort to force for the redress of grievances or to overthrow a regime, a regularized and peaceful means of doing so is provided. We call it an "election." Modern democracy, then, may be viewed as having given us a new set of instrumentalities for the promotion of political and social change. To make use of such instrumentalities is quite in the spirit of Luther's ethic, even if he himself, at that period of history and within the limitations of his own late-medieval world view, did not envision such alternatives.

Lutheranism was accused by Niebuhr of having too cynical an attitude toward the political realm. But in fact it may more often have fallen into the opposite error, an overly positive attitude toward the political state of things. Karl Holl and other interpreters of the heritage of the Reformation have pointed out how much more natural it is for Lutheranism than for Calvinism to take an affirmative attitude toward the achievements of human culture, as well as toward the natural basis of human life. Thus Lutherans (except for the Pietist tradition) have seldom had the "hang-ups" about sexuality that Calvinists, and especially Puritans, have had. The Lutheran appreciation and utilization of art and music may be cited as another example. In fact, an honored place in the Lutheran scheme of things has been given to all three -- wine, women, and song! But when it comes to the sphere of politics, this appreciative or accepting attitude often betrays Lutherans into an uncritical endorsement of the status quo. Here, then, Lutherans need to gain something of the Calvinist spirit of suspicion of all things human, especially of that which "vaunts itself" or is "puffed up" (I Corinthians 13); while Calvinism, in turn, could benefit from an infusion of the Lutheran acceptance of the natural.

* * * * * * * * * * *

"Eternal vigilance is the price of liberty" is a familiar slogan from the Revolutionary period (commonly attributed to Thomas Jefferson). This is indeed a lesson to be remembered by any people who would continue to enjoy the blessings of democracy. This vigilance is needed not primarily against those who would attack democracy from without -- this usually is the least of our problems -- but rather against perversions of democracy from within. The democratic structure may grow creaky; the democratic process may be clogged; and there are always those who would misuse the democratic system for their own purposes. Therefore constant alertness on the part of the citizenry is called for.

This, in fact, must become a major emphasis of our interpretation of the meaning of good citizenship. In past centuries, the central motif in the exposition of the Christian's political responsibility was often that of obedience, and this was understandable in the light of the prevailing social situation. St. Paul reflects this kind of background when he advises Roman Christians, as in Romans 13, to "be subject" to the governing authorities. But these authorities, he makes clear, have no autonomous power, but rather are "ministers of God" for the punishment of evil and the promotion of good. Therefore we are in accord with Paul's deeper theological intention when we view those who hold office in the political realm not as authorities to be obeyed, but as stewards with a mandate to discharge. And it is up to us to hold them accountable for their stewardship, as well as to fulfill the civic tasks that fall to us, whatever our placement in the social order. There is, of course, an element of obedience in civic life, but this obedience is to the laws, and not to men. The primary motif of the Christian's role in the political realm ought not to be obedience, but rather alert and critical participation.

In fulfilling this task of vigilance, one of the most important tools available to the citizenry of a democracy is a free press -- and this must be interpreted today, of course, also to include radio and television. As was seen in the Watergate affair, the press has an invaluable watchdog function to perform. The media can be used to misinform or manipulate the populace; they can also be used to inform and educate. This is an instrument of democratic process about which the founding fathers already were concerned: witness the First Amendment to the Constitution, guaranteeing freedom of the press. And we have reason doubly to be concerned today.

Also of great significance for the health of democracy are the innumerable action and agitation groups which spring up from time to time, some of which endure only through a particular crisis, but others of which survive to become an important part of the consensus-forming and decision-making process over a period of years or decades. Through such groups, the concerned Christian or other conscientious citizen can vastly multiply his or her power to influence the course of events.

None of what we have said should be taken to imply that democracy is a perfect system! In fact, we may make our own Winston Churchill's reported comment to the effect that "democracy is the worst form of government on earth -- except for all others that have ever been tried." The democratic system is based, as we have seen, on a very realistic view of human

nature, a view that is well expressed in one scholar's effort to put into words
the assumptions that are implicit in the Constitution of the United States:

> All men are fallible and likely to blunder because of their failure
> of knowledge or their lack of objectivity face to face with issues
> that affect them closely. Let us limit the extent of their blunders;
> and, above all, let us keep open the channels by which their
> blunders can be pointed out, explored, and condemned. Let us
> also see to it that the blunderers will be replaced, in due course,
> by other men, who will in their turn compose the government
> temporarily. [3]

We have tried to make the point that the Lutheran tradition, as one of the
carriers of this realistic doctrine of man, can be an important resource for
the maintenance of a viable democracy today, even if it was not a major
source for its rise historically. But in so doing, Lutheranism needs to
guard against lapsing from realism into cynicism; and it needs also to
learn to apply its realistic analysis to the high and mighty -- to the clout-
wielders and image-makers of this world -- as well as to the common
citizenry.

Most of the foregoing remarks have dealt with questions of political
democracy, and there is no space remaining to give the theme of social
democracy the attention it deserves. Suffice it to say that insofar as the
problems in this realm arise out of the unchecked operation of an unmod-
ified capitalistic system -- the exaltation of the pursuit of profit over the
pursuit of justice -- Lutheranism is in a fairly good position to present a
critique and a corrective, since it never became so entangled with the spirit
of capitalism as did Calvinism (as the studies of Max Weber and many others
make clear). No doubt the term "welfare state" has negative connotations
for many Lutherans in America today, but in fact it was in a Lutheran land
-- Bismarckian Germany -- where the "welfare state" was invented, through
the provision of the first social insurance schemes protecting individuals
against the ravages of illness, unemployment, and old age. And it is the
even more thoroughly Lutheran lands of Scandinavia, as we have already
noted, that have become the model social democracies of our time. Lutheranism has a deep social memory of a time when a more organic conception
of the community prevailed, when it was taken for granted that fellow citizens
would care for one another. This heritage, when properly understood, should
make Lutherans today vigilant not only for the protection of liberty, but also
for the promotion of justice for all, making their due contribution to the
perennial project of closing the gap between the democratic vision and the
democratic substance of our society.

NOTES AND REFERENCES

[1] James Hastings Nichols, Democracy and the Churches (Philadelphia: Westminster, 1951), p. 108.

[2] See Franklin Sherman, "Christology, Politics, and the Flacian Heresy," Dialog, Vol. 2, No. 3 (Summer, 1963), pp. 208-213.

[3] Adrienne Koch, Power, Morals, and the Founding Fathers: Essays in the Interpretation of the American Enlightenment (Ithaca, N.Y.: Cornell University Press, 1961), p. 132.

Part Three

PHILOSOPHICAL AND RELIGIOUS
FOUNDATIONS OF BELONGING

CHAPTER VII

THE FOUNDATIONS OF BELONGING IN A CHRISTIAN WORLDVIEW

by
Philip Hefner

I.

Preliminary Considerations for Constructing a Worldview

This essay is purely speculative, it is an exercise in thought, focusing upon one question that seems central for the future of human life. The question: What worldview seems to be called for if human beings are to live adequately in this world? It might appear arrogant at worst and irrelevant at best to raise a question that is so large, so ambiguous, and so difficult of evaluation and demonstration. If it were not that such a question is both helpful and necessary, one would never summon the courage required even to embark on the speculation that follows. Worldview is necessary, that is to say, a comprehensive world of meaning is essential for adequate human existence, because not only our more ordinary day-to-day activities, but also the critical perceptions, decisions and actions of our lives require a context of whole meaning. It is not that people do not or cannot on occasion act without such a world of whole meaning, but that their acts are apt to be less wholesome. Without such a vision of larger meaning, human beings simply cannot sustain action for very long. Meaninglessness is not conducive to life. The formation and re-formation of worldviews is also of strategic value, if we accept the thesis that reform of social structures is a pressing challenge for us today, but that such reform follows rather than precedes reform of worldview.

Where does one begin with the speculation upon worldview? This particular exercise takes as its starting-point certain issues that are currently emerging and which have been of central importance for the seminar which led to this volume. My assumption is that these issues have emerged as neuralgic points of human life, precisely because they point to fundamental elements of human existence which stretch our previous worldviews beyond their ability to order these elements within our existing frames of meaning.

161

As the title of this volume suggests, belonging is the issue that has arisen again and again in the discussions of this seminar, both as it is fundamental for human existence generally and also as a pressing concern for human life precisely in our time. In this, we are part of a larger movement of thought in our time which focuses on the painful struggle that has marked our perceptions of belonging and its place in human life. Today we have a renewed sense of: (1) our belonging to our fellow human beings, across all barriers -- racial, sexual, economic, geographical, national, and age; (2) our belonging to the ecosystem of which we are a part, the natural environment which is the womb of our emergence and the support system for everything human; and (3) our belonging to the matrix of evolutionary development out of which our total ecosystem has unfolded.

The essential place of belonging in our lives comes to light forcefully when we are sensitive to the emptiness caused by its absence and to the general indifference to it in important sectors of society. Belonging is illumined by our awareness that human being is characterized by receptivity, as well as by the hurt we suffer when we deny that receptive dimension of ourselves. Our keen sense for the limits and destructiveness of technology and the instrumental reason which is its cornerstone grows out of the insight that in the reasoning behind technology man may be regarded as only aggressive, self-initiating, and active, fabricating and contributing to the world, and not as a recipient from the world about him. The demonic potential of technology and instrumental reason is manifest when the human beings employing them do not acknowledge that man receives his life from the very nature that is the object of his technology and lives out his life in partnership with that nature.

To speak of man as receiving from nature is another way of uttering that primal word of belonging, just as depicting technological man as the aggressive, self-made, independent fabricator of nature is to portray a man who suffers from his insensitivity to belonging as an essential characteristic of his own being. In short, I interpret the widespread current uneasiness about technology and instrumental reason as a reflection of our sense that we belong fundamentally to and with that very world of nature our technology acts upon.

This sense (I do not speak of our "knowledge" or "insight," because our awareness in this area is not susceptible to the kind of structuring that we ordinarily insist upon for knowledge, nor are we sure enough about it, en masse) of belonging surfaces again in our uneasiness with the suggestion that human nature is infinitely malleable and alterable. We are, to be sure, mindful of the artificial and defensive definitions of human nature which have served as instruments for sex discrimination and chauvinism, and for racial repressiveness. And we are more and more compelled to acknowledge that consciousness can be altered by drugs, by discipline of body and mind, and by technologies of various sorts. Nevertheless, we have misgivings about

the naivete and overt danger of espousing the view that human nature, sexual identities, and consciousness are without boundaries and open to almost
endless permutations and manipulations. Unworthy motives often underly
these misgivings, but their sound instinct lies in the sense that there are
structures to which we are beholden for our very nature, to which we belong,
if you will, which can be repudiated or ignored only at our peril.

Consistent with these signals of belonging which I have mentioned
is the interpretation of current history within the context of the physical,
biological, and cultural evolution of the world. These interpretations give
human belonging a historical dimension. What we are today and what our
civilization intends and accomplishes receives breadth and depth, as well
as more relevant interpretation when that civilization is understood as a
phase of this planet's total evolution, when our cultural development is seen
in connection with biological evolution. The increasing dissatisfaction with
older assumptions about the dichotomy of mind and body, history and nature,
spirit and nature is again a testimony to our sense of a dimension of belonging that runs counter to those dualisms.

Human beings know, however, that if they belong to each other, to
the ecosystem, and to the process out of which that ecosystem was born,
they belong as human beings, and that means as a species that is self-
conscious and consequently able to plan, receive feedback, alter its plans,
and act upon the wisdom it has accumulated in the process. To be human
beings includes the possibility and the responsibility to create and to share
in the creation of our own world in a manner and to a degree unknown before
in the history of this world. If we are to speak of our sense of belonging,
therefore, that must not be construed as a diminishing of human beings as
initiating and self-creating. Receptivity and activity are correlative in
human existence, and belonging must include them both as polar realities.
We underline the correlative importance of man as active creature when we
exhort him to remember that he belongs, that he is receptive and dependent,
and then urge him to act upon that recollection!

If we are to speak, then, about the worldview that is required for
human existence and about the issues that give us clues to that worldview,
we point to man's belonging as a receiver and as an actor in his ecosystem
as the fundamental issue, within which the most important clues for worldview are to be found.

A. An Ontology of Belonging

A worldview construction that takes the issue of belonging as a
prime datum is in fact providing an ontology of belonging. What we observed
earlier about the need and desirability for a comprehensive world of meaning
is nowhere clearer than with respect to belonging. One cannot simply decide
to belong. Belong to what? To oneself? To one's fellow human being? To

society? To God? To the Universe? Rather one needs to know deep down
that we human beings and our daily lives belong to something, to something
greater than ourselves and our immediate world and our present time in
history. We need to know that belonging is essentially a part of "the way
things are." Lesser foundations for belonging have proven their superfici-
alities in recent years. Popular psychology, for example, which tried to
fabricate instant belongingness, and transient political, racial, and other
groupings aiming at social reform have shown that their claims for solidarity
were not well-grounded, since they have disappeared from the scene or failed
in their attempts to draw people together. Alienation has its roots in a doubt
that this is "the way things are"; alienation is inescapable when we are un-
persuaded that belonging is ontologically grounded. The demonic use of
technology, disregard for continuities in human nature, and a disregard for
the ecosystem grow out of an inadequately grounded sense of belonging.

B.   Elements of a Worldview of Belonging

We suggest five elements of a worldview that can provide a context
of meaning within which human beings can live adequately. These elements
become the grounds for the possibility and necessity of such a worldview
and also the criteria for the adequacy of any worldview.

1.   This world and our own lives unfold within the divine life.

Belonging is ultimately not conceivable, to the mind or to the heart,
unless our world and our lives are part of something larger. The ontolog-
ical ground of belonging is not secure unless this "something larger" is
itself ultimate, God himself. We choose to speak of this in the terms of unfolding within the divine life. Besides rooting our own lives in ultimacy,
this term suggests that that ultimacy is itself a living reality, with the implication that our relations to ultimacy will be those of one living reality
with another. The term also suggests that the ultimacy within which we
live itself possesses purpose. Without the sense that our human and terrestrial enterprise itself transpires within the ambience of a living God who
possesses purpose, full and wholesome human life is impossible. This
element is difficult for those who see the world separated from God, who
see the finite incapable of possessing the infinite and conversely the infinite
incapable of possessing finitude within it. Some facets of this vision are
widely held now. There is a broad awareness that we are part of cosmic
and terrestrial evolution, for example, which puts it in the context of that
which is larger than ourselves. But the doubt whether this larger cosmos
is possessed of any purpose and the question of how we can speak of it as
living have a generally depressing effect on this wider context of our lives.
The older image of Sir James Jeans is still relevant: that life on planet
Earth is like a match struck in the night that flames gloriously for a few

seconds and then goes out in a charred mass. Here a sense of belonging is strong, but it is intertwined with deep alienation, since the very system to which we belong is without purpose and quite possibly, in the long run, dead.

2. There is a point of contact, with a definite character, where the divine life grasps us.

How does the "something larger" of which we are a part make its incursion into our lives and our world? What is the point of relationship? These questions must be dealt with clearly and forcefully by any worldview that would provide the basis for adequate human life. Without such a point of contact, belonging is an empty category. Mechanistic and non-purposive worldviews do speak clearly at this point, hence their depressing effect. There is not much doubt as to how the universe described in Sir James Jeans' comment relates itself to us. Genetic and environmental entree to our lives is real and overwhelming. Traditional Western religious world-views are frequently unclear at this point, and this is one reason for their general loss of credibility.

3. What is the significance of distinctively human being within the divine life?

No worldview can long escape the issue of purpose. Those that deal with it negatively, such as the absurdism of some existentialists, the Marxists, and some scientific worldviews (like Jeans') work in the final analysis against belonging and reinforce alienation. This element of the worldview asks not only the question of purpose, but the question of the pur-pose of the human species. This question is rendered all the more difficult by some recent opinions that the human species has overstepped its bounds and in a kind of species-ethnocentrism thinks more highly of itself than it ought. These opinions go too frequently hand-in-hand with a denigration of the distinctiveness of the species that takes our attention away from the crucial question of what the species' real niche is in the ecosystem. The clarification of this distinctive niche is the only real safeguard against the egregious arrogance that many fear. An answer to the question of what the purpose of the species is enables us to affirm belonging without compromis-ing human distinctiveness; the active pole of belonging is embraced in this portion of the worldview.

4. Despite our intimate relatedness to the divine life and its unfolding, evil is real and unavoidable.

A worldview by its very nature has difficulty dealing with evil, because a worldview aims precisely at providing wholeness of meaning, whereas evil by definition is the antithesis of meaning and wholeness. A worldview that takes seriously both the world and also the intimate

relationship between world and God, which places the world within the unfolding of God's life, has special difficulties with evil. Evil, in many respects, becomes the basic question for such a worldview and theodicy the
major undertaking. In recent times, evil has been so indelibly impressed
upon us in its egregious, malignant, persistent, and demonic (in that it
turns the good against itself) aspects that no worldview can be credible unless it speaks persuasively about evil. The question of evil is another
point on which any worldview today must stand or fall. Belonging cannot
be strong without an adequate understanding of evil.

5. What concrete image have we to shape our action in the world so that
we may be in accord with the career of the divine life in which our world
unfolds?
        The description of what "things are really like," the elaboration of
the "is," turns immediately into the most important basis for the "ought,"
the imperative to action that will conform us with reality, in this case with
the divine life. Worldviews clash exactly at this point, but at the same time,
they make their deep incursion into the lives of persons according to the
cogency with which they can present an image for shaping action. This concrete image gives content to the style or form of belonging.

        The five elements just described deal with essential human ques-
tions, and therefore they point to both the possibility and the necessity of a
worldview. That people raise the questions indicates that they are capable
of entertaining the answers, just as it indicates that they sense a need for
answers. These elements are also criteria, since they form the basis upon
which we would assess the adequacy of any worldview that purports to provide a world of meaning within which humans can live adequately. These
are also the elements of the ontology of belonging, the criteria assessing
whether a worldview is a sound and credible base for a life of belonging.

                                II.

                  An Exercise in Worldview Construction

        There are existing attempts at worldview construction that can be
useful in meeting the requirements that we have laid down. Some of these,
to which I will refer, are set forth in the thought of Alfred North Whitehead,
Martin Heidegger, Hegel, Schelling, and Teilhard de Chardin. In what
follows, I suggest the most adequate worldview, with the five criteria in
mind that I have just elaborated. My primary concern is to show how the
Christian faith and theology are able to engage in worldview construction.
Although influences from certain philosophies will be apparent, what follows

is an attempt to build a Christian worldview not on the basis of an existing philosophy, but rather on the basis of the Christian tradition itself.

A. Our World Unfolds Within the Divine Life

1. Concept of Nature.

Why must we speak in terms of the world unfolding within the divine life? Simply because our present understanding of the world based on the most solid scientific information that we possess, does not provide us with a concept of the "outside." It is not comprehensible to us that the world could be "outside" God, because there is no outside for him or us to inhabit. Furthermore, the "inputs," or sources of insight and knowledge and powers that guide human beings and their history, manifest themselves as internal, rather than external with respect to the ecosystem in which we live. The inputs or sources of knowledge and power that we have traditionally called "revelation," "redemption," and "Holy Spirit" are resident within the system, otherwise, they are simply inconceivable to us. To assert this internal character of the inputs is in no way to degrade them or to make them subject to the autonomy of man. Rather, what we are acknowledging is that our understanding of nature demands that the relationship of what we call "the world" and "God" be dramatically recast. (I pre-suppose here what Burhoe has discussed about nature in much more detail in his contribution to this volume). For many, this recasting will seem to be an alteration of the religious realities themselves and a loss of traditional meaning. On the contrary, a refusal to recast doctrine at this point is misguided, since it implicitly raises a concept of nature to ultimate status and ties our understanding of the world and God to the worldview dictated by that concept of nature.

We cannot discuss in detail the concept of nature which the current state of scientific knowledge suggests. Professor Burhoe has provided a much more extensive summary in his article (see Chapter I). Several characteristics of nature, as presently understood, do undergird our worldview construction, and they are to be kept in mind, even though we cannot here elaborate upon them. (1) Nature and everything in it is process. "Matter," for example, is very nearly an unusable word, because matter is what matter does (to quote C.G. Collingwood) and as a consequence, matter is not distinguished from life as in the older dualistic modes of thought. Everything in nature finally resolves into energy states, that is, process, which means that every facet of nature, whether human, biological, physical, subatomic, psychological, has a way of opening onto all the other facets of nature. (2) Every object in nature is interrelated dynamically with everything else in nature, even if only in an infinitesimally faint way. Collingwood has put this point vividly:

The idea of nature is the idea of a reality thus doubly broken up, spread out or distributed over space and time. This characteristic affects not only the idea of nature as a whole, but every idea of any thing in nature. The idea of a material body is the idea of a number of particles distributed in space; the idea of life is the idea of a number of characteristics distributed in time. Hence there is no one place at which the idea of a body can be locally exemplified, and no one time at which all the characteristics of life can be actualized. You can nowhere say the body is here; you can never say, I am now, at this instant alive. Even if you indicate a cubic foot of space when you say here, and a span of eighty years when you say now, you still cannot say that the being of the body is wholly contained within that region, or the being of the organism within those eighty years; in both cases the being of the thing overflows beyond these boundaries; the body makes itself felt by its gravitational effects throughout space, and the organism, whether you look at it physically, chemically, biologically, or morally, is only a temporal and local concretion in a life-stream stretching vastly beyond it on all sides, and what we call its peculiarities are really characteristics pervading that life-stream as a whole. [1]

If we understand this statement by Collingwood, we have grasped much of what our contemporary knowledge tells us about nature. (3) All of nature is self-transcending. Self-transcending refers to an activity of a thing in itself and at the same time to an effect of a power that is larger than the thing that continuously raises it beyond its limitations and thereby grants it the ability to be what it is. We shall refer to these characteristics of nature as process, interrelatedness, and self-transcendence.

The picture of nature that corresponds to the most objective knowledge we have of our universe allows for no realm "outside" from which God can enter into relationships with our world. Furthermore, the unfolding of this world through physical, biological, and cultural evolution follows the interplay of information already encoded genetically and culturally on the one hand and in the environing ecosystem on the other hand. This picture of nature requires an understanding of our own lives and our own contemporary world as unfolding within the larger life of the ecosystem. The ultimate "environment" of all things is God (to recall Teilhard de Chardin's term the "divine milieu.").

Several thinkers of the recent past have been attentive to the demands of this concept of nature and have attempted to erect comprehensive systems of meaning accordingly. Hegel and Schelling anticipated the contemporary scientific advances in their philosophies. Hegel attempted to forge a concept of nature that was ahead of his time, but was hindered by his captivity to the science of his day. Hegel's basic dialectic of reality,

in which Geist or Spirit unfolds in the passage through its opposite lays
down a view of the world unfolding within the unfolding of God himself.
Schelling accomplishes the same task with his philosophy of the divine
energies, which constitute both world and God's own becoming.

In more current thinking, S.C. Alexander, Alfred North Whitehead, and Charles Hartshorne have carried worldview construction much
further in the light of contemporary knowledge about the world. They have,
as summarized in Whitehead's notion of the consequent nature of God, established in a determinative manner how this world's processes can unfold
within God without compromising his divinity.

2. The Christian Doctrine of the Trinity.

The traditional Christian conceptuality for dealing with the relationship of God and the world is the doctrine of the Trinity. It is significant
that this doctrine of the relationship between God and world is also the most
fundamental Christian doctrine of God. The conclusion to be drawn is that
Christian theology has wanted to make the career of God and that of the
world inseparable. The doctrine of the Trinity represents the spiritual and
intellectual effort of Christian theology to bring order to the Christian experience of what had to be acknowledged as three archai or first principles.
The Christian commitment to monotheism left the Christian mind with no
alternative but to relate these three fundamentals in such a way that Christian faith could speak of one ultimacy, one God. The three archai of the
Trinity correspond to the three so-called "persons" (a term that is quite
misleading in English and should be supplanted by a term such as "three
ways in which God is God"). The First Person (God the Father) represents
the Christian encounter with the source and ground of all possibilities. This
is God in his primal, impenetrable being, the God of whom Rudolph Otto
spoke as the mysterium tremendum et fascinosum. In this arché, God is
scarcely able to be discerned in any detail, let alone subjected to the categories of human experience. The processions of the Trinity from this
primal being trace the career of the world and its meaning. Traditionally,
the Second Person (God the Logos, the Word) represents the expression of
the primal being of God in articulatable form. The process of creation is
an action of the Second Person, just as revelation is. Revelation renders
intelligible the meaning and purpose of the creation and God's intentions towards it. The Second Person includes, but is not limited to, the historical
figure Jesus of Nazareth. It is of considerable significance, for our discussion, that the Christian mind insists that the expression of God in the
act of creation is a first principle, an arché.

If the First Person of the Trinity is arché as the causa princi-
piumque rerum and the Second Person is arché as the ordo intellegendi,
the Third Person (God the Holy Spirit) is arché as the ordo vivendi, that
is, as the first principle of the order of nature, life, and history. As

Third Person, Christians point to God as the ground of the order of movement that constitutes the created world since its beginning, whether that
movement be the evolution of the geosphere, of the biosphere, or of the
culture of man.   The Third Person is of particular significance for our
present concern because it is the Christian proposal that, firstly, God is
present as God and as fully God (totum dei) in the earthly, historical realm
that he has created, the realm of nature, and secondly that both this presence in the world and the original creation are intrinsic to the unfolding of
God's very Godness.   These two aspects of the Third Person possess a
significance for contemporary worldview construction that cannot be over-
estimated, because they establish that the world of nature need not undergo
transformation in order for God to be present as God within it and they also
interpret the ordo vivendi as internal to God's life and not external.
        The difficulty that Christian theology has had in understanding the
importance of the Third Person lies largely in the failure to comprehend
that what appears in the conventional view to be a realm of non-transcendence
or even anti-transcendence is in fact a realm in which God can be fully himself and still be present.   The idea that nature is the realm of anti-transcendence is rooted in an older, obsolete concept of nature that is to be
identified with the medieval and Newtonian eras.   This concept of nature did
not comprehend either process or self-transcendence, as we have observed
these characteristics in our earlier discussion.   As a consequence, the only
way in which Christians could take the Holy Spirit seriously was to identify
it with the "supernatural" action that transpires in the church.   Here we
have a classic case of what C.G. Collingwood has pointed to as the entrap-
ment of the human mind and imagination by the prevailing concept of nature.
The contemporary scientific understanding of nature liberates us to appreciate the fullness of the Third Person of the Trinity, even as that doctrine
presses us to explore more fully the depth of nature which the scientific
view facilitates.   The new concept of nature is only now making an impact
on the general consciousness, although some scientists and philosophers
have been conversant with it for the better part of a century.   Having experienced the liberation to perceive the compatibility of nature and divinity,
it is still a very great challenge for us to comprehend the wisdom of the
traditional Christian teaching in taking this compatibility up into its normative doctrine of God by asserting that God's being as ground of the created
order of nature and history is essential to the process of his being God at
all.

3.   The Meaning of the World.
        The Christian doctrine of the Trinity performs another important
function, however, in addition to proposing that the world unfolds within
God's own life.   The doctrine also makes an assertion concerning the intentions of God toward this world.   This intention provides the meaning of the

processes of nature. This assertion is embodied in the Second Person, the
archē of intelligibility. In the revelation epitomized in Jesus Christ, the
proposal is made that God intends good and not ill for the world, that, at
whatever cost, he intends to fulfill the world, bring it to a consummation,
and not destroy it. It is significant that this, too, was considered by the
Christian tradition as an essential for the doctrine of the Trinity. In other
words, it is not adequate to speak about God unless one also conceives of
his action in which he makes himself and his intentions intelligible as part
of his unfolding his Godness. The Second Person, then, not only provides
the Christian response to absurdism and meaninglessness, but also lays the
foundation that is necessary if the basic alienation that threatens belonging
is to be overcome. We have observed that a worldview of belonging to an
absurd world (à la James Jeans) carries with it an excruciating contradiction,
since belonging to that which is indifferent or hostile to the human species
makes human existence intrinscially one of alienation. The Christian doctrine of the Trinity conveys the wisdom that not only must belonging be
grounded in the world's being a part of the divine life, but also in the divine
intention to work goodness and fulfillment for that world.

B. The Point of Contact with the Divine Life and the Significance
    of Distinctively Human Being within the Divine Life

    The question of the point where the divine life grasps human beings,
impinges upon their lives, is inseparable from an interpretation of what
human being is about in the total ecosystem. To put it succinctly: The
human species has been unleashed within the ecosystem of terrestrial evolution as a species that is bounded by that ecosystem and defined by God's
working in that ecosystem, but the species, bestowed with self-awareness
and the ability to act upon it, must actively seek to discover its bounds and
its definition, and thus is driven to self-definition within the context of its
already having been defined. Put in naturalistic terms, the unconscious
process of evolution has eventuated in a species that is able to be aware of
the process that has produced it and is compelled to discern the nature of
that process and act accordingly, in the process discerning its ecological
niche and defining itself by its action in that niche. Man is evolution become
aware of itself, as Teilhard observed. In theological terms: God has created a creature that can understand itself, and he has given that creature the
ability to define the creation and act responsibly upon that definition. God
has created the human species as his co-creator, and demands accountability in that role.
    It is in the experience of this self-definition within the broader con-
text of having already been defined that the divine life grasps us, and it is
in this experience that we understand the significance of the distinctively human within the divine life. We can only sketch here what this implies.

1. Self-definition.

Self-definition is a function of the complex self-awareness which has appeared in the evolutionary process in the human species. Self-definition in its most general terms is described by the model of a self-aware, cybernetically functioning system. By a cybernetically functioning system, I mean a system that sets its goals and judges its performance by these goals, even as it alters its goals on the basis of its experience and performance. The system entertains feedback and modifies both its goals and performance accordingly. Every living system does this, but the human system does it self-consciously, as well as unconsciously. My conceptuality implies that this cybernetically functioning human system represents a stage in the ecosystem's evolution.

Self-definition is both reflective and political. It involves human feelings as well as the mind and action. The "self" in "self-definition" is the human being. It is the individual human being, and individual self-definition is largely synonymous with the process that we call identity formation. The "self" is also the group (small or large) and group self-definition is largely synonymous with the process that we call politicization, or what has been surveyed in the emerging field of "organizational development." By this I refer to the process in which a group which has formed, for whatever reason, takes stock of its own internal interests and fixes the order of its priorities, assesses the situation in which it exists, its friends and its foes, attempts to understand the interests of both, and then embarks upon action which will enable it to achieve what is necessary for its own self-interest. If we tend to associate individual self-definition with the work of Erik Erikson, we might associate group self-definition with that of Saul Alinsky.

One of the distinctive features of our present time is that the human species has moved toward a "global village," that is, one planetary community. This movement is still at a very early stage, but it is certainly increasing. There is not very much knowledge about or literature on the species' self-definition. This paucity of literature itself tells us that we are dealing with a dynamic historical process in which our understanding of the self changes, and the challenges which face the self change.

It seems to me that our present situation in history may be best described as one in which we stand approximately midway in the history of life, which originated 5,000 million years ago and which will possibly become extinct in heat death 5,000 million years from now. We cannot account for the fact that at this point evolution has eventuated in a creature who is responsible for defining what the entire process is about and acting on that definition, but the facts seem to support this interpretation.

2. Self-definition as Encounter with Transcendence.

It is against the background of the Holy Spirit affirmation, within the trinitarian scheme of classical Christianity, as I have interpreted it, that I approach the whole question of definition and self-definition in the human species and the ecosystem. What I have called self-definition of the ecosystem through the human species is one of the most significant processes that we see in this world, in this realm that bids fair to be autonomous and even anti-transcendent. I believe that this process of self-definition is the challenge of our times and that it is also the locus of the Holy Spirit's most important activity today -- the place where we can point to the Spirit at work in a significant way. The self-defining process is authentically this-worldly. One need not be a theologian, a Christian, or even a philosopher to see it in our world today and to feel its impact. It is without question a leading event in the anti-transcendent realm, and many persons would insist that it is an anti-transcendent process.

Just as the Christian affirmation of Holy Spirit insists that the world is more than it seems to be, and thereby does not mean to denigrate this world or draw us away from it, in the same sense we emphasize that the process of self-definition is not to be underestimated; it is a place of holiness; that is why we associate it with the working of the Holy Spirit. Self-definition is an event and a process in which we stand eyeball-to-eyeball with the deepest-reaching questions of our own personal and corporate existence. In the attempt to define ourselves, we are reaching into the deepest recesses of our own being for wisdom so that we can understand ourselves, while at the same time we try to muster the insight and courage to act upon whatever measure of wisdom we can obtain. Finally, the stake we have in self-definition is immense, because this adventure is not just a joyride that may entertain us or divert us, but rather it is the journey that makes us what we are, that makes us or breaks us. We might say with considerable justification that to be a human being is to engage in the defining of ourselves.

In other words, we say that the self-definition process is itself a place of encounter with the transcendent; that is why it qualifies as a Spirit-process. Let us look briefly at this meeting with transcendence -- it takes place in several dimensions. First, self-definition, by its very appearance in the evolution of life, represents a transcendence within that process. The evolutionary process has moved with great momentum until it has gathered the force to reach self-consciousness. The ecosystem is transcending itself when it questions its purpose in man. From the big bang that simply banged away, to the subtle questioning that is now going on in the self-defining process is a long step, and it is a manifestation of transcendence within the evolutionary career of the world.

Second, the very fact that human beings name the world and its elements and correlate to those names a set of uses, brings a difficult-to-imagine but nevertheless real transcendence to the non-human world, through human definition. When we name a substance "iron-ore" and use it accordingly, a transcendence has taken place. Quite apart from the

misuses of the non-human world, what man has done with the world has been
a transcendence for the world. The misuses, abuses, and faulty naming
attempts point, as we shall say later, to the presence of evil and negation
even within the transcending movement. In any case, nature is functioning
in a way that was unthought of prior to the human phase of evolution. But
not only has nature transcended itself; out of the concourse with nature humans themselves gain a broader sense of their environment and their own
definition within it. The ecological crisis has come about through nature
transcending itself, and it has opened up a whole new understanding for
human beings of themselves, a new understanding that is an encounter with
transcendence within their own self-awareness.

Third, with respect to the individual and the group, there is yet a
higher level of transcendence that opens up for us as in the process of defining itself. As we try to understand ourselves as individuals within groups
and as groups who must include individuals, our gaze is directed not only
outward toward the ecosystem, but also inward, to understand the inner
dynamics of our lives, toward understanding our psyches and our bodies,
so that we can understand what we are for and what the group is for. Who
has not returned from an intense group meeting, or an intense encounter
with wife and children asking, "Just who am I? What am I called to become
if I have to live with these people?" Or what group has not asked questions
like these: "What is this family all about, if it is to respond to husband and
father, wife and mother, or to teenager who is going through this growth
process?" What group of whites has not had to reexamine its whole reason
for being when a black person became its member? These are questions of self
definition, and every one of them is also a meeting with transcendence.

Fourth, when we move to the level of humankind, the species, all
of these transcending questions are raised to a higher and more difficult and
complex level. Each of us finds four elements in his or her nature that may
have gone unnoticed before: nature, individual, group, and humankind.
Taking nature seriously, for example, raises questions as to who I am, who
my group is, and what my species is, and each of these questions opens new
vistas and new depths of problems that we can deal with only if we transcend
ourselves. Furthermore, all of our smaller identities are relativized and
made more complex by the recognition that we belong to a planetary species.
When the astronauts looked back upon planet Earth and saw it in its aloneness
and in its relatedness and its smallness, and saw that the Earth and its people
were one planetary group, it changed our consciousness. Race, nation, sex
-- these are still crucial identities for us, but they are not enough -- we are
humankind, a species, a global village.

Finally, there is another sort of transcendence that we encounter
in self-definition: the transcending of our own future. When we consider
who we are and attempt to act upon that consideration, we look over our
shoulders to recapture and understand who we have been, our past, and we

look around us to take account of the present in which we live and act. But
it is the future that we must stare down most terrifyingly and sensitively.
In the unflinching defining process, we take on that future and cast ourselves
upon it -- and in the act of doing so, we transcend our own future and we
discover a new future just beyond it, at every moment.

To sum up, we encounter transcendence in the self-defining process,
inasmuch as in the attempt to know and to actualize ourselves we find at
every point that from within what seems to be a "natural" thrust that is every
bit "ours, " which we own as ours, at every moment we come to the brink of
what is MORE, the transcendent, and although the process is very much
this-worldly, we find ourselves in touch with the MORE than this world, in
its depths. We are ourselves continually altered and enlarged as we define
ourselves. We surpass ourselves, and thus we are pulled and pushed towards
newness. This is an unsettling state. Yet, being unsettled by the push and
pull of transcendence is also very profoundly sustaining and consoling, because the disturbance that belongs to our attempt to be who we are, and the
effort to be what we are called to be is the most comforting and sustaining
moment of life. In the vernacular, God's strokes come to us in the struggle,
because there is no greater comfort than to be struggling to actualize our
self-definition in accord with what we feel moved to become. The Holy
Spirit is both troubler and comforter at the same time.

3. Human Beings as God's Co-creators -- God Transcendent within Us.

This affirmation, that God's Holy Spirit is present working transcendence in the ecosystem's definition takes on particular meaning when
it is related to the three topics I have spoken of previously. Fundamentally,
to suggest that the ecosystem is defining itself decisively in Homo sapiens
is to suggest that the human species stands in a special relationship to God
-- a relationship that I designate as "co-creator." To interpret the current
situation as I have, with human beings poised as individuals, groups, and as
a species on spaceship earth, bearing responsibility for discovering what
"it is all about, " and acting upon that discovery -- this is to suggest that the
human species has become an agent in the creative process in a way that cannot be attributed to any other species -- either in quantity or quality.

Traditionally, the Jewish and Christian traditions have spoken of
this special relationship as man's being created imago dei, in the image of
God. Scholars and preachers have reached no consensus on what this
phrase, "in the image of God, " means, except in very general terms. In
the light of this ambiguity, I feel perfectly free in suggesting that to be created in the image of God means that humankind shares in God's activity of
defining and determining the creation. And in this sense, co-creatorhood
is the form in which transcendence manifests itself within the human species.
Co-creatorhood, God within us.

This assertion of co-creatorhood does not mean that humanity has created itself nor that we have total control over ourselves and the world. Co-creatorhood does not mean autonomous power for man. The term does mean that the human species has been created for this, to assume co-creatorhood, and in this sense it is by nature co-creator. Co-creatorhood involves what we noted earlier -- the responsibility to define ourselves and therewith the ecosystem itself, to define what a human being is for and what the ecosystem is for. Discernment, decision about the accuracy of that discernment, and the actualizing of that discernment -- that is what human beings are here for, and that is co-creatorhood.

To assert co-creatorhood, then, is not a statement of arrogance. We are co-creators because God has made us so, and not because we ourselves merited the status. Co-creatorhood is bound up with God's prevenient action. He unleashed the process of evolution, and it has come to this -- a species with the capacity for self-awareness and ecosystem-defining power and responsibility. This we share with God himself, since this defining power and responsibility are his. By his grace, he has determined, or at least permitted, that his creator-power of defining, naming, and using shall be advanced and carried out through the agency of Homo sapiens.

4. Defining and Being Defined -- God through Us and beyond Us.

In recent generations critical methodology has come to the fore with increasing prominence. One thinks, for example, of the neo-Marxist philosophy of the Frankfurt school. From one angle, this is the ultimate in sharpening our self-awareness, honing sharp our self-defining faculty, so that hidden agendas, ulterior interests, and the consequences of those agendas might be unmasked, with the purpose of bringing our actions and their consequences into harmony with our intention to survive humanely. From this angle, the process of critical self-defining seems to be an aggressive human activity, with a great deal of autonomy and responsibility. I would not wish to tone down or soften this emphasis. To be co-creator means to be aggressive and fully responsible. But there is another angle from which critical self-awareness must be viewed. Namely, the element of critical self-awareness also throws light on the sense in which man and the ecosystem are already defined, the sense in which Homo sapiens discovers his definition (and the ecosystem through him) more than he invents that definition. Here co-creatorhood takes on another nuance. The powers and responsibilities of co-creatorhood unfold under the pressure and the gracious gift of beholding the new, deciding what is fruitful in the new and acting responsibly to perfect the new. On the other hand, newness unveils itself in the context of the invariant which has always existed, but which man has yet to discover. Furthermore, the invariant unfolds itself in ever-new forms and processes.

The definer of the ecosystem, the co-creator human species, then, is aware of a two-fold experience -- the experience of being the meaning-giver to the ecosystem and yet finding that that meaning is one that he only partially forged himself, it having already been forged in its fundamentals before him. This experience does not negate the creativity and the defining responsibility of man, but it does remind him that creativity and defining take place in a context that provides both ground for his efforts and also a limiting set of rules.

It would be a fundamental error to emphasize man's self-defining co-creatorhood in a way that weakens our recognition of how we are already defined. To do so would be to drive us to extinction, since we must adjust to the order of nature if we are to be human beings in our ecosystem. Professor William Cooper, zoologist from Michigan State University, has made this point vividly in describing human life in this world as a card game: "We play the game to see how many hands we can play before we lose, but you lose once and then you're a fossil."[2] On the other hand, it would be equally a disastrous mistake so to emphasize the rules of the game to which we must conform, the sense in which we have already been defined, as to cut the nerve of man's morale, destroy his sense of freedom and negate his co-creatorhood. Without the most energetic and aggressive playing out of his role as definer-for-the-ecosystem, man will not serve his function in God's plan or the ecosystem's further career. It will take every ounce of energy and every bit of insight and courage for Homo sapiens to discern what this spaceship earth is for, what its needs and possibilities are. In other words, if man is less than the full co-creating definer he was created to be, the spaceship will be the worse for it, and this phase of the God-given evolutionary process will be aborted.

Transcendence is present in both aspects of this human experience I am describing. The power of the Spirit is at work in human self-definition, but the power of God is equally present in the invariant structures and processes of life which our self-definitions must discover and to which they must conform. When, therefore, we speak of the human being as definer and yet being defined, we speak of God through us and God beyond us. Critical man is aware that God is present through him, but man in the experience of sensing his own being defined recognizes that the God who is present through him is also beyond him.

C. The Unfolding of the World and the Divine Confronting Evil

The worldview that we are suggesting cannot explain evil, either its origin or its purpose. We confess with this admission that we stand where all human beings have stood and stand today. We do acknowledge evil, however, and the worldview does attend to the place of evil within the world of meaning. Even though we do not understand evil, we do understand that the divine life itself penetrates the reality of evil in order to undo it, in order, that is, to accomplish the purpose of the consummation of God and his world. This being so, the human being participates in the divine penetration of evil.

My general reliance upon the evolutionary model and the ecological imagery might mislead one to suppose that I picture the unfolding of the human story as an easy development. The very term "evolution" seems to imply this for people. They tend to equate it with "progress, " in a liberal optimistic sense. Nothing could be farther from the truth. Teilhard understood this when he likened human development to neither "millenary tranquillity nor bourgeois felicity, " but rather described progress in human affairs as a "way of the cross, " in which success is achieved only if the powers of hatred and warfare are "sublimated" to brotherhood. Those powers could never be eliminated or glossed over, he believed, but they could be sublimated. 3

The philosophy of Hegel and Marx, which underlies much of critical thinking today, has also accepted conflict and negation as intrinsic to the process of life. Whether speaking of God, of the human self, or of nations, Hegel understood that authenticity involves a going out from oneself to encounter and embrace that which is really different and separate and working through to a corporation and mutual incorporation that gives birth to the new. This dialectic is essential, fundamental, to life. God cannot be God, man cannot be man, apart from this way of negation, conflict, acceptance of the different into himself, and suffering synthesis. Fulfillment moves by way of this famous dialectic.

The way of the ecosystem is also a continual ingesting of that which is different, separate from ourselves and through the ingestion we become new and richer for it, or else perish either in the attempt or in the refusal to undertake the adventure. The self-definition of the ecosystem moves through this dialectic, universally.

The Christian theologian has no difficulty in recognizing this aspect of the definition process as an encounter with transcendence. Indeed, he is inclined to recognize that Jewish-Christian patterns of belief influenced Teilhard, Hegel, and Marx at this point. There are several predispositions that the Christian theologian brings with him that incline him to chart this dialectic as a movement of God. For one, the theologian recognizes the eschatological dimension of God's Kingdom, that is, the finality of God's definition of the world, that calls into question every proximate definition. Our specific definitions are continually giving way to new ones, to corrections of the old ones, and this giving way never comes easily. It comes by way of extinctions, by way of suffering and death, by way of the negation that accepts the unexpected and utterly different and overcomes the hatred of the tensions by sublimating them into a new kind of peace. This is what many theologians

today call the eschatological proviso. Earlier theologians spoke of a
"Protestant Principle" that implied continuous, rigorous critique, the continual unmasking of ideology and deception in the name of the God who
grounded the entire process.

A more vivid motif for the Christian theologian is the cross and
the crucifixion of Jesus. On the cross, the conflict between critical truth
and masking ideology is revealed at its sharpest. As J.S. Bach embodied
the story in one of his chorales, "Es war ein wunderlicher Krieg" -- it was
a terrible battle -- between truth, embodied, as it always is, in a concrete
life, and that which is other than, separate from, truth. For the Christian
theologian, the resurrection symbolizes that untruth was not only unmasked,
but that it was itself negated and redeemed.

The human species that stands midway between the 10, 000 million
years of life's career on Earth recognizes the struggle that accompanies
the process of definition and self-definition. It was thus, he now knows, in
the millennia before Homo sapiens, and it is so now in the Age of Self-Aware
Definition and Critical Definition of Man and the Ecosystem. Defining ourselves requires the kind of lucidity, discipline and courage that can only be
counted a struggle and an acceptance of negativities into ourselves, in the
hope that something new and more adequate will emerge. That is true
whether the self-definition is that of a teen-ager passing through to adulthood, a racial or sex grouping defining its liberation, or the species defining
itself and its ecosystem. If we accept that the human species is the first to
be critically aware that its specializations can lead to extinction and that a
vast shifting of gears is now necessary, then we have no difficulty at all in
recognizing the validity of the dialectical, struggle-and-conflict oriented
image of the definition process. The Christian theologian sees this process
of negation as a manifestation of God Suffering with Us, the crucified God,
who did not count it an insult to enter the fray, because it is his own creation
that is at stake, the suffering God, who demonstrates in the process that he
can take negativity into himself and thus be God as the Spirit that is in, with,
and under the forms of this anti-transcendent world.

D. A Concrete Image to Shape Action in Conformity with the Divine Life

If on the one hand the divine life itself must penetrate the reality
of evil and on the other hand we and the world participate in the divine life,
then the concrete image for our lives must encompass our penetration of
evil. This much is part of what it means for us to be defined within our ecosystem. But since we have also been defined as the self-definers, the co-
creators, that penetration of evil must be intrinsically our decision and self-
definition. The centrality of the Christian understanding of the sacrifice and
resurrection of Jesus of Nazareth, the Messiah, comes into play here, and
its pivotal significance for worldview construction becomes clear.

Jesus' sacrifice is not simply model for our action, although it is that, nor is it simply an action in our behalf, although it is also that. More profoundly, his sacrifice is an epitome of what it means for human existence to participate in the divine life which is its ultimate ecosystem. In summary form we can elaborate as follows: Jesus' sacrifice was an action in which his own powers of discernment and decision shared fully in God's will for him. His vocation and God's providence were coterminous. His sacrifice was not an accident, but rather an intentional act in which he laid down his life in an attempt to confront the powers of evil so as to elicit from them a human response. He risked death, and it came. His total act -- risk and death -- became the arena within which power was released which could transmute evil into redemption, alienation into reconciliation. The resurrection is the seal of validation that this was in fact the case.

As a concrete image, Jesus' sacrifice thus becomes a shaping force for our own lives. Sacrifice for us, as for Jesus, is not an exercise in violence or masochism. Rather, it is a calculated effort to lay our lives down in such a way as to elicit authentically human responses in the situations in which we live. Our sacrifices do not effect redemption, nor are they assured of success. Rather, we live in the hope that they become the occasions for the release of divine power for transmutation of alienation into reconciliation and redemption.

This concrete image gives shape to belonging. Belonging, in the ultimate analysis, is both an assurance that we are part of God's life and also a commitment unto death for that life. The worldview we have elaborated here makes such belonging possible.

NOTES AND REFERENCES

[1]R. G. Collingwood, The Idea of Nature (New York: Oxford University Press, 1960), 127.

[2]The source of this quotation is lost to the author.

[3]Pierre Teilhard de Chardin, The Future of Man (London: Collins, 1964), 153.

CHAPTER VIII

RELIGIOUS INSTITUTIONS AND HUMAN SOCIETY: A Normative
Inquiry Into the Appropriate Contribution of Religious Institutions
to Human Life and to the Divine Life

by
W. Widick Schroeder

Introduction

This essay is more normative than descriptive, for it delineates
the appropriate contributions religious institutions ought to make to human
life and to the Divine Life. It does incorporate a descriptive dimension in
one section. In that section the broad structure of the contemporary American social order is characterized and correlated with normative forms of
social organization outlined in a preceding section.

The term "religious institution" is used in the title for a specific
reason. Religious institutions, whose constitutive acts center on worship
of the Divine Reality, are ubiquitous in human history. They are a genus
of which the Christian Church is a species. The Christian Church bears a
tradition through which most people in the West in general and the United
States in particular have been led to develop interpretations of the Divine
presence in human life. Most of the illustrative material cited here will
be drawn from Christian thinkers, but analogous patterns are discernable
in other religious traditions.

Christianity is a species of the genus "religion." No categorically
unique qualities are ascribed to the Christian Church or to its founder, Jesus
of Nazareth; nonetheless their contributions to a network of feeling and meaning evoking sensitivity and theological reflection are gratefully acknowledged.[1]
In its origins Christianity does differ substantially from the other great world
religions. The other great world religions emerged with full-blown metaphysical interpretations of God and His relations to the world; Christianity
has always been a religion seeking an adequate mode of interpretation. Its
founder's teachings were direct and intuitive sayings and observations. His
utterances were concrete and usually commonplace. His person is a salient
factor in the emergence of the Christian movement, and He has evoked people
in that movement to reflect on God-world relations.

The term "human society" is used to indicate the presence of an
entity -- or more properly, a complex clustering of entities in patterned

181

relations to one another through a multiplicity of social institutions with a variety of defining characteristics -- characterized by the presence of religious institutions and of institutions in the other spheres of the social order. Taken conjointly, the social institutions in the several spheres of the social order, in conjunction with the human beings from which the spheres are abstracted and with the defining characteristics embodied in the past and present of human beings, constitute human society.

Theologians in the Christian tradition have held various views of appropriate relations between the church and institutions in the other spheres of the social order.[2] Some have held that a sharp contrast ought to exist between the church and the world. Significant segments of the early church and various withdrawing sects, such as the Mennonities, saw such contrasts and urged their adherents to have as little to do with non-believers as possible.

Others accepted a sharp contrast between life among Christians in the church and life among Christians and others in the world, but they saw a paradoxical relation between the church and other social institutions. Hence, as in the case of Martin Luther, they counseled for participation by Christians in both spheres, but they saw different leading principles manifest in the two spheres. In Luther's view, for instance, love (understood as outgoing concern for others, kindness, sweetness, and charity) was the leading principle in relations among Christians in the church, but power (understood primarily as the use of force, physical or psychic, to establish the superiority of one will, individual or collective, over another) was the leading principle among people in the state. The strange work of God's love was manifest through the state.

Still others sought to effect a coalescence or a movement toward an identification of the church and the world. Thomas Munzer in the Reformation and some protagonists of contemporary "liberation" theologies illustrate interpretations in which the sword was or is to be used to bring forth an increased harmony of life with life under the conditions of existence. Others, including many twentieth century "liberal" Protestants, have urged the extension of the suasive power of love to the public spheres to enhance the harmony of life with life under the conditions of existence.

In both of these instances, some vision of the harmony of life with life rooted in a Christian experience provides the basis for efforts to effect a radical transformation of the world. Current protagonists of a radical transformation of the social order are more apt to locate the crux of the problems increasing disharmony of life with life in the economic or cultural spheres than earlier proponents did, but they all share a common vision of a sharp contrast between the existing rather miserable state of disharmony of life with life and a potential future state of an enhanced harmony of life with life. They relate such a possibility to changes in the religious, cultural, political, economic, social, and/or familial spheres of life.[3]

Although not as frequently manifest in the Christian tradition, a more conservative reading of the possibilities of human life may lead proponents to seek to restore some past state of the social order or to defend the status quo as that situation most likely to maximize the harmony of life with life possible under the conditions of existence. [4]

Classically, social conservatives related the doctrine of the Fall to a vision of the perfect harmony of life with life under the conditions of an earlier state of affairs. Affirming the persistence of sin among humans, they rejected a perfectionist vision and sought to conserve existing institutions as the best possible under the conditions of existence. Sometimes they supported the existing political forms as the best possible ones, granted the persistent inordinate self-centeredness of humans; sometimes they supported existing economic forms. In other instances a more inclusive model was defended, incorporating social institutions in most or all the spheres of the social order.

All of these views have one thing in common; they involve a rather sharp contrast between a vision of perfection and the current condition of humankind. In spite of this common element, they differ markedly in their assessments of its implications for present and future human life. The Lutheran vision is the most conservative, and the "radical transformation" vision is the most innovative. The Anabaptist vision develops the most clarity about church-world and Christian-non-believer distinctions, and the "radical transformation" vision develops the least clarity.

One other broad view remains for consideration. Proponents of this view discern an overlap or a point of contact between the vision of the harmony embodied in the beatific vision of the Good and the degree of harmony of life with life possible under the conditions of existence. Protagonists vary in their assessment of the contribution of the forms embodied in human experience to the harmony of life with life.

The possibility of a necessary contribution of a priori static forms to human life represents one polar view. The possibility of an emergent and dynamic context providing the basis for the emergence of forms represents the other polar view. In this instance, all forms are constantly being outgrown and outrun by the emerging present. [5]

Whether anyone is guided unequivocally by a view of a priori static forms or an emerging dynamic context is a moot question. Historically, Catholicism has had the most formalistic bias (natural law, causistry, natural theology, etc.), Calvinism a moderate formalistic bias (natural law, ambivalently positive relations between love, justice, and forms of social organization, emphasis on third function of the law, i.e., a positive contribution of the law to human life, and a rejection of natural theology), and so-called "contextualists" the most dynamic bias (no natural law, strong emphasis on God's freedom, no natural theology, principles emerging from context, strong emphasis on novelty of contexts). The strongly formalistic versions

of this "overlap" or contiguous view of love-justice relations have close
relations with the more conservative or "contrast" interpretations discussed earlier; the strongly dynamic versions have close relations with the
more innovative "contrast" interpretations.

The view elaborated in this essay has more in common with this
"overlap" perspective than with any of the others. Because it holds that
forms are necessarily included in every experience, it has some affinities
with the more formalistic versions of this "overlap" interpretation. Because it holds that the emerging present subject surpasses the past and
appropriates novel forms as well as forms embodied in creatures lying in
its causal past (implying the ultimacy of a category of creativity), it has
some affinities with the more dynamic versions of the "overlap" theory. In
sum, the view developed here is intermediate with a moderate dynamic bias.
It is more Catholic than classical Protestantism, and more Protestant than
classical Catholicism.

Because of the relations envisaged between the formal, dynamic,
and unifying components of experience, some will see the normative connections suggested here between the church and social institutions in the other
spheres of the social order as standing between a "two kingdom" view and a
transformative view. In relation to church-state connections, the view advanced here is more Lutheran than classical Calvinism, and more Calvinistic
than classical Lutheranism.

The "Isness-Oughtness" Contrasts in Human Life

Humankind has been haunted by the lure of perfection. The vision
of the perfect harmony of life with life is manifest in many cultural contexts.

Augustine envisaged a perfect harmony of life with life in a literal
Garden of Eden. Adam and Eve had been so created that their wills were
perfectly united with the Divine will. This perfect harmony led to a harmony
of their reason with the Divine reason and the perfect harmony of the components of their bodies. A similar harmony of sub-human and supra-human
creatures in relation to the whole prevailed.

In his formulation of a hierarchy of nature, angels, creatures with
minds and wills but without bodies, were intermediate between humans and
God. An angel turned away from God before humans did, so there was some
prior propensity toward disharmony -- evil being a privation or lack of being
-- in the cosmos. Nonetheless, though the action was foreknown by God,
Adam and Eve through inevitability but not necessity turned away from the
Divine will and centered their lives upon themselves. This disruption led
to the cleavage between Divine reason and human reason and subsequently
disrupted the harmony between the body, the mind, and the will. Consequently, because of the sin of Adam and Eve, death entered the human situation

and disrupted the harmony of creation.

In the present context, the point warranting emphasis is the Augustinian vision of a perfectly created and harmonious world disrupted by human and trans-human agents. The Fall is contrasted with the vision of a pre-existing harmony and a future restoration of that harmony for some but not all creatures.

The Stoics' notion of a pre-existing Golden Age from which humankind had fallen, Plato's envisagement of the Good, and Aristotle's notion of a supreme Being reflexively thinking thoughts about itself all illustrate the persistence of a vision of perfection among humankind.

In the present epoch, Karl Marx's view of the enhanced harmony of life with life to be attained by an appropriate reorganization of the social order, Jean Jacques Rousseau's vision of the harmony of nature, and Sigmund Freud's entertainment of the possibility of understanding the forces and factors shaping human behavior in order to live in conformity with them may all be interpreted as responses to a pervasive intuition of perfection.[6]

Contemporary Protestant theologians have frequently rejected the cosmological side of Augustine's interpretation of the "isness-oughtness" contrast embodied in human experience, but they have usually affirmed the inner spiritual and existential dimension of that analysis. The wretchedness or estrangement of humans is contrasted with their reunion with the Divine reality effected by Divine initiative. They often differ in their views on sanctification, leading them to contrasting views on the extent to which the harmony of life with life may be attained under the conditions of existence. The broad shape of these alternatives has been discussed in the introduction, and it is not necessary to elaborate them further in the present context. It is important to note, however, that alternative assessments lead to differing diagnoses of and remedies for the disharmony and the injustice discerned in the social order.

At a more everyday level of less fully interpreted experience, people are constantly contrasting a projected or experienced "better" state of affairs with an existing "worse" state. These widespread experiences of humans suggest the pervasiveness of an experience of harmony and intensity of feeling in emerging creatures.

These experiences of perfection do not float into the world from nowhere; they must find their locus in a subject-object whose qualities are objectified in human experiences.

God's primordial envisagement of all potentiality constitutes such a locus for the human experience of perfect harmony. His subjective aim orders and harmonizes all of the forms and lures creatures to aesthetic satisfaction and enhancement of feeling. The forms constituting His primordial nature are not internally related to each other; they are related through their common participation in His subjective aim. In this sense, the forms do not constitute a class but are a multiplicity.

Because of this relationship an unequivocally convincing and self-evident rational proof for the existence of God cannot be developed. A religious intuition that there is a relational essence to the universe sustains and supports the rationalistic faith that the relational essence can be illumined by reason. A metaphysical system may enhance human religious feelings, but it cannot -- on its own -- create them.

This view of God's subjective aim seeking satisfaction through the evocation of creatures in a world is closely related to the Platonic understanding of the Good, but the lack of internal relations of all the forms means that philosophy cannot lead one to a vision of the Good as directly as it does for Plato in Books V-VII of The Republic.

This view of the relation of the forms to each other through their common envisagement by God also provides a coherent explanation for the becoming of some creatures without eliciting the becoming of all creatures. If the forms were internally related to each other, the actualization of one form would elicit the actualization of all forms. Potentiality and actuality would coincide; the result would be a static universe in which all that could become would have become. There would be no contrast between that which is and that which might be but is not; hence, there would be no consciousness.

The "isness-oughtness" contrast, the reality of which is expressed in common history of humankind and to which illustrative references have been made earlier in this essay, is rooted in the perfection of God's harmonization of the forms in His subjective aim and the limitations necessarily imposed by the finitude of actuality. As they become, creatures cannot actualize everything; some selectivity, some exclusion, and some limitations are unavoidable.

The "oughtness" of the perfect harmony of God's subjective aim is experienced with varying intensity by the creatures of the world. In certain of the occasions which in serial order constitute the life history of a human being, the intensity of this perfection is unusually strong; in other occasions, it may be markedly diminished. The rather exceptional experiences of great intensity are what are termed "mystical" or "ecstatic" experiences. In such occasions the subject-object structure of the experience, which is always embodied in the structure of the world, is not overcome, but the human subject-object is in an especially intense way experiencing the objectification of a facet of the Divine Nature in his experience. [7] This experience is interpreted frequently as the "oughtness" of perfect harmony.

The limitations of existence impose themselves upon creatures as an "isness," a givenness which necessarily precludes the actualization of the perfect harmony embodied in God's primordial nature. When conscious creatures, such as human beings, compare the "oughtness" of the intense experience of God's subjective aim with the "isness" imposed by the limitations of existence and, through the exercise of negative judgment imagine the possibility of the actualization of that which is necessarily only potentiality, they experience an "isness-oughtness" contrast.

The confusion of potentiality and actuality has led some people to seek an inordinate harmony of life with life under the conditions of existence. Because of the intensity of their convictions, many have considered them to be religious fanatics and have been concerned about the dangers to social, economic, and political stability embodied in their views. From the constructive view informing this essay, there is substantial wisdom in such popular assessments of proponents of radically transformative visions.

The inexorable and inviolable foundation for the contrast, as has been noted, is the limitation which actuality imposes on potentiality. Other factors also contribute to the "isness-oughtness" contrast. These factors are discussed in the following section.

The Factors Contributing to the "Isness-Oughtness" Contrast

As noted above, the "isness-oughtness" contrast in human experience is rooted in the difference between the harmonization of all potentiality in one facet of the Divine Life and the necessary limitations on the infinity of potentiality imposed by the actualization of some but not all potentiality in the finite becoming of a particular creature in the world. There is no such thing as a single mode of perfection in the cosmos. Each actualization must be assessed in relation to the context in which it emerges. The actualization will be more or less appropriate to its context, but "best" is always a relative term and the "best" is possible only from the Divine perspective. Other creatures have to settle for a relative better or worse.

In addition to this foundational limitation on the degree of harmony possible under the conditions of existence, other secondary factors may intensify the "isness-oughtness" contrast embodied in human experience. Finitude imposes other limitations on the degree of harmony of life with life possible in a particular context in a particular cosmic epoch.

The capacity of organisms to respond novelly to their past is intimately related to the limitations of finitude. Their freedom may lead them to seek, consciously or unconsciously, the actualization of new and novel forms of potentiality in the present. These actualizations may prove to be evil if they are born out of season; on the other hand, without the actualization of novel forms, the complex development of societies and the emergence of organisms with enhanced capacities for intensity of feeling could not have taken place in the evolution of the cosmos.

Often two potentially meritorious actualizations are mutually exclusive. For example, it is not possible for a human being to actualize all of his potentialities. Granted some relative differences due to ability and

temperament, no one person can actualize numerous professional compe-
tencies. If one chooses to become a physician, it will be almost impossible
for that person to become a distinguished musician. Who can say which is
"better" and which is "worse"?

In addition, decisions now lying in the causal past of emerging
creatures may limit the degree of harmony possible in a given locus. For
example, a network of decisions made by preceding generations of Americans
has contributed to the emergence of a society in which the influence of technical rationalism and high technology is very substantial. Granted the need
to modify technical rationalism and to restrain the multiple impact of high
technology, it is impossible to effect many qualifications on the shorter run
without very substantial disharmony.

In addition to finitude in its primal and secondary manifestations,
ignorance and sloth and lethargy contribute to human experiences of the
"isness-oughtness" contrast. Emerging creatures do not possess fully adequate knowledge of creatures lying in their causal past, and contemporary
creatures actualize themselves in causal independence of their contemporaries. Both factors contribute to the inability of emerging creatures to actualize themselves in such a fashion as to maximize the degree of harmony
possible in a given context.

Inadequate knowledge of the creatures in one's causal past may
cause one to do things which are at cross purposes with what other contemporaries are deciding to become, thereby attenuating the richness of future
creatures. For example, a lack of awareness of certain traumas in the life
of another, such as intense fear of automobile accidents because of experience of a terrifying crash, may lead a person to drive more aggressively
than his companion would desire.

Even if one had a fully adequate knowledge of the causal past, one
could not know for certain what an emerging creature was going to become,
for contemporary physical events happen in causal independence of one another. Two emerging creatures may share much of a common past and may
appropriate and respond to that past similarly. These responses may enhance the harmony and intensity of feeling of future creatures, but there is
no way to be certain of such compatible responses. Indeed, the independence
of contemporary creatures from the causal influence of each other provides
some "elbow room" in the universe. Without such independence, novel
creatures could not emerge. [8]

Sloth and lethargy also contribute to disharmony by fostering inordinate creaturely self-interest. The point of view elaborated here, as noted
earlier, does not appeal to a doctrine of original sin in either its classical
or contemporary forms. Nonetheless, the persistence of the doctrine suggests it is pointing toward a recurrent and pervasive aspect of human experience, i.e., inordinate human self-interest. Self-interest is grounded in the
necessity to actualize something, for there must be "selves" who are aiming

their becoming at their "interests." The vision of the larger whole to which the parts are contributing may qualify and modify self-interest, but the vision cannot eliminate self-interest. Indeed, any whole which does sensitively sustain its parts is pernicious. A whole ought to foster some diversity in its parts.

Finitude, ignorance, and sloth and lethargy in their interrelatedness and inter-penetration create the "isness-oughtness" contrast embodied in human experience. This contrast cannot be eliminated, but there are principles of justice which can give some guidance to the shape of structures which may enhance the possibilities of increased harmony of life with life and to the appropriate relations between human social institutions in the familial, ethnic, social, economic, political, cultural, and religious spheres. Subsequent sections address these issues.

Form, Dynamics, and Unification in Human Life

Human experience begins with the appropriation by an emerging creature of creatures lying in its causal past. From the human point of view, the past is never fully objectified in an emerging creature; the objectification involves some loss. Nonetheless, every creature in the causal past contributes <u>something</u> to the structure and the feelings of a novel emerging subject-object. Eternal objects, those forms of definiteness embodied in God's primordial nature and representing potentiality capable of being actualized again and again in the creatures of the world, provide the basis for the objectification of creatures in the past in emerging creatures. Some of the eternal objects contribute forms and feelings to an emerging creature; all of them contribute feelings, including the negative feeling of elimination from the definiteness of a particular creature.

The importance of necessary relations of the causal past to the emerging present inherent in this view should be underscored. Cause and effect are intertwined in human experience. In the appropriation of the creatures of the world, the body functions as a giant amplifier, feeding data into the organizing center of the human being. The organizing center is an ultimate percipient occasion, sometimes conscious and the locus for all our data about ourselves and the world. Humans do not merely impose their categories of understanding on the world; the patterns embodied in the order of nature are appropriated by humans in the initial phase of their experience. [9] Facts and values are interrelated, for the "facts" contribute their share of feeling, meaning, and form to an emerging creature.

This initial physical phase in the emergence of a creature is "succeeded" by a mental phase, in which novel eternal objects embodied in the Divine Life are appropriated directly by the emerging creature. The verb "succeeded" is placed in quotation marks to indicate that the emerging subject-object being discussed is literally out of physical time, for such time itself is measured by the sequence of occasions which become. The "movement" of eternal objects constitutes the passage of time. The emerging entity can only be separated analytically into earlier and later phases. In fact, it is an inextricably interrelated entity unified by its own subjective aim.

In this supplemental phase, contrasts between the initial data appropriated in the physical phase of the becoming of a new creation and the eternal objects appropriated in the mental phase develop. The emerging creature aiming at esthetic satisfaction and intensity of feeling synthesizes and contrasts its physical and conceptual feelings. The more complex the organism, the more salient the conceptual phase, and the richer the contrasts emerging in the later phases of the creature's becoming. The peak of consciousness is the negative judgment, when a creature contrasts what is with what might be but is not. In this sense, God is the supremely conscious creature, for He contrasts all that might be with all that is. He Himself is becoming more conscious in the evolution of the cosmos; for, as more and more creatures become, He has more actual subject-objects to contrast with what might be but is not.

The emerging creature unifies its physical and conceptual data and their concomitant feelings as it seeks its satisfaction. Its initial subjective aim, through which it is able to unify its feelings and objects, is derived from God's overarching subjective aim. God's subjective aim, as noted earlier, involves his unification of the forms of definiteness in his primordial nature. God is a suasive force in the universe; for He is an evoker, luring forth creatures seeking esthetic satisfaction and intensity of feeling.

Three components-in-relation are all pervasive in experience. The first component is a formal component, involving both creatures who have become and, hence, are objects for all subsequent creatures, and also forms of definiteness embodied in God's primordial nature.

The second component is a dynamic component, involving the process of the appropriation of objects, the emerging synthesis of those objects and related feelings into an evolving subject, and the process of the objectification of that subject into the Divine Life. The rhythm by which the many in the cosmos first become an integrated unity and then become one more of the many is perennial. The ultimate category is the category of creativity. All creatures, including the Divine creature, are subject to the emergent process. [10] In affirming the ultimacy of this category one can appeal only to intuition, for the category is more inclusive than any other one. Creativity is manifest in all creation, and appeal to nothing more general than it can be made to illumine it.

The third component is the unification of the formal and dynamic components in concrete, actual entities. Emerging creatures aiming at their satisfaction synthesize and harmonize the feelings and objects constituting their data into an emerging unity. This unification is dependent upon God's subjective aim.[11]

Form, dynamics, and unification are three-in-relation. No one
component of experience can be understood except as it is set in the context
of the other two. There are differences in the priority of the components
in various dimensions of experience. These differences permit a characterization of the leading dimension in various facets of life and the development of normative views about principles of justice and forms of social
organization. They also permit a formulation of the appropriate relations
between religious institutions and institutions in the other spheres of the
social order. Such relations guide the assessment developed here of the
contribution religious institutions ought to make to human life in the present
and in the future.

The Priority of Justice, Power, and Love
in the Dimensions of Human Experience

As form, dynamics, and unification are three-in-relation, these
components are present in every sphere of human life. In spite of these
necessary interrelations, a leading component, a secondary component, and
a tertiary component are discernable in the various spheres of human life.
The saliency of a particular component in one or more of the spheres of
human life permits an assessment of the potential contributions of social
institutions in the several spheres of the social order to human life. It also
permits an interpretation of the appropriate relations of social institutions
to each other.

There are six possible sequences of relations between these three
components: dynamics, unification, and form; form, unification, and
dynamics; form, dynamics, and unification; dynamics, form, and unification; unification, dynamics, and form; and unification, form and dynamics.

Before relating these components to human life, these symbols
referring to basic metaphysical processes need to be correlated with more
familiar ones. The form component of human life embodies the notion of
justice, for it entails the rational side of things. The dynamic component
embodies the notion of power, for it entails both causal influence and self-
determination. The unification component embodies the notion of love, for
it entails the harmonization of formal and dynamic components into a unity
and the sensitive responses of creatures one to another.

The first sequence of priority, power, love, and justice, refers to
the basic process of the emergence of the novel creature per se. Any
emerging creature under the necessity to actualize itself (power) is able to
do so through the derivation of its subjective aim from God's subjective aim

(love). As it emerges, it synthesizes form (justice) and feelings derived
from the causal past and from God's primordial nature into a whole.

   The second sequence of priority, justice, love, and power, refers
to the relations between human beings in face-to-face relations. The form
of the person can be most fully respected in such relations; for, at least
potentially, one can be more fully accepted and understood in such small
group contexts than in any other context. Love, involving sympathetic and
empathic responses to the needs of others, is second in emphasis. Self-
determination is third in emphasis; for, at least in principle, one's own
aims are intimately related to the aims of the other.

   The third and fourth sequences, "justice, power, and love" and
"power, justice, and love," relate to human groups and social institutions
in their abstraction from the concrete network of social relations in which
human beings are enmeshed. These abstractions refer to intergroup relations in the racial, ethnic, status, economic, cultural, and political spheres
of the social order.

   The justice, power, and love sequence is predominant in all of these
spheres except the political, for the values shaping these relations are defined by cultural forms. These cultural defining characteristics are themselves the product of the response of the shaping capacities of human beings
to factors inherent in the conditions of human existence. These forms shape
the way people are lured or coerced to participate in the social institutions
in these spheres.

   The state may enact and enforce laws which reinforce or run counter
to the forms predominant in one or more of these spheres. As this law-
making and law-enforcing function of the state suggests, the sequence of
priority in the state is power, justice, and love. Power considerations are
predominant; the state acts to shape and to enforce laws helping to define
the character of the social insititutions in the other spheres of the social
order. If a state is to endure, its citizens must participate in some commonly
shared values and give at least tacit approval to the political leaders of the
state. Leaders seeking to impose their wills upon a citizenry without regard
for justice or for the expectations of the citizens may be able to do so for a
time, but eventually such leadership will modify its views or be deposed.
The "better" the state, the greater its reliance on suasion and the less its
reliance on force.

   The state seeks to develop forms and patterns to facilitate both
domestic and international order and harmony. Within a state, understood
as a geographical territory with some common shared values in which an
organizing center has a monopoly on the legitimate use of force and on the
shaping of domestic and foreign policy, a consensus formation process is
often successful, for the members of a state share enough common values
to accept or to acquiesce to the policy decisions developed by the leaders in
the organizing center of the state. If members do not share enough common

values to permit the consensus formation process to evolve, internal strife and civil wars will develop.

The nurture of order and harmony in the domestic side of a state's life is often difficult, but such nurture is even more difficult in international affairs. There is little consensus about justice and a minimal participation in common values among the peoples of the several national states on this planet, so the dimension of power looms even larger in international affairs than in national affairs.

This reality limits the capacity of any nation state to shape policy which will enhance the harmony of the whole. Political leaders must always consider the expectations of their own citizens in the formulation of foreign policy; the predominance of self-interest among all peoples suggests only those policies fostering the common good of all humankind which also clearly enhance the welfare of the peoples of particular nations have any chance of adoption. Any view of the human future fostering the adoption of policy which ignores the pervasiveness of self-interest among the nations of the world will not only create internal discord but also will increase rather than diminish the fragile order currently extant among the nations of the world.

The sequences "love, power, and justice" and "love, justice, and power" refer to God-world relations. From the Divine point of view, the sequence of priorities is love, power, and justice. God manifests his love by sensitively responding to the becoming of the creatures of the world and by then seeking to evoke the becoming of new creatures who will maximize the harmony and intensity of feeling of which they are capable. He does so by providing them with seasonally relevant forms of definiteness from which the creatures may appropriate those which they "decide" to incorporate in their emerging selves. These creatures are then objectified in the Divine Life, and the sequence is repeated for emerging creatures. In His totality God functions in the universe as a locus of potentiality, a lure for feeling, a mediator of experience, and an ultimate receptor of all that has become.

From the human point of view, the sequence of priorities is love, justice, and power. Love refers to the development of the emerging creature's subjective aim evoked by God's subjective aim. Justice refers to the emerging creature's appropriation of creatures lying in its causal past and of forms of definiteness embodied in God's primordial notion. Power refers to the dynamic process of self-development and to the actualization of the creature who then becomes a "power" which all subsequent creatures must take into account. [12]

Religious institutions are grounded in human religious experience and in interpretations of that experience. The priority of love in the love, justice, power sequence provides the basis for the development of criteria to guide the relations between religious institutions and institutions and groups in the other spheres of the social order.

The Divine Reality functions by persuasion in the cosmos, and institutions lured forth by that reality should do likewise. Religious institutions should not use physical force or threat of physical force either to attract participants or to relate to people. Except in the most extraordinary circumstances, they should not be involved directly in the conflict of political group with political group in the political sphere. The necessary inclusion of form in human experience implies that reason contributes positively to human experience of the Divine Presence, but the saliency of love means that religious experience is more fundamental and elemental than any analysis of it or of the supreme subject-object of religious devotion. Faith is prior reason in human religious experience, but reason may enhance faith.

Because justice and love are more salient than power in interpersonal relations and because social institutions involve abstractions from the concrete net of relations to which humans are bound, the fullest dimensions of human life are realizable only in interpersonal relations. Some forms of social organization are more consonant with human nature than others. When a given society can sustain them, these forms should be supported; but it is a mistake to criticize inordinately forms of familial, ethnic, status, economic, political, cultural and religious organizations on the grounds that they thwart the fulfillment of human life. Those forms of social organization which offer the possibilities of more adequately enhancing human life should be fostered, but the most any form of social organization can ever do is to provide a more favorable environment for the cultivation of richer, fuller, and more harmonious life.

Because human actualization involves some loss of the past, even the most congenial forms of social organization and the most satisfying interpersonal relations cannot provide an ultimate fulfillment. Religious institutions should seek to evoke human intuitions of an ultimate fulfillment beyond the temporal. In the Christian tradition, this non-temporal locus of fulfillment has been characterized by the symbol "the Kingdom of God." These symbols bear witness to the everlasting objectification of the creatures of the world in the Divine Life. The creatures are objectified in God's consequent nature and then flow back into the world -- the Kingdom of God is with us now and forever more.

Temporal fulfillment of human life surpasses social institutions and historical groups and is embodied in individual human beings in their concrete relations with other creatures -- human and non-human; eternal fulfillment of human life surpasses the perpetual perishing of the temporal and is embodied in the everlasting full and complete objectification of the creatures of the world in the Divine Life.

The contrast between the priority of power in political life and the priority of love in the religious life is the foundational reason for the similarity between this view and the classical Lutheran "Two Kingdom" interpretation of church-world relations. The necessary embodiment of form in

all experience, the universality of general principles of justice, and the
ambivalently positive contribution of desirable forms of social organization
to human life are the foundational reasons for the similarity between this
view and classical Calvinism and Catholicism.

The question of the appropriate contribution of religious institutions
to human life is inextricably related to an understanding of the principles of
justice and desirable forms of human social organization in the several
spheres of the social order. The subsequent section of this essay addresses
these issues.

Human Principles of Justice and Desirable Forms of Social Organization

Human Principles of Justice -- The process of creaturely actualization involves the unification of data derived from a given creature's causal past
and from God's primordial nature. The "power" component involves both
the givenness of data and the dynamic decision by which an emerging creature becomes what it is to be. Power in human social systems involves the
actualization and implementation of decisions made by various participants
in the system.

"Justice" involves the forms which give shape to creaturely actualization. Justice in human social systems relates to the principles of justice,
to the rules and regulations of justice informed by the principles and shaped
by the decisions of people in the organizing center of a state, and to the
application of the rules and regulations of justice in a particular situation
by seasonally relevant participants in that situation.

"Love" refers to the unification of power and justice in a particular
context. In human societies, the unification of power and justice takes place
in a twofold manner. First, people have to make decisions to embody the
principles of justice through particular rules and regulations of justice in a
specified context. Second, people have to apply the rules and regulations of
justice in a particular situation. The power component, as noted earlier,
is the leading component at each level, so the encounter of wills with wills,
both individual and collective and also domestic and international, is characteristic of political life.

The form, dynamics, unification triad inherent in the actualization
of all creatures provides the basis for the formulation of the principles of
justice. The rational component of form provides the basis for equality
appropriate to form as a principle of justice. The rational component initially
gives rise to the recognition of odd and even. The recognition of even and the
intuition of the idea of congruence entail the idea of equality. Differences
among creatures require some limitations on the principle of equality, for

the principle can apply only to equals. Thus the qualifying phrase "appropriate to form" must be added to the notion of equality. [13]

The dynamic component of power provides the basis for self-determination informed by excellence as a principle of justice. The dynamic bias inherent in the cosmos in general and human beings in particular limits the fit of forms to facts. As befits high grade organisms, the shaping capacity of human beings is substantial. The lure for harmony and intensity of feeling, both within and between creatures, qualifies self-determination; for it is informed by the excellence of harmony and intensity of feeling. Thus the qualifying phrase "informed by excellence" must be added to the notion of self-determination.

Some humans have greater shaping capacities than others, so self-determination modifies and qualifies equality among humans. Some social differentiation is necessary and desirable, but protagonists disagree on the degree of differentiation that ought to be sustained within and between nations.

The problems inherent in efforts to harmonize the principles of equality appropriate to form and self-determination informed by excellence lead to a consideration of order, peace, or harmony, the third principle of justice. Both equality and self-determination must be manifest, but they cannot be harmonized perfectly. A tolerable balance is obtained in a healthy society, but the precise integration cannot be determined a priori. It depends on contextual factors and the give and take that is part of the life of a living community.

Protagonists of either excessive equality or excessive self-determination are apt to ignore the principle of order, but its saliency in human life should not be underestimated. In its political organization, humankind is also imperiled by the danger of tyranny on the one hand and anarchy on the other hand. The excessive disorder of anarchy encourages the excessive order of tyranny, and vice versa.

Equality appropriate to form, self-determination informed by excellence, and order are thus universal principles of justice. These principles taken in conjunction with the sequence of priorities of form, dynamics and unification discussed earlier and with the characteristics of human beings, can inform the development of forms of social organization most likely to permit -- but not to guarantee -- the maximization of the harmony of life with life under the conditions of human existence. The next portion of this section elaborates these forms.

Normative Forms of Social Organization -- The capacity of human beings to surpass their pasts and to shape their emerging present is substantial, compared to other organisms on this planet. This freedom is limited by destiny, for the human past and the conditions of nature combine to place limits on what is possible in the present. Human capacity to shape the defining characteristics giving form to human social institutions in the spheres of the social order is more substantial than human capacity to shape the defining characteristics of nature, but even these capacities are not unlimited. The multiplicity of forms of familial, racial, ethnic, social, economic, political, cultural, and religious institutions underscores the interplay of human decisions and historical destiny. Even though these forms are the product of human intentionality, such intentionality becomes a causal factor limiting the freedom of expression of future creatures.

As a consequence of the interplay of freedom and historical destiny, the forms elaborated here are not seasonally relevant in many human societies now or in the foreseeable future. In spite of this limitation, the vision of normative forms of human social organization in the several spheres of the social order can serve as a lure for people to seek such forms in societies where they are not institutionalized and for people to sustain and to enhance them in societies where they are institutionalized.

The family is grounded in biological and social necessity. It is the elemental and fundamental unit of the social order. The diadic nature of human procreation, the needs for intimacy, and the prolonged maturation process for humans all encouraged the emergence of the monogamous family. Human self-determination plays a role in the initiation of the family unit, but this freedom occurs in the context of structures which qualify it. The monogamous family is most apt to harmonize self-determination informed by excellence and equality appropriate to form, and it is the most desirable form of family organization.

The problems centered around the notions "equality appropriate to form" and "order" in the family are manifold. As the visibility of women's liberationists indicates, there is no full consensus on the forms which give the proper equality in family life. Age differences qualify the relations within the family unit, but neither age nor sex differences provide definitive directives about intra-family relations.

It is doubtful if the plasticity of human nature is sufficiently great to permit humans to redefine radically traditional sexual roles. Certainly, the predominant role of women in the procreation process is not changeable now or in the foreseeable future. This basic elemental biological and psychic reality limits the extent of familial "equality."

In spite of this limitation, human ability to surpass natural forms permits some modifications of traditional patterns. Radical revisions must be challenged, based on the forms to which human organizing centers are intimately related, but gross inequalities must also be challenged.

Self-determination informed by excellence centers on the promise-giving and promise-receiving embodied in the public aspects of the marriage ceremony. Persons exchanging promises are under substantial obligation to honor such promises.

In spite of such intentionality, marriages do cease when partners no longer feel married. Divorce, though scarcely a desirable action, is sometimes necessary. People who will to dissolve their marriages should be forgiven, but the guilt involved should not be trivialized. [14]

Awareness of the relations between potentiality and actuality raise major problems with abortion. However the issue is rationalized, there is no question that in most instances an evolving fetus would become a human being. It is life, and it bears the potential of a more complex form of life. It is beyond the scope of this essay to explore this issue in detail, but the understanding expressed here occasions serious reservations about the sanction of abortion on demand. [15]

Other primary groups besides the family frequently emerge in human life. They incorporate relatively inclusive relations, and they permit a fuller recognition of the person than institutions in which technical rationalism is predominant. Often the net of interrelations in social institutions in these latter spheres elicit primary friendship groups. [16] A reasonable number of such groups to supplement primary groups shaped by familial relations is desirable. Due to finitude, a person may participate in only a small number of primary group relations.

Human creating, shaping capacities especially related to self-determination informed by excellence combine with biological and social necessity to produce social groups including racial, ethnic, and status groupings in human societies. Social identity based on real or imagined racial differences, regional or nationality characteristics, and/or style of life is very widespread in human societies. A "good" society will harmonize these groups into a contrasting whole in which the parts enhance the complexity and richness of the whole. Such a synthesis requires a harmonious blending of freedom informed by excellence and equality appropriate to form. It is not possible to stipulate the precise range of pluralism that is desirable except in a given context. There are limits to the diversity any society can sustain, but those limits are shaped by the historical destiny of a given people.

Equality appropriate to form in the social sphere suggests the desirability of varied racial, ethnic, and status groups in a particular society blended into a harmonious whole. In a "good" society, overarching commonly shared values encourage mutual respect and tolerance among the several racial, ethnic, and status groups, groups sharing a measure of equality in economic, political and cultural life.

Human rational shaping capacities, particularly those associated with technical reason, and biological necessity combine to foster the emergence of economic institutions. The biological bases for the production of goods and services are primary human needs for food, fiber, and shelter. These basic needs are elaborated through the free play of imagination into endless varieties of means to produce products to satisfy these primal needs and an array of other needs related to human life. Some of the other "needs" are incidental and become the basis for critical assessments of inordinate production and consumption.

Every economic system seeks to harmonize people's demands for goods and services (the shape of self-determination informed by excellence in the economic sphere) with available resources and the provision for responsible growth (the shape of equality appropriate to form in the economic sphere). Some pricing mechanism based on supply and demand is necessary, but there is no "best" form of economic organization.

The propensity of humans to abuse their power suggests that government ownership of all the means of production is undesirable and that unbridled private ownership is undesirable. In the first instance, too much power would be concentrated in the hands of the government bureaucracy, and political opposition would be impaired. In the second instance, too much power would be concentrated in the hands of owners, or, as is more likely in contemporary America, in the hands of a managerial elite. In neither instance would service to the common good be maximally enhanced.

Social necessity is more human than biological necessity, so the state, grounded in the human rational shaping capacities and social necessity, has the right to intervene in economic affairs; but the shape of the intervention cannot be decided except in a given context. Government incomes redistribution policies can modify markedly an enterprise economy without radically changing it.

As just observed, human rational shaping capacities and social necessity combine to produce political groups and have fostered the emergence of complex entities termed nation-states. The government, which is the organizing center of the state, is the co-ordinating, integrating, and directing center of a society. It cannot attain a perfect harmony between the principles of self-determination informed by excellence and equality appropriate to form, but it must seek to sustain a tolerable harmony between the two principles as they are embodied in the complex interplay of individuals and groups in the life of the living community.[17]

Democracy is the form of political organization most able to order the other two partially contradictory principles of justice. The principle of self-determination (albeit not always informed by excellence) is inherent in the democratic process. The principle of equality appropriate to form is enhanced by the participation of large numbers of citizens in political processes, but this participation may sometimes foster moves toward policies that are too egalitarian. A federated form of democracy is better able to balance self-determination and equality than forms offering the electorate a more direct role in policy formation. The electorate should have a voice in giving direction to public policy, but the specifics should be left to smaller and more coherent bodies.[18]

Granted human propensities toward inordinate self-interest, the balance of power and multiplication of faction doctrines informing the American democratic structures have much to commend them.

The free play of human imagination (rooted in the substantial capacity of humans to contrast what is with what might be but is not) and human shaping capacities combine to produce cultural objects, of which education, science, and art (including music, literature, and visual arts) are salient. For the same reasons as were cited for the social sphere, cultural diversity and pluralism are desirable, but there are limits to the degree of pluralism a particular society can sustain without disintegration. Generally, the greater the differentiation within and between the spheres of the social order, the greater the degree of pluralism, for the very presence of the differentiations suggests that mutual pluralism and tolerance are foundational values in such a society.

Human awareness of the Divine Presence in the world and human rational shaping capacity combine to produce religious institutions. The insistent particularity of human existence ties humans inextricably to special lived histories, including particular religious traditions. On the conceptual side, one may envisage the possibility of an emerging world theology which will co-ordinate and harmonize the theologies developed thus far in human history. On the physical side one must note the enmeshing of people in particular matrices of religious feeling and meaning.

This particularism and the multiplicity of alternative interpretations of the Divine Reality practically present and theoretically possible among humankind suggest the desirability of religious liberty and religious pluralism set in the context of some overarching unity.

Worship, education, and the cultivation of socialibility constitute the primary internal facets of religious institutional life. The articulation of principles of justice and of desirable forms of social organization constitute its primary functions in relation to institutions in the other spheres of the social order.

In sum, monogamy, racial, ethnic, status, cultural, and religious pluralism and tolerance, economic organizations permitting a rational allocation of resources based on a supply - demand mechanism, and democracy are the forms of social organization most apt to maximize the actualization of the three principles of justice. The following section discusses the public faith of America and the religions of America to permit an assessment of the relation between the public faith of America, the religions of America, and authentic religion.

America's Public Faith and the Religions of America

Introduction--Religious institutions, such as temples, churches, monasteries, shrines, and synagogues have been part and parcel of the fabric of social life in all human societies. The modern occidental historical epoch is distinguished from all others by the sharper separation of the religious sphere from the other spheres of the social order. It is also distinguished by the widespread questioning by the people in many social strata of interpretations of life affirming the reality of the Divine presence in the world.

   This section is focused on foundational notions or grounding assumptions Americans hold about the bases for the values associated with America's public faith and the several religions of America. Many of the observations will appear to be "self-evident" -- once they have been brought to consciousness. The reason for this self-evident character is rooted in the nature of human experience. We habitually think by a method of difference. Sometimes we see a giraffe, and sometimes we don't. Our awareness of the presence of the giraffe is heightened by our recall of those experiences in which we did not see a giraffe.

   To discover a component of experience that is always present, one must employ a negative judgement, imaginatively considering the absence of the omnipresent component. This is the method used in this section to examine those foundational notions shared by most Americans. These notions are characterized under the rubric of "America's public faith." They are generally presupposed in discussions of religious beliefs and values. In a very significant sense then, the religious communities are not ultimately foundational, for the notions informing particular religious traditions are shaped and directed by ideas somewhat more general and pervasive -- ideas presupposed but rarely discussed explicitly.

   The public faith of America, as the term is being used here, is composed of three diverse value components. The first complex component is the "Religion of America," a common religion shared by most Americans. This common Religion of America is to be contrasted with the religions of America, the multiplicity of faith communities commonly understood as "religious" groups. The second component of the public faith of America is "technical rationalism," the idea that human reason should be used to calculate the most efficient means to attain a given end. The third component is "secular humanism," the notion that emerging human beings are worthy of concern, dignity, and respect. Certain moral notions, such as the values sustaining the forms of social organization in the familial, social, economic, political, and cultural spheres, shade into the Religion of America.

   The religions of America are embodied in the familiar tripartite structures of faith communities in America -- Protestant, Catholic, and Jewish. Within Protestantism and Judaism, there are a number of sub-communities. People may move from one such sub-community to another

without undercutting their basic identities as Protestant or Jews. Within
Protestantism, a White Protestant - Black Protestant division is also part
of sub-community differences.

The Emergence of the Voluntary Religious Institution in the American Experience -- A sequence of events that was one of the most significant in the
history of Christianity transpired in the United States in the latter part of
the eighteenth and the early part of the nineteenth centuries; the federal
government, and subsequently all the state governments, affirmed the principle of religious liberty by disestablishment of all religious institutions.
Some voluntary sectarian religious groups -- among whom the Mennonites
and some left-wing Calvinist groups are salient examples -- and Jewish
faith communities had existed in Europe, but an officially established state
church had long been the practice in Europe. Now, in the Age of Reason,
the Bill of Rights of the new republic affirmed the principle of church-state
separation at the national level.

In human affairs, critical actions of leaders in an epoch-forming
period shape the feelings, customs, habits, social institutions, and cultural
values of succeeding generations, for their decisions become causal components contributing to the decisions of others both in their own time and in
later historical periods. In this sub-section, salient aspects of America's
past are retrieved to enhance the understanding of contemporary church-
state relations and to illumine the factors shaping the emergence of the voluntary religious institution to a position of preeminence in the United States.

American churches and synagogues are rooted primarily in Europe,
for the vast waves of European immigrants brought their own religious institutions with them. Unable to transplant their social, economic, or political
institutions in the new world directly, they were able to implant their religious institutions with fewer modifications. Some American Indian and some
Oriental religious institutions have resisted assimilation, but the overwhelming majority of religious institutions in America are related to some facet
of the Christian movement. The most influential minority religion in America
is Judaism, which has some shared history with Christianity and with the
European tradition. Black religious groups, rooted both in the American and
in the African heritages, are, in some senses, a minority group within the
Christian movement in America.

The early post-feudal period during which the first white settlers
migrated from Europe to the new world was scarcely conducive to the idea
of religious liberty. With the notable exceptions of Rhode Island and Pennsylvania, the early colonists established their versions of established
churches in the colonies they settled. These early settlers may have had
doctrinal disputes with the established churches of Europe, but they did not
repudiate the idea of establishment per se.

Social and cultural realities, however, made the maintenance of the established church difficult in the American colonies. Immigrants to a given colony came from different parts of Europe with different established state churches. This religious diversity made the establishment of one state church difficult and contributed to the trend toward disestablishment.

This sociological reality was augmented by ideological trends, for both non-Christian thought forms, particularly French Deism and various forms of naturalism and romanticism, and also various Christian views of the Believers' Church rooted in the left wing of both the Lutheran and Calvinist versions of the Reformation, led more and more people in the colonies to question the wisdom of an established church.

The framers of the Constitution were very aware of the potentially devisive effect of religious sects upon the body politic, and they were determined to mitigate such possible conflicts by minimizing the involvement of the government in religious matters. The First Amendment to the Constitution, prohibiting Congress from enacting any law establishing a state church, reflected this concern.

The Supreme Court held that the amendment applied only to the federal government and not to the state governments, but its suasive power was considerable. By 1833 the last of the states had disestablished the church, and the separation of church and state in America was substantially completed.

The importance of this historical development for the style and shape of the religions of America can scarcely be overemphasized, for it minimized the hostility toward religious institutions manifested so frequently in Europe. It also reinforced the emerging norms of religious liberty, religious tolerance, and religious pluralism. It provided the framework for the mass evangelism of the frontier era and made the voluntarily gathered congregation the normative form of religious organization in the United States.

This vision of the intentional gathered church as normative had been fostered by various groups related to the left wing of the Protestant Reformation. Neither 16th century Lutheran nor Calvinist churchmen had supported this view of the church; they had sought to substitute an established Protestant church for an established Catholic one in the areas where they were predominant.

The sociocultural homogeneity of the small European principalities of the late feudal period and the elitism of both state and church made this transition from an established Catholic church to an established Protestant church possible in parts of Europe, and groups emphasizing the Believers' Church were subject to various forms of persecution in most of Europe.

The First Amendment to the Constitution contributed to the development of a radically different situation in the United States, for the left-wing vision of the church as an intentional gathered fellowship of believers was sanctioned politically in the United States. Religious voluntarism, religious

pluralism, and religious tolerance, inevitable correlates of the doctrine of
the separation of church and state, were evolving into a central place in the
emerging public religion of America. The denomination, representing an
amalgamation of the more inclusive, less evangelical, less intentional, and
less demanding church with the more exclusive, more evangelical, more
intentional, and more demanding intentional fellowship, was destined to
emerge as the predominant form of religious organization in the United
States.

Jews, long subject to various forms of persecution in Europe and
already having a voluntary religious association, readily affirmed the separation of church and state and the related notions of religious voluntarism,
religious tolerance, and religious pluralism. At the time of the founding of
the nation, the few Roman Catholics in the United States -- forty thousand
out of a population of about four million -- did likewise.

By the time of the Civil War, something of a consensus on this issue
had been attained in America, but the consensus was challenged between 1865
and 1915 by the large numbers of Roman Catholic and Lutheran migrants
coming from European lands where these faith groups were established
churches.

These migrants altered markedly the religious composition of America. By this time the separation of church and state had become a core integrative value in American society, a central part of the Religion of America.
Consequently, if the national consensus were to be sustained, separation of
church and state, religious liberty, religious tolerance, and religious pluralism had to be accepted by these more recent migrants. Since these notions
were alien to many of the migrants, especially Roman Catholics from eastern
and southern Europe, considerable disharmony and conflict about church relations developed in the United States during this period. The continued debates about state aid to church related schools and some issues of public
morality and public policy show that these issues are not completely resolved,
but a broad consensus has now been attained on the basic idea of state neutrality in these affairs.[19]

The separation of church and state precluded the use of government
monies for the support of religious institutions and their salaried professionals. The implications for the religions of America are far-reaching.

Religious professionals in America have had to be more sensitive
to the needs and interests of their members than have their European counterparts. A simple explanation for the much higher religious institutional involvement of American lay people than European lay people is impossible,
but the long-established voluntarism of American churches and synagogues
is certainly a most significant factor. In order to sustain their institutions,
American clergy have had to develop much more innovative and often more
imaginative programs than their European colleagues.

Voluntarism, coupled with the pragmatism and the lack of intellectualism in the nineteenth century American ethos, contributed to the activistic and programatic emphases of American religious institutions, looked upon with such disdain by many European church people. The fund-raising aspects of the church socials of American Protestantism, the bingo nights of American Catholicism, and the sisterhood activities of American Judaism all reflect this pragmatism and activism.

The lack of any significant feeling of anti-clericalism in the United States is also related to religious voluntarism, pluralism, and tolerance, for no ecclesiastical group was able to impose either its teachings on any significant segment of the learned community or its socioeconomic views on large segments of the country. The dependence of the clergy on voluntary lay contributions had ameliorated potential lay-clergy conflicts, for the lay people could readily withhold their talents and their money. Suasion was the only means by which church people could seek members or pursue matters of public policy.

In relating to their lay people, religious leaders in America have had to pay much more attention to the consensus formation process, for in the final analysis -- regardless of polity or of doctrine -- a person in America is a member of a church or synagogue because he wills to be a member. If a given person finds a particular church or particular denomination unsatisfactory for any reason, he can probably find some religious institution which will welcome him to membership without undue difficulty. He can also become inactive in his given faith community or he can withdraw from any and all religious institutions at will. Consequently, most local clergy focus on adjustive and integrative issues, seeking to attract and to keep members in their fellowship.

In this situation it is easier to be a priest than a prophet, for comfort is less disruptive to the life of a church or synagogue than challenge. The relative balance one envisages between priestly and prophetic functions depends ultimately upon one's understanding of the nature of religion, the principles of justice informing one's view of the social order, the forms of social organization considered to be normatively desirable, and one's assessment of the current situation. The point deserving emphasis in the present context is the necessity for an adjustive, integrative style of leadership in the voluntary church.

The only alternatives are either an established church, funded by tax monies, or a multiplicity of highly intentional communities sustaining values in substantial opposition to the predominant culture but on which the members concur. In such an instance, clergy are "prophetic" externally but "priestly" internally. The first alternative is unacceptable to those who think religious liberty is one of the hallmarks of high civilization, and the second, coherent with the basic values of the Religion of America, will result in small groups relatively isolated from the center of American life.

As a result of religious voluntarism, people tend to join churches and synagogues whose constituents reflect their own ethnic and social situation. This self-selection process contributes to the status and/or ethnic exclusiveness of many churches and synagogues. Insofar as exclusiveness obscures people's visions of the inclusiveness of humankind, it is evil. At the same time, insofar as exclusiveness enhances the novelty of the parts of a whole and gives rise to contrasts contributing positively to the whole, it is good.

Technical Rationalism and Secular Humanism-- Before turning to a discussion of the major substance of the Religion of America, the other two components that are part of the public faith of America, technical rationalism and non-theistic or "secular" humanism, should be noted.

Technical rationalism seeks the most efficient means to attain a given end; secular humanism affirms individual dignity and the value of the human personality. Both motifs of the public faith of America had their genesis in elements of the Judeo-Christian tradition. Technical rationalism is a product of the transformation of the inner worldly asceticism and the truncation of redeemed ontic reason of Calvinism; secular humanism is a truncation of the value of the human personality as a child of God, a salient value in portions of the Judeo-Christian heritage.

The two motifs cannot be perfectly harmonized with each other, and some conflict between them is inevitable. Technical rationalism tends to atomize people and to foster competition, but secular humanism tends to unify them and to foster cooperation. In spite of this conflict, the two motifs. are interrelated, for a person appropriating technical rationalism is apt to challenge traditionalist views of life. Such traditionalist views restrict the potentiality of some groups, such as women, beyond the limits placed by nature. Thus, an uneasy alliance exists between proponents of technical rationalism and secular humanism. They both reject theistic interpretations of life and seek to minimize the limits which history and nature place upon human life.

These facets of America's public faith also have their impact on the religions of America. Technical rationalism has given impetus to the proliferation of ecclesiastical bureaucracies and the concerns with "efficiency" within the churches and synagogues. Non-theistic humanist notions, such as are embodied in the Human Potential Movement, have encouraged the development of a multiplicity of small group emphases within churches and synagogues. In the public realm, secular humanism, technical rationalism, and the public Religion of America interplay, partly reinforcing one another and partly conflicting with one another. No strong coherence exists, and the same person may emphasize different motifs at different times and in different contexts. Indeed, the co-existence of piety and secularity in the context of the American experience, a phenomenon of great interest, is dependent upon the capacities of people to appropriate these differing motifs without sensing undue disharmony and incoherence between them.

Technical rationalism has fostered the transformation of America from a folk society to a large-scale technological society, for technical reason knows nothing of history and of social honor. It only asks "What are the most efficient means to attain a given end?" In this way technical reason supports the pragmatism and activism which are deeply embodied in the American experience. The transition from a folk society to a large-scale technological society has altered the shape of the religions of America, for it has contributed to the separation of the religious sphere from the other spheres of the social order and to the segmentation of human social interaction.

Over the past two centuries the scale of social organization in the United States has increased tremendously. At the time of the first census in 1790, the population was slightly less than four million. Farm and rural residents comprised 95 per cent of the population, and the two hundred thousand urban dwellers lived in what would now be considered small towns.

At the present time over two thirds of the nation's population of over two hundred million live in urban centers. They live in a society shaped by big business, big labor, and big government. Without the mind set encouraged by technical rationalism, the large bureaucracy -- corporate or governmental -- would not have emerged. This emergence was coterminous with the industrialization and urbanization of America. Technical rationalism was the foundational value fostering the vast extension of urbanization, bureaucratization, and industrialization that characterized the transformation of America from a folk society to a large-scale technological society.

Prior to this transformation, people knew each other in many different contexts. Church-goers on Sunday saw the people with whom they dealt every day in social, economic, and political activities. The gradual disestablishment of state churches and the influx of different immigrant groups increased the number of religious institutions. This increase reduced the likelihood that people worshipping together on Sunday would interact in other social contexts during the week, but these non-urban people still encountered each other in many different circumstances.

The vast extensions of urbanization, industrialization, and bureaucratization in the late nineteenth and twentieth centuries have greatly segmented human social interaction. Today the likelihood that a person attending a given church or synagogue would encounter a fellow member in other social contexts during the week is much less than earlier periods. This is especially true in the urban centers where the majority of Americans live. This segmentation of social interaction reinforces the privatization of the religious sphere, i.e., the separation of churches and synagogues from direct participation in public life and from direct contributions to public policy issues.

The church-state separation discussed earlier gave impetus to the privatization of the religious sphere, for no doctrine associated with a particular religious group could hold sway in the public spheres. Religious beliefs became private matters not directly pertinent to the public realm. Thus technical rationalism and the separation of church and state factor in the Religion of America reinforced the privatization of the religions of America. This privatization of the religions of America, in turn, has contributed to the emergence of a technological society par excellence in the United States, for it largely freed the market place from the restraints of religious convictions. The demise of Sunday business closings in the past two or three decades is evidence of the continued erosion of the impact of particular religious values in the economic sphere.

The small group emphases associated with secular humanism have also contributed to this privatization, for the introspection and focus on group processes not infrequently leads participants to excessive preoccupation with themselves and their small groups.

The Emergence and Substance of the Religion of America -- Most Americans share America's public religion and also identify with one of the major faith groups. The separation of the church and state and the correlates of religious liberty, religious tolerance, and religious pluralism discussed are one aspect of the Religion of America. In this subsection the emergence and the development of the central core of the Religion of America, a common faith in which members rooted in different religions of America may participate, is elaborated.

In order for the members of a society to sustain themselves over an extended period of time, most of them must share some common integrative values. Coupled with the privatization of particular religious beliefs fostered by the emergence of the idea of separation in church and state and the notion of technical reason, a Religion of America emerged in the seventeenth, eighteenth and nineteenth centuries. This Religion of America does not monopolize the faith of the public realm, for as already suggested, it shares this domain with non-theistic or "secular" humanism and technical rationalism. America's public faith, somewhat inchoate and amorphous, is a blending of motifs drawn from these three sources.

The broad contours of America's public religion have been shaped by the epoch-making events in American history -- the settlement of the country, the Revolutionary War and the unification of the colonies, the Westward expansion and the doctrine of manifest destiny, the Civil War and the assassination of Abraham Lincoln, the mass European immigration between the Civil War and the First World War, and, in the first half of the twentieth century, the emerging consciousness of a national vocation to extend democracy to all people.   This analysis is concentrated on major national holidays and major cultural heroes, for these events and figures elucidate the major components of the Religion of America.

The analogue between the early colonists and the people of Israel is striking.   Old Testament imagery was frequent in public references in seventeenth and eighteenth century America.   The early settlers saw themselves carving new colonies out of the wilderness of the Atlantic seaboard. Many of them believed they were a chosen people, freed from the bondages of Europe and starting afresh in the land which had known no feudal period. [20]

An unduly romantic reading of this historical epoch is clearly unwarranted for, as previously noted, most religious leaders intended to establish their version of a state church in the American colonies.   In addition more people probably were drawn to the New World by economic motives than by religious vision.

In spite of these cautionary observations, the novelty and freshness of the New World were facts of major importance in shaping colonial America and in the interpretative retrieval of that period made by later generations of Americans.

George Washington, seen as the one who led his people to liberty from the oppressor, is the Moses of the Religion of America.   As the "father" of his country, he helped unify the colonies into a new nation.   In these formative years, liberty, equality, and brotherhood in a democracy under God, a notion reflecting the Deistic influences drawn from eighteenth century European thought, particularly French, began to emerge as another central motif in the evolving Religion of America.

The notion of manifest destiny, giving divine sanction to America's Westward movement, emerged as an interpretive motif in the Religion of America between the time of the Revolutionary War and the Civil War. Manifest destiny gave an overarching theological rationale for activities and practices shaped in large part by self interest and desires for economic betterment, and it contributed to the popularity of the doctrine of progress, also a part of the public religion.

During the fusion of Deistic and Christian motifs in the period between the Revolutionary War and the Civil War, the idea of a transcendent creative, and judging God, shorn of Christocentric emphases, emerged into a central position in America's public religion.   This concept was personified in the public theological interpretation of life offered by Abraham Lincoln.

Just as George Washington may plausibly be interpreted analogically as the Moses of America's public religion, Abraham Lincoln may plausibly be interpreted as the Jesus of Nazareth of that religion.   In his December, 1862, message to Congress, in his Gettysburg Address, and in his second Inaugural Address, Lincoln powerfully reinforced the idea of a transcendent, creative, and judging God in the public sphere.

Lincoln's sacrificial death sanctified what he had said and done. His life and death gave impetus to the emergence of the value complex "liberty, equality, and brotherhood in a democracy under God" to a central position in the American moral order and in the Religion of America.

The great symbolic importance Americans attach to the birthdays of Washington and Lincoln and to Independence Day and Thanksgiving Day give credence to this symbolic interpretation of Washington and Lincoln and of the emergence of America's public religion.

The vast immigration of persons from southern and eastern Europe in the period between the Civil War and World War I engendered considerable disharmony in the United States. It produced the melting pot vision of American society, for no society in history sought to assimilate so many diverse groups in so short a time.

As Americans sought to interpret and to adjust to this increasing internal diversity, the Statue of Liberty began to attain symbolic significance. America was to be the recipient of the poor and oppressed from other parts of the world and to be a model of democracy for all the world.

During the first half of this century, America's sense of national vocation came to fruition. Earlier America had sought to become a new nation, free from foreign entanglements. During this period, people began to suggest that America was called to extend democracy to all people. In World War I, Woodrow Wilson proclaimed that America sought to make the world "safe for democracy"; in World War II, Franklin Roosevelt sought to extend the "four freedoms" to all people. It is too early to be certain, but the Vietnam War may mark the end of this expansionist era; new imagery may now be developing to interpret the end of this era.

Shifting and unstable "prophetic minorities" are also components of the Religion of America. In recent times Martin Luther King, Jr., William Fulbright, Eugene McCarthy, and their followers illustrate the prophetic utterances and unstable character of these minorities.

Presidents serve as high priests of the Religion of America and the Constitution serves as its Bible. Presidents are especially apt to evoke ideas embodied in the Religion of America in their inaugural addresses, in addresses and proclamations related to Memorial Day, Independence Day, and Thanksgiving Day, and in periods of national crisis.[21] The death of major national heroes also evokes aspects of the Religion of America. This public religion -- vague, diffuse, and only fitfully self-consciously held -- is shared by almost all Americans and serves to unify diverse and conflicting values.

The dark underside of human experience symbolized in the Christian tradition by the doctrine of original sin accentuates the element of inordinate self interest and conflict in human life. It is a subdued motif in the Religion of America, but it is not absent.

For instance, one finds such a motif clearly manifest in the writings of Nathaniel Hawthorne. It is embodied in the political life of the American experience through the multiplication of factions and balance of power doctrines incorporated in the Constitution and articulated most forcefully by James Madison in The Federalist Papers. It also is entwined with the life and death of Abraham Lincoln.

This interplay between America's public faith and the religions of America constitutes the context in which Americans respond to the Divine Presence in their lives. In the final portion of this essay, a normative interpretation of this situation is undertaken.

Religious Institutions and the Human Future: A Normative Interpretation

Human beings are inextricably intermeshed in a complex network of societies and hierarchies of societies. The insistent particularity of existence and the historicity of human experience interject a note of caution about discussing the "human future," for there is no such thing as a "human in general." Each of us is what he is because of the context in which he is set, including his relations to his own past and his more immediate net of societies. Americans approach the future in a different way than Chinese, Russians, or Indians. There is no way to discuss the human future in the economic and political spheres except in the context of particular lived histories of the several peoples of the world.

Because of the privatization of the religions of America and the separation of church and state discussed in the preceding section, it is extremely difficult for Americans in particular religious traditions to address directly matters of public policy and to receive a hearing unless they are able to appeal to values and notions embodied in America's public faith. Because of its relations to the principles of justice and to normative forms of social organization, the assessment of the public faith of America advanced here is ambivalently positive. This view runs the risk of making idols out of the nation and of underplaying a prophetic critique of facets of American society. Nonetheless, if one is prepared to affirm constructively the desirability of the separation of church and state and the related values of religious liberty, religious tolerance, and religious pluralism, one cannot be unambivalently negative about the relation of religious institutions to American society. Those periods in history when the Christian church had more direct influence and power than it does in contemporary America did not suggest that church people possessed peculiar political and economic acumen.

Similarly, if one believes that monogamy is the most desirable form of family life, that racial, ethnic, and social pluralisms are desirable, that a modified free enterprise system is a viable form of economic organization, that democracy is the best possible form of political organization, and that cultural pluralism is desirable, one cannot make an unqualifiedly negative assessment either of American society or of American religious life.

The nature of the Divine Reality and the sequence of priority of the form, dynamics, unification triad discussed earlier permits a delineation of appropriate functions and activities of religious institutions.

The priority of unification in the form, dynamics, unification triad in God-world relations accentuates the suasive role of religious institutions and indicates that worship, which is human response to the awareness of the Divine Presence in the world, is the constitutive function of religious institutions. In worship humans are led to an increased awareness of the Divine Presence. God is always immanent in human experience, but human awareness of His presence varies from person to person and from time to time.

Human awareness of God is enhanced in three interrelated ways, as the unification, form, dynamics triad would suggest. The first -- and in some ways the foremost -- is through aesthetic sensitivity. Beauty in art, beauty in music, beauty in thought, and beauty in expression all can serve to heighten the human sense of the Divine.

The second way in which human awareness of the Divine is enhanced is through reason. The quest for truth is not all-important, but it is very significant in human experience. Because of its contribution to human apprehension of the Divine, rational discourse as well as aesthetic attainment is important in worship.

The third way in which human awareness of the Divine is increased is through the doing of good. Issues involving justice and the common good are interwoven in worship services. Aesthetic sensitivity, rational understanding, and the good act reinforce and evoke each other. Beauty, truth, and goodness in their interrelation ought to be interwoven in worship services.

Other activities of religious institutions flow from these relational qualities. The educational aspects of the life of religious institutions focus on the quest for truth, but beauty, involving feelings and sensitivities, and morality, involving an appreciative respect for people, are also important in the educational process.

The whole pastoral side of ministry -- professional and lay alike -- is rooted in the sharing and caring concerns of people seeking to do the good. The enrichment of life through the fostering of close interpersonal relations and through group activities is an important aspect of the life of religious institutions.

Sharing and caring are not only an internal aspect of the life of religious institutions. They are bound to a concern for others beyond the immediate fellowship. Love of others and interest in the common good ought to lead participants in religious institutions to seek justice in the social order and in relations between groups and between nations.

It is at this point substantial problems emerge, for there are a multiplicity of views about the proper relation between religious institutions and the public sphere. Further, justice is much more difficult to attain in intergroup relations, due to differences in the sequence of priorities in the form, dynamics, unification triad discussed earlier. According to the view developed here, religious institutions should seek to accentuate the principles of justice and to affirm normative forms of social organization, but religious institutions qua religious institutions should be wary about issuing directives to a society.

Too close an identity with some of the protagonists in most complex social, economic, and political issues compromises the religious institutions' unique position among social institutions. Obviously, no such stricture should be made with reference to individual participants in religious institutions, but they are likely to be found entertaining conflicting views on complex policy issues. Informed by a sense of cause, a sense of proportion, and a sense of responsibility, members of religious institutions may hope to make some contributions to the quest for justice, but they cannot expect undue success.

Strife and conflict are a perennial aspect of the human situation, and they are especially salient in the political realm. Without some sense of a peace surpassing this realm and suggested by the idea of a Kingdom of God beyond the temporal world, people cannot sustain their spirits in the face of persistent strife and turmoil. The religious institution which loses its balance and proportion by confusing its constitutive and derivative components and/or by becoming too preoccupied with issues of morality and justice is in danger of losing its life for the wrong reasons. Conversely, the religious institution ignoring issues of morality and justice is perverse.

NOTES AND REFERENCES

[1] It is obvious from these observations that the assumptions shaping this essay differentiate the author from the vast majority of Christian theologians, who emphasize more forcefully the categorical uniqueness of Jesus of Nazareth, and, frequently, of the Christian church. Similarly, they accentuate the discontinuity of Divine-human relations and entertain a "one-way" immanent-transcendent God-world relation. God is immanent in the world, but the world is not immanent -- at least not in accord with the structural principals they develop -- in God. The emphases on the Christian movement as a sub-conscious matrix of feeling and meaning and a self-conscious affirmation of that matrix as a locus for feeling the Divine Pres-

ence and for interpreting God-world relations are the bases on which the author affirms his allegiance to Christianity.

[2]Although the epistemological assumptions in this essay differ from those of the theologians of "typical" groups cited here, there is a common factor relating all these perspectives. In spite of differing assessments about the means by which humans become aware of the Divine Presence and in spite of different interpretations of the implications of this awareness for God-world relations, common experiences of a beatific vision more fundamental and elemental than the abstractions made from it underlie all these assessments and interpretations.

[3]In Being Free, (New York: Macmillan, 1970) Gibson Winter centers his critique of contemporary American society on the cultural sphere. In A Theology of Liberation (Mary Knoll, N.Y.: Orbis Books, 1973), Gustave Gutierrez centers his critique on the economic sphere. These differences are a matter of degree rather than of kind, for both analysts note the interrelatedness of the spheres of the social order. Both are critical of high technology and capitalist forms of economic organization.

Jurgen Moltmann's Theology of Hope (New York: Harper and Row, 1967), J. Deotis Roberts' A Black Political Theology (Philadelphia: The Westminster Press, 1974), and Letty M. Russell's Human Liberation in a Feminist Perspective -- A Theology (Philadelphia: The Westminster Press, 1974) illustrate this general perspective.

In contrast to most classical theologians, these interpreters relate Christian "liberation" quite directly to the social, economic, and political spheres of life.

[4]Richard Baxter represents such a perspective in his A Holy Commonwealth. Some of James Madison's essays in The Federalist Papers may be read in this way. Persuaded that human beings are inordinately motivated by self-interest, Madison elaborates balance-of-power and multiplication-of-factions doctrines to evolve structures to blunt and deter the efforts of humans to attain inordinate power. Once such structures have evolved, they ought to be supported and sustained.

Those seeking to defend a capitalist enterprise economic system on theological grounds (see, for example, William Lawrence, "The Relation of Wealth to Morals," The World's Work, Vol. 1, No. 3, January, 1901, pp. 286-292) reflect a similar conservative perspective.

[5]T.S. Eliot's The Idea of a Christian Society (New York: Harcourt, Brace, and Company, 1940) illustrates a Christian social theory with a formalistic bias that seeks to life up the medieval period as a model of a "good" social order. Thus he moves toward the perspective of those accentuating the past as "good." H. Richard Niebuhr's The Responsible Self (New York: Harper and Row, 1963) illustrates a Christian social theory with a dynamic bias that seeks to transform the present social order. These figures do not

attack the existing order as sharply as the more radical visionaries; hence they are more centralist in their interpretations of the created order.

[6]Of course, it is not being suggested that these thinkers would concur with the assessment being made here or that they shared either a common interpretation of the world or the view informing this essay. From the constructive viewpoint elaborated here. it is held that they were attracted by the lure for truth and for harmony embodied in the Divine Nature.

[7]We reject the notion of Tillich and others that God is beyond the subject-object structure of experience. Because of the priority of the mental pole in His experience, God is unique subject-object, but He is not beyond this structure. He is, rather, the supreme exemplification of the subject-object structure of existence. As the supreme subject who never "closes up, " He is able to receive into Himself all the subject-objects of the world who have become. For this reason, Tillich wrongly concluded that God was beyond the subject-object structure of the world.

The subject-object structure of the world involves a two-fold character. First, all objects, i.e., creatures who have become, are data for emerging subjects. Second, every creature is both a subject and an object. As it is becoming it is an emerging subject aiming at its own satisfaction. After it has become, it is an object which is objectified everlastingly in the Divine Life and is a datum for all emerging subjects which "succeed" it.

[8]It should be noted that the lure for harmony is in partial contradiction to the lure for intensity of feeling. Harmonies involving minimal contrasts, and, hence, minimal intensities of feeling, may be less "good" than the temporary increases in disharmony needed to attain richer and more complex harmonies, and, hence, greater intensities of feeling. For example, the disharmonies engendered in America by the resurgence of the civil rights movement in the 1960's were a necessary prerequisite for the attainment of higher harmonies with richer and more complex contrasts among the component parts. Such an emergence is not guaranteed, but without some risks more complex societies and hierarchies of societies needed to sustain the mix of breadth and depth required for rich and complex harmonies could not have evolved.

[9]This affirmation of philosophical realism separates this perspective from Hume's understanding of cause - effect relations. Humans do have some sense of antecedent causes contributing to present experiences. The appropriations of forms from subject-objects in the causal past necessarily relate human reason to forms and patterns embodied in the external world. The Kantian bifurcation between pure reason and practical reason and its attendant fact-value disjunction does not accord with our foundational experiences. H. Richard Niebuhr's distinctions between internal and external history and between speculative and practical reason are based on this Kantian understanding of perception. This view is pervasive in contemporary Protestant theology.

[10]Because of this view of the ultimacy of the dynamic dimension in experience, the perspective elaborated here has a Protestant bias. Nonetheless, the necessary presence of formal components in every experience implies a rejection of the notion of the radical freedom of God and the transcendence of forms in the height of human freedom fashionable in contemporary neo-orthodox forms of Protestantism. In this sense, this view has a Catholic bias. This is the basic reason for the possibility of progress in morality; each "moral act" incorporates forms. Some of these forms enhance morality. The evolution of better forms provides the basis for some "progress" in morality.

[11]From this point of view, the frequent appearance of trinitarian modes of thought in the Christian tradition is based on factors rooted in the nature of things. The symbol "God the Father" is rooted in the dynamic dimensions of experience, the symbol "God the Son" is rooted in the formal dimensions of experience, and the symbol "God the Holy Spirit" is rooted in the unifying dimensions of experience. Protestantism has tended to emphasize the Father and to set the Son and Holy Spirit in relation to the Father. Catholicism has tended to emphasize the Son and to set the Holy Spirit and the Father in relation to the Son. The perspective developed here emphasizes the Holy Spirit and sets the Son and the Father in relation to the Holy Spirit.

[12]This sequence of priority is the basic reason for the rejection of the classical Protestant idea of justification by grace through faith. God's grace is manifest in his overarching subjective aim, but the saliency of structures in the emergence of an entity permits the use of reason to illumine facets of the Divine Nature. Indeed, God-world relations are not intuitively self-evident. They require rational interpretation.

[13]In human life, differences in age, sex, ability, and social functions are salient limits on equality. A continued discussion about the forms legitimately limiting equality occurs in the life of a living community. The current struggle in the United States about the Equal Rights Amendment to the Constitution illustrates the ambiguity inherent in the notion "appropriate to form." Interestingly, opposition to the amendment is greatest in the South, the region of the country most influenced by the Anglican tradition. Conservative seventeenth century English divines, persuaded that the medieval social theory having a formalistic bias was true, implanted notions related to that tradition in the South.

[14]In American society, social forces contribute to an inordinately high divorce rate. The contract theory of marriage, minimizing the organic side of marriage, reflects the widespread popular understanding of freedom as the ability to do what one wants to do.

The predominance of technical rationalism and an inordinate emphasis on achievement, upward social mobility, and geographical mobility accentuate the pressures on marriages, particularly among white collar people. The inordinate emphasis among such groups on the conjugal family accentuates the problem, for humans need the sympathetic support of relatives in the extended family.

A theological critique of facets of American life based on its negative impact on the family is certainly legitimate. At the same time, religious institutions should do all they can to sustain and to support wholesome family life in the midst of these environmental pressures.

[15]Complex problems focused on the need for substantial reductions in the birth rate cannot be explored here. Limitations on conception are a much more acceptable means of birth control than abortion.

[16]In societies in which the spheres of the social order are markedly differentiated from each other, such as in contemporary American society, substantial disharmony may be induced in primary group relations by the network of secondary relations fostered by membership in a bureaucracy in one of the other spheres of the social order. For example, a manager who is asked to evaluate the productivity and the competence of a colleague may feel substantial pressures in evaluating a colleague who is also a friend.

[17]The use of the term "organizing center" to refer to the political leadership empowered to act in the name of the state is based on an analogy between the individual and the state. The state itself is an abstraction from the nexus of individuals who participate in it. It is not a living organism in the sense a person is. Therefore, there are limits to this analogy; the state is not an organism, and the individuals who participate in it surpass the state in their individuality. The state cannot claim the individual as a part in the same sense that the individual person can claim its constituent parts. Even in the person, some of its societies function in relative independence from the organizing center. At the same time, in both instances all of the constituent parts are qualified by their participation in that particular whole.

[18]Democracy is obviously not seasonally relevant in many human societies. Religious institutions should seek to foster governmental concern with the common good rather than the good of the rulers, whether the government in a given society is predominantly a rule of one, of some, or of many.

[19]In a recent study, lay people in three Roman Catholic parishes in a cross section of suburban Chicago overwhelmingly supported the proposition that the government should be neutral toward religious institutions (Schroeder, W. Widick, et. al., Suburban Religion (Chicago: Center for the Scientific Study of Religion, 1974) p. 20.

[20]This imagery was particularly prevalent in New England. These Puritan motifs were not salient in the South, where, as observed in an earlier note, conservative Anglican influence was very pervasive in the seventeenth century. It is interesting to speculate on the relation of the English civil war between the Royalists and the Puritans in that century

and the American civil war in the nineteenth century. Certainly, the medieval legacy Anglicans left to the South contrasted sharply with the Puritan influence in the North and exacerbated the contrasts between the two regions of the country.

[21]The intense agony of the Watergate experience for Americans is deeply rooted in the character of the American presidency as shaped by the American experience. Not only is the President a political leader -- he also is the high priest of the public Religion of America. The emotions, the wounds, and the divisiveness engendered by the Watergate events are grounded in the failure of the President to perform satisfactorily either as high priest or as political leader. The dishonesty, the deceitfulness, and the failure to observe the constitutional processes all stain the public Religion of America. The positive aspect of the experience is also rooted in the Religion of America -- the Constitution was preserved and the wisdom of the multiplication of factions doctrine and of the principle of the separation and balance of powers was illustrated.

The ambivalences of technical reason in the context of the American experience were also manifest in the Watergate phenomenon. The expediency, the willingness to use highly dubious means to attain a desired end, the calculation, the hair-splitting, the circumvention embodied in the legal order, the efforts to avoid the spirit of the law -- all of these factors were present. The unique character of the individuals involved points to the episodic aspects of the Watergate phenomenon. The use of calculating reason and inordinate concern with self-interest point to the systemic aspects of the phenomenon.

Clergy and lay people did not speak with a clear voice on the Watergate problem -- a reflection of the complexity of the issues, the diverse understandings they have about the relation of the church to the public sphere, the privatization of the religious sphere, and the predominance of adjustive and integrative activity in church and synagogue life.

CHAPTER IX

SYMBOL AND SOCIETY: THE RENEWAL OF FOUNDATIONS

by
Gibson Winter

There is a search for foundations in our time that is indicative of the seriousness of the present crisis. Some see promise of moral and spiritual renewal in the Jewish and Christian heritages of the West.[1] Others do not.[2] Christianity was, of course, implicated in the emergence and legitimation of the technogenetic society--the society in which everything is reduced to means. Christianity expanded hand in hand with the global spread of the Western way of life, legitimating the modern domination of nature and humankind.[3] Why then should anyone hope to find resources for a renewal of morality and spiritual life in this religious heritage?

The Western story is far more ambiguous than it sounds when we first consider the identification of Christianity and the technogenetic city. Christianity is a powerful current flowing through Western life. Like any great stream, it has given rise to many forms of life, sheltered various species, and washed away some niches that had supported others. It would be too simple to say that Christianity gave rise to the technogenetic society, whether in the "Spirit of Capitalism" or the spirit of science and technology. On the other hand, Christianity was implicated in the ethos and institutional life of the West, spawning a variety of movements and cultural trends that played subordinate roles in the Western development, yet nurturing and legitimating a commitment to autonomous rationality as the path to mastery of the world. Scientific exploration of nature and technological domination are best seen, in these terms, as subordinate aspects of this drive to mastery.

It seems paradoxical to suggest that Christianity contributed importantly to the emergence of this Western drive to autonomy and mastery, for Christianity never extolled human powers. Yet this paradox lies at the heart of the Western development. Christianity loosened the human connection to earthly life, weakening the tie to nature. Christianity also weakened the bonds of sex, kin, tribe, and people, substituting a heavenly promise for this earthly vale of tears. Christianity replaced these earthly forms with a communion of saints, the eternal Church. Whatever forms of life Christianity nurtured in the subterranean flow of Western life, and they were many and diverse, its major thrust was to weaken the ties to earth, community, and history.[4]

Recent theological work has emphasized the idea that Christianity was an historical fulfillment of an historical faith of Israel. Yet from the outset Christianity was an eschatological faith--envisioning history as already finalized in the life, death, and resurrection of Jesus, the Son of Man.[5] In this context, "eschatological" refers to the last or final things, and the "eschatological figure" refers to the heavenly deliverer who inaugurates the final age.

Weakening the bonds with earthly life was no great trick for slaves and outcasts! It only became problematic as Christianity began the conversion of upper strata of Hellenistic and Roman society.[6] Yet Christianity was from the outset a vision of a final redemption. The old, earthly, corrupt, politically divided Jerusalem was superseded. The true Jerusalem was Above.[7] With the return of the Son of Man the Church would be revealed in all its martyred splendor.[8] Jaroslav Pelikan caught this sense of a heavenly destiny in his brief study, The Shape of Death: Life, Death and Immortality in the Early Fathers.[9] He used geometrical images to convey the different conceptions of the significance of earthly life. The important point for our purposes is that the early Church Fathers had a real problem making sense of earthly life. If the true life is Above, what sense does it make to be on earth--a punishment for sins, a time of trial, a period of education for the true life? These and other notions are explored in this fascinating study by Pelikan. Whatever the views of the various theologians, the real and true life was located Above. And however much Christianity tempered its vision of finality, which it did in myriad ways, awaiting the other world remained the Christian way. The ties to earth were weakened if not severed; only grappling lines could hold the Church to its earthly commitments. Christianity in the West struggled for centuries to come to terms with an earthly life already "finished": thus, in different dualities of dwelling it maintained a link to earth--the Two Cities, Nature and Supernature, the Two Kingdoms, the Inner Life of the Spirit and the Outer World of Law and Death. Christianity made peace with the earth in different ways. The vision of finality freed a Saint Stephen and a Saint Francis for heroic witness and care of the neediest, yet its essential impact was to juxtapose this earthly history to a real transcendent history.[10]

Weakening the human connection was even more paradoxical than dissolving the tie to earth. Christianity exalted love and human community. Ernst Troeltsch took this vision of love as central in his interpretation of the struggle of the churches to come to terms with social and political life in the West.[11] This radical sense of a community of love would always live in tension with laws, punishments, imperial powers, and the harsh inequalities of economic struggle, inspiring and empowering monastic and sectarian movements. This communal sensibility was uprooted, for it was detached from human life in sexual, familial, economic, local, tribal, and later, national life.[12] National churches emerged through the weight of historical development, but the essence of religious community was an ecumenical gathering of souls saved in Christ, <u>communio sanctorum</u>. The loving community was exalted as the true vision of the Kingdom, yet the actual communities of conflict and affection, struggle and reconciliation, alienation and forgiveness, were viewed as at best transitory and at worst a bad lot. [13] One put up with these communities, making the best of them, while preparing for the Kingdom.

The meaning of history in Western experience is the most troubling issue we are raising. As the historical consciousness emerged during the 18th and 19th centuries, Christianity began to come to terms with its historical development. [14] After a long struggle with historical relativism and the shattering impact of the historicizing of the figure of Jesus, Christian thought moved into a neo-orthodox phase in which Jesus was interpreted as the fulfillment of a history of salvation begun in the dim past of the Hebrew religion. [15] Hence, the historical character of Christianity was taken seriously, but the finality of the revelation in Jesus as the Christ was reasserted. It was acknowledged that this was not the linear history of the positivistic historians, but this salvation history was taken to be the inner, irrefutable meaning of the Scriptures. Corollary to this finality of the figure of Jesus was the assimilation of Greek philosophy in the Church Fathers which ensconced the God of the Scriptures in an eternal, immutable world of forms, untouched and unaffected by the course of history. [16] Hence the finality of the figure of Jesus was fused with a metaphysical theism of an immutable deity.

From the outset, Christianity in its various forms was struggling to come to terms with historical and sociological realities. Even though believers continued to work and suffer in the world, the true meaning of history had already been disclosed and concluded in the appearance of Jesus as the Christ, and his return would consummate all things as his Kingdom. [17] In contrast to this finality, Hebrew Scriptures and religion were plunged fully into history, awaiting a Messiah but not celebrating a Messiah already come. [18] Christianity was ambiguous on this issue, since its sacramental world included various forms of association that image the divine society. A figural imagination controlled the interpretation of historical events, transposing their real meanings to a heavenly screen. Biblical events before Jesus and crucial events in the life of the Church were taken as figures of the Christ event, as figures of heavenly transactions. [19]

In this broad interpretation, Christianity may be understood as playing a negative role in the triumph of an ethos of mastery in the West. Despite its vision of a community of love, or perhaps because of the radical character of that vision, Christianity treated human communities as transitory in comparison with the eternal community. Although its monastic and sectarian strands were to embody a much more vigorous communal life, these communities were somewhat separated from the established societies. Although

Christianity celebrated an incarnate Lord of History, the very finality of the ministry of the Lord opened the way to two histories--one figural and the other real.

The Greek heritage furnished a framework of rational thought for this Christian vision.[20] Western development might have oscillated between millennial expectations and earthly compromises had it not been for this powerful heritage of rationality. The logic of knower and known that had gained hegemony in Greek thought gave the Church a framework within which to rationalize its final, revelatory vision. Yet the logic of knower and known is unstable, for truth is interpreted as a correspondence between the knower's knowledge and the known, and the known is always established by principles of self-evidence or authority. Once the taken for granted character of the known or the authority which sustains it comes into question, the tower of cards falls. At this point, the knower is left with his "knowing."[21] Once the authoritative world of the Church was shaken in the late middle ages, in part through the venality of the religious institutions, the metaphysical structure began to crumble. Rationality, once dislodged from its objective position, was driven back upon the knowing subject for certainty.[22] This turn toward the subject, sometimes called the subjective turn in philosophy that is associated with the method of Descartes, set Western development on a course of autonomous rationality of the subject.[23]

Two major phases of Western development came together in the late middle ages, thus setting the stage for the domination of nature: (1) Christian anchorage in a final, historical fulfillment severed the bonds with earth, community, and history, though the Church maintained these ties by its authoritative discipline; (2) the heritage of rationality, a logic of knower and known in which the knower re-presents in consciousness the object known, gradually foundered and collapsed into the knowing subject. Thus, a project of boundless mastery over nature was born. The knowing subject and the will of the subject to grasp reality in clear and precise ideas became determinative for truth.

In this context, the struggle for mastery emerged slowly. It found its classical spokesman in Francis Bacon. The Church resisted this tremendous historical impulse to knowledge of nature, intimidating and oppressing pioneers of this project.[24] But this was a rear-guard action that would go on for centuries while the new knowledge swept over Europe and later America.[25]

This is not intended to be a rewrite of the "Decline of the West." Meanings are given ambiguously in human history. This dispensation of the West has important disclosures of human meaning and destructive distortions in its development. The West inherited great powers from the rationality of the classical world. No one who enjoys the commonsense world of today would wish to be cast back into a world of darkened understanding. We see no need now to track down some scapegoat to suffer for the terrors of a

thunderstorm. Rational interpretations of natural and social processes contribute, or can contribute, to the enhancement of human life. Our problem
is not with the rationality of the West, nor even with its scientific and technological powers. Our problem is with the displacement of all meaning on
the knowing, willing subject, whether individual or collective, and with the
reduction of all truth to proven knowledge of science. This is not a time for
recrimination but for searching out our foundations, for asking whether we
are not more dependent upon earth, others, and disclosures of meaning than
our science has imagined.

A Post-Religious Age

The most radical question about our religious heritage is the one
raised by those who claim that ours is a post-religious age. They do not
deny the religiousness of various peoples, but they argue that such religiousness is a private affair. The public world can no longer be informed and
guided by religious powers, for the gods have long departed. In this perspective, the metaphysical world with which Christianity was inextricably
interwoven has collapsed. The only world we treat as credible is the empirical, earthly realm. The only access to that world which we trust is empirical science. The only history we have is the one history for which we are
responsible. Whether as polemic or nostalgic regret, this post-religious
mind has been gaining ascendancy since the mid-nineteenth century. Nietzsche
gave it decisive expression in the statement of Zarathustra, "But now this
God has died!"[26]

This is not a time for pious counter-assertions to Zarathustra's
announcement. We do better to locate his utterance within our Western
history, the same history which we have been tracing from the eschatological vision of early Christianity. In locating the post-religious age within
this history, we begin to ask questions about a post-religious consciousness.
A sense of the sacred is a universally attested dimension of human experience
with its own significance. We can assume, therefore, that the departure of
the gods tells us something about the technogenetic city, for the eclipse of
the Holy does not erase the religious dimension of human species life; at the
most, it transmutes the expression of the religious.[27]

The "death of God" or departure of the gods can be seen as the other
side of the divinization of the human subject. Once truth and certainty come
to rest upon the knowing subject, once the world of meaning is assimilated to
the will of the subject, once history has become an artifact of humanus faber,
the horizon of grace is eclipsed. Nature and persons still confront us with
mystery and otherness, but the mystery is reduced and overlooked. Awe,
wonder, mystery, and even beauty are relegated to feelings having no truth-
value. They are confined to the private zone of experience. The realm of

interpersonal community, especially in its bureaucratic forms, can no
longer be healed with repentance and forgiveness, since human relationships
are determined by efficiency. This is a world without forgiveness or grace.
How can grace exist in a world fashioned by the human species? There can
be error, weakness, and even malfeasance, but certainly not ineradicable
fault, repentance, and forgiveness. If relationships are a matter of more
and less control, errors can be corrected, weaknesses can be overcome
and malfeasance or disloyalty can be punished, but there is no room for
grace.

Arthur Koestler portrayed this bureaucratic condition of humanity
in his novel about the trial of the generals under Joseph Stalin, Darkness at
Noon.[28] The generals were tried to satisfy the suspicions and even paranoia
of Stalin. Perhaps some were disloyal, but clearly not all. After their
interrogations, they stand under the judgment of the regime to which they
devoted their lives. They can go down protesting their innocence, resting
their case on some higher authority than the decision of the regime. But it
becomes evident that there is no higher court. The truth of historical events
is determined by the regime, for the regime in power is the sole source of
authority and truth. And the generals agree! They duly make their confessions and accept their execution at the hands of the only "god" which they
have served. There is no other authority to which appeal could be made or
to whom a plea for forgiveness could be addressed. When the world is the
project of the human subject, individual or collective, grace and forgiveness
are meaningless, or, as Franz Kafka would have it, purely arbitrary.[29]
There can, of course, be the necessary accommodations of exchange where
one pardons another in expectation of some reciprocity, but grace is another
order of reality which cuts through these mutually beneficial arrangements.
Arthur Koestler caught this merciless force of the technogenetic city in his
account of the trial of the generals.

We know that the deeper, religious dimensions of the human cannot
be erased from our language and foundational symbols, for our experience
is constituted and guided by such symbols.[30] More recently we have witnessed the power of such symbols in the Soviet experience. The protests of
Solzhenitsyn, Sakharov, and many others draw upon a myth of Russian destiny.
They are appealing to a destiny in which the human spirit transcends bureaucratic powers and state authority. Even though they are declared disloyal
to Soviet Russia, they define themselves within their heritage as serving the
true interests and meaning of Soviet Russia. Even in our post-religious age,
the deep lying claims of the human to a world of truth, freedom and higher
loyalties persists in the infrastructure of our linguistic heritage. The announcement that "God is dead!" could better be formulated, "God has gone
underground!"

Ours is an age of forgetfulness of Mystery and grace. Yet deep
lying experiences of our world are borne day by day in the foundational

symbols and mythic structures of our heritage. Whether we recognize this
heritage or not, we live from it. We are bound by it, which would be a way
of understanding the meaning of the term religious, binding to the Mystery.
On another occasion we traced certain primordial symbols of our American
religious heritage--sense of the open space, sense of the free, sense of a
new beginning. These motifs or symbols continue to shape and inform the
American experience, albeit in distorted form. And even amidst the distorted experience of these symbols, we live by their originary powers. It
is the character of such primordial symbols that we live in them rather than
entertain them as problems. They constitute a world which we take for
granted, even though there is nothing self-evident about that world. There
is nothing self-evident about the land as an open possibility. Many peoples
have lived in closely confined cycles of growth and decay. The same holds
for the free and the new beginning. Some peoples have understood the free
within a tight network of obligations. Some have denied any new beginnings,
experiencing the world as an endless cycle of births and rebirths. The world
in which a people lives on this deepest level is first a world given by the
grace of heritage, by public and religious symbols.

Our religious heritage liberates as well as binds us when it is
appropriated critically. Receptivity to our past, appropriation to it, releases its healing powers and opens its alienating distortions to question.
This is the paradox of foundational symbols, even as it is the paradox of our
own personal histories. Decisive events of our past, especially the traumatic
ones, distort our existence; thus, we repeat the distortions endlessly like
scenarios run again and again on a screen. They cripple us unless we find
our way back into critical reinterpretation of those events, recognize them
for what they are and appropriate them critically to our present "real" situations. If we treat our religious past as irrelevant, we live with alienated
symbols that dominate rather than liberate us. This does not mean that we
have to be "religious" in the private sense of that word which we now employ.
We have the power and right to reject authoritative claims of our heritage
whether they be religious, political, or social. The one thing we cannot do
without suffering the consequences is thoughtlessly and forgetfully ignore
our heritage. This is the state of the technogenetic city. It is not post-
religious by conviction but by forgetfulness, a forgetfulness rooted in its
pretentious claims to autonomy. Thus, now in the United States we are
chained to a reenactment of the distortions of individualism and novelty when
we need renewal of our common life. We act out of distorted symbols unless
we can recollect the full possibilities of those foundational disclosures.

What we have called foundational symbols are a giving of a world
in its depth structures. [31] This primordial giving is not a once and for all
matter but undergoes change, unfolding in various ways over time. Again
like a personal history, certain symbolic events, Exodus or Declaration of
Independence, become foci of expanding and enriching meanings rather than

deposits that persist unaltered. Our moods and cognitions about "home" for
example, emerge in childhood experiences, undergoing extensions and distortions throughout our lives. But the primordial character of this symbolic
process is one of giving, of a world being given to us, a world into which we
are received and to which our responses are primarily receptive.

In a religious understanding of receptivity, the giving is viewed as
gracious, however ambiguously that giving may be understood in various
religious traditions. Nature in its cycle of birth and decay graciously brings
forth life and sustains it, though pollutions may require rites of purification.[32]
The primordially religious moment is one of receptivity, of abiding in the
gracious giving of a world. Celebration of cosmogenic events in sacral rites
assumes a responsibility for the continuation of the world but also underscores human acquiescence in a process not of human contrivance.[33] Sacrifice which characterizes religious rituals throughout the ages, discloses
human responsiveness to the gracious giving of a world. However distorted
the element of sacrifice at certain points in the religious history of humankind, in its depth it points to the cost of giving in which our world comes to
us. Sacrifice points to the giving, graciousness, and forgiveness which found
and sustain the human community.[34] If events arising out of our past are
destructive, and many of them are, then we are simply given over to destruction unless there is a way to a new beginning. If the past is a finished, grace-
less thing, we have no future.[35] Religious traditions in various ways have
attested to the gracious overcoming of evil, guilt, fault, and pollution, thus
indicating possibilities of a new beginning, of a forgiving at the heart of the
giving of our world.[36] Forgiveness of the sinner, receiving the prodigal
son, forgiving seventy times seven, forgiving the adulterous wife (Hosea),
all point in different ways to the graciousness of the Mystery. On a primordial level, this graciousness is the source of the giving of our world in
foundational and mythic symbols. Whether in devotion of a parent, protection by a community and its laws, or attention from a friend, the grace of
giving, and implicitly the forgiveness and sacrifice that undergird it, bestows life. Receptivity into our world and the forgiveness that sustains it
do not eliminate critique. Symbols obscure as well as reveal. They constitute our source and invite our critique.

Receptivity, giving, and forgiving disclose our human possibilities.[37]
When receptivity is excluded by the drive to mastery, our foundational symbols no longer empower the common life. We have experienced this impov-
erishment of life in the question of amnesty after the Viet Nam War. Amnesty
was a powerful healing force in America's past. Following the Viet Nam War
Richard Nixon declared himself against any but a conditional amnesty; consequently, amnesty meant confession of fault and imprisonment for deserters
and defectors. When Richard Nixon was forced to resign, Gerald Ford
pardoned him, attempting through a kind of amnesty to restore public health.
However, the amnesty offered to those who had protested a war that most

citizens now firmly believe to be wrong continued to be conditional and was
accepted by relatively few. Thus, the alienation of tens of thousands of men
and women from their homeland, many of them morally right about the war,
continues. The scars from the war fester in our body politic.

What is the real issue? The issue is one of coming to terms with
our past as a people, recollecting the injustices that we perpetrated. The
deserters and defectors, not to speak of thousands in the ghettos who received less than honorable discharges, are witnessing to this past. How do
we come to terms with that past? We can ignore it, laying down conditions
for participation in American life that mean accepting and legitimating that
past. This is conditional amnesty! Or we can recognize the distortions of
that past, accept it for what it was, penitently hoping for grace, welcoming
back into this community those who for many different reasons protested
this evil. Thus we become receptive to that past in its distortions and in
confidence that acknowledging it for what it was will not destroy us, resting
upon the graciousness by which we live every day of our lives. Our forefathers did not hesitate to declare and share in a day of penitence when they
reckoned that events warranted stock-taking, for they knew a giving and
forgiving grace at the heart of things which their worst faults could not
erase. When this deep sense of the grace at the heart of things fades, the
technogenetic city becomes a wasteland. It becomes post-religious and post-
human. There is no possibility of honest critique of our national life for
what happened in Viet Nam so long as we conceal from ourselves the evil of
that past, keeping at a distance those who protested so that they do not raise
questions about our past. Receptivity, giving, and forgiving are not avoid-
ance of critique but liberation from the past for critique and judgment, for
true appropriation of our heritage.

Coming to terms with the past, the religious note of grace, is one
side of the Mystery of our abiding in this linguistic world. The other side
is our encounter with the future. The technogenetic city comes to terms
with the future through its notion of progress. Each advance in mastery
over nature is taken to mean progress toward human liberation. The future
is assimilated to the process which we have called technogenesis. However,
the future is an open horizon with two aspects--one luring us to new possibilities, the other threatening us with disasters. Technogenesis assimilates
the future as progress only by taking over human possibilities and promising
to stave off disasters. In this sense technogenesis takes on a "religious"
character, for futurity and our human possibilities constitute a realm of
trust or mistrust, not a realm of manageable projects. We comprehend
this when we subject a notion such as progress to critique. There is nothing
self-evident about such a notion. We may well be in the final stages of a
5,000 year experiment with urbanization which will terminate in global disaster. The human species may well be one of the many dead-ends that we
have found in the evolution of life. The future is never something at hand or

determinate. The future is our own way to be as human, a way given to us in our linguistic world. In our linguistic powers we can conjure up many futures, some more beneficent than others. On a deeper level, in our foundational and mythic symbols, the future comes to us as promising and threatening. We live in those possibilities as coming to us, opening horizons of possibility and closing off various paths that other peoples and cultures have tried. Receptivity in the future tense is answering, taking responsibility. Though we do not have the future in hand, we are always in process of taking it upon ourselves, receiving it and being appropriated to it. This is the risk of answering to futurity. No doctrine of progress can conceal this risk. Appropriation to the future which opens before us as possibility is always taking the risk of our own possibilities.

Receptivity of our heritage and appropriation to our future in responsibility constitute a dialectic or dialogue in the life of a people. This dialogue is the source of critique. The heritage is not something finished. It opens up richer, fuller, more expansive worlds of possibility. Foundational symbols open ever richer meanings, bestowing new possibilities and bringing judgments upon older appropriations. The wilderness has never been one thing in the American heritage; in our time, it challenges us to conservation rather than mastery. Futurity beckons us with the lure of new possibilities out of the very heritage which graciously sustains us, beckoning us to risk that heritage for its fuller and deeper possibilities. Over against the threats of disaster, fears of change and anxieties of loss, the future lures us to the enrichment of our humanity, unfolding possibilities in our heritage, challenging and correcting distortions in that heritage, restoring our heritage in a new beginning.

The foundational myths and symbols that give us our world are fraught with possibilities to be discovered. This is true of the work of art, the poem, the myth, or symbol. It is likewise true of creative scientific insights. The heart of the linguistic world is a giving that opens possibilities, a receptivity that bears a promise of fuller disclosure to come. Contrary to the positivist spirit, a thing is never just what it is and not another thing. Even "things" lure us with infinite possibilities as artists and poets have demonstrated. This promise in things, symbols, meanings, and the whole range of our linguistic world opens a future that is both enticing and threatening. And not the least of the threat of this enticing future is the critical appropriation of the past which it demands; entertaining new possibilities always means risking a world already known and accepted for a promise of things to come.

The promise of futurity has often been muted in religious traditions which were preoccupied with threats of disaster. The brilliant astral speculations of so many religious cultures undoubtedly stemmed in part from preoccupation with future dangers. The chthonic, vegetative cults and rituals of agricultural peoples evidence this concern for assuring the future, since

the future was bound to the cycle of life. The linguistic way to be bears a
promise of futurity which can easily be obscured by such fears of disaster.
The dialogue of future and past, critical appropriation and recollection,
seems more often to have fallen on the side of repetition than critique. [38]

The technogenetic city reveals a strange "religious" quality in a
post-religious age, for it has institutionalized futurity, concealing the threats
of the future. Rather than a repetition of the past, it is bound to a repetition
of its projected future. For this reason, theologies of hope have been particularly attractive in these critical years of that darkening city, restoring
confidence that the future which now looks so threatening still bears promise. [39] The dimension of promise which is fundamental to the linguistic
world finds one or another expression in the foundational myths of every
people. In our Western heritage the aspect of promise was accented to the
highest degree by the eschatological vision of early Christianity. When these
religious foundations eroded under the shaping power of the technogenetic
project, the religiously founded promise was assimilated under the name of
progress. In the name of progress, technogenesis is bound to a repetition
of its destruction of earth and community.

The religious moment of futurity, even when secularized to a notion
like progress, depends upon trust and commitment. Whether that trust is
evoked by hierocratic pronouncements on the course of the stars or technocratic assurances that energy will be available, our linguistic world rests
upon trust in the future--a trust which is never reducible to something at
hand. Such trust and commitment are evoked by the foundational symbols
of a religious heritage, even when that heritage is suppressed and forgotten.
And where the promise of futurity is creative and powerful, as it has been
in the Western Hebrew and Christian traditions, a critical appropriation of
the heritage is possible. Change is institutionalized. When trust and commitment wane, as seems to be happening throughout the technogenetic city,
the threats of the future become almost unbearable, anxiety rises to dangerous levels, and leaders promise a secure future on condition that the people
acquiesce to their authority.

The promise of futurity is an integrative moment in linguistic experience and religious symbolization. The vision of futurity, how it unifies
past and present with human possibility, how it envisions the unfolding of
species life, this symbolization is the other side of the gracious giving of a
world in the heritage. In our Western religious heritage the symbol,
Kingdom of God, has been the paramount religious expression of promise.
This symbol has borne multiple meanings in various stages of Western
religious history, but at each point it has integrated the hopes and threats
of futurity in such a way as to evoke trust. [40] In the uttermost extremity,
Job could say "I know that my Redeemer liveth and will stand at the latter
day upon the earth." In the desolation of the Cross, Jesus is reported to
have uttered the words, "Father, into Thy hands I commend my spirit."

St. Augustine could anticipate the fruition of the divine plan in the heavenly
city. St. Bernard could anticipate the heavenly vision after the arduous
course. And so through our Western history, in different ways that foundational promise has borne our history, evoking trust in the darkest times,
and reducing pride in the most arrogant moments.

     To say we are in a post-religious age, a time of forgetfulness, is
only to say that we have repressed the sources of our faith, assimilated the
grace and promise of our heritage to the technogenetic process. Such forgetfulness is dangerous. The gracious giving of our heritage can easily be
transmuted to a wasteland without forgiveness or mercy, a wasteland in
which torture or bureaucratic chill become means of silencing the human
spirit, when dictatorial leadership displaces the promise of an open future,
demanding submission rather than responsibility. The danger of the post-
religious age is not its loss of nerve or its moral deterioration, though these
are serious matters. The extreme danger is the loss of the renewing power
of the heritage, the obliteration of the critical power of the future. When
the future becomes a mere project of the cybernetic society, it is eclipsed
as symbol. The linguistic species lives by grace and promise, dynamically
appropriating and anticipating out of the symbolic power of an integrative
vision. When that dynamic giving and luring of the Mystery are reduced to
mere repetition, the horizon of possibilities is eclipsed.

     It does not seem important to haggle over whether we shall call
ours a "post-religious age" or a religious age in transition to death or to
a new integrative vision. We have argued only that the religious moments
of grace and promise are integral to the linguistic character of human
species life. We have argued further that various religious traditions have
symbolized these deep lying structures in particular ways. And we have
argued that the technogenetic city is living out of the grace and distortions
of its religious heritage, dangerously forgetful of its true source and thus
immune to the critical powers which that heritage could bestow. In turning
now to some major possibilities of that heritage, we are recollecting our
heritage in its distortions and creative possibilities. In this sense, we are
taking our place within the technogenetic city and asking about its forgotten
symbolic depths. We make no claim that such foundational symbols require
a particular religious institutionalization. We only claim that such symbols,
myths of origin and rituals of renewal are at the roots of our common life,
informing our public world whether in distorted modes or in creative, liberating power. In forgetfulness, such symbols are chained to their distortions.

The American Religious Experience

     The American experience, as we traced it in another context,
constitutes an important epoch in Christian history. Whatever the defections

and betrayals of divine covenant in our heritage, the settling of the colonies and the establishment of the Republic drew upon an historical vision of Exodus, a vision whose roots were more Hebrew than Christian. This "almost chosen people" believed the land would be their place of liberation. That sense of promise found expression in the Declaration of Independence, the Constitution and the Bill of Rights. Here in America, the Exodus was a far more compelling image than the Crucifixion, the chastisements of the people of Israel a far more integral motif than the apocalyptic vision of the end of time. [41]

It would distort the American story to portray its religious experience as Hebrew rather than Christian, for certainly the two were synthesized in this American vision. Yet an important relocation of the Christian story in its Hebrew matrix was underway from the start, in part borne by Calvinist theology and discipline. Translating this American experience in terms of the struggle with earthly life, communal bonds, and historical responsibility, we can see the founding of the Republic as part of the movement of Christianity toward earthly, historical responsibility.

One has to say this with care, for the eschatological strand in American religious experience has been very powerful, sweeping over the land in waves from epoch to epoch. [42] Yet Christianity in its various denominational forms wedded its vision of Exodus and Land of Promise to the settlement of the continent, the fashioning of a Republic and the building of a public happiness. The Covenant of the Republic in this new world was through and through a Covenant of historical life.

Even the distortions of the American religious vision stem from this Hebrew sense of a chosen people in a Promised Land. Americans have always found it difficult to distinguish between their calling as the "almost chosen people" and their racist, exploitative, and imperialistic existence. Manifest Destiny easily became a legitimation of economic colonialism and global expansion. This is a familiar story in the Hebrew Scriptures, but it gained a certain absoluteness in the American experience, since it founded its claims on the finality of the Christian story. [44] The Americans were living a Hebrew vision of emancipation under the aegis of a Christian absolute. When the finality of Christ is fused with such an earthly historical embodiment, the spotted actuality of this project is obscured. Any project of the "chosen" gains divine legitimation.

We simplify this story too much by reducing it to the interplay of the Hebrew and Christian heritages. We have seen in another context how a Puritan vision and an Enlightenment heritage played into this complex American story. We reviewed the degradation of this vision of liberation in the drive to dominate the earth, advance individual greed, and elevate novelty to an absolute. Enslavement of Black peoples stands at the very threshold of this Land of Promise, imprinting the mark of Cain on this covenanted people. Yet deep in this experience was a promise of liberation, a promise of public happiness to which Blacks as well as Whites could aspire. These possibilities are rooted in the American religious heritage. The relation of the Christian story to those Hebrew roots in the American experience is still far from clear, though Abraham Lincoln wrestled with these questions throughout his tortured career.

We have unfinished business in relocating our Christian heritage more fully in this Hebrew context. Until this is accomplished, we shall continue to waver between a worldly realism and an absolute legitimation of American destiny. These Hebrew roots are proper to our Christian heritage as our forefathers saw in turning to the imagery of Exodus, Land of Promise, and Covenanted Law. We are at another turning, and a turning is also a turning back to the source of grace and promise. We are part of the Christian pilgrimage, coming to terms with earthly life. This is no merely "intellectual" exercise but a new way of life, a new reciprocity with nature, a new commitment to global community. It is a work of liberation in which thought and action join, but it is founded in a new receptivity to our foundational heritage, a creative, critical recollection of our beginnings.

We explored in another essay the major moments of the work of art--receptive, expressive, and integrative. We determined that these are temporal moments which constitute the possibility of any experience, structuring the event of meaning that we call human species life. Receptivity is appropriation to possibility, to meaning, in species life, being within the realm of meaning. Articulation is giving expression in word, act, and work to those possibilities within which we stand. We used earlier the example of Michelangelo chipping away as he conspired in the coming forth of the figure of David which slumbered in the marble. Without the receptive moment there are no possibilities but without word and act there is only waiting before slumbering possibilities, unless, of course, the silence be the depth of listening speech. The integrative moment was earlier designated the moment of recognition, the abiding in the open that is truth, unconcealment, including a public space in which the meaning is preserved, cherished and borne beyond itself. We took these moments of the work of art as indicative of the primordial coming to pass of a world of meaning. Other modes of experiencing, other ways of being and orienting to the world such as handling or analyzing arise from this primordial structure. However, they may, and often do, obscure and conceal this primordial structure of experience. We have argued throughout these reflections that the technological world is precisely that forgetfulness of primordial giving of meaning, a preoccupation with articulative tasks of analyzing and handling by which receptivity is suppressed and integrative vision eclipsed.

The suppression of the receptive moment is also indicative of the loss of primordial expression and recognition. When thinking and acting become alienated from their primordial relatedness to things and persons, speech and language no longer convey depth and richness of meaning. The only language that has currency is the debased coinage of information and feedback. Truth is reduced to logical coherence, now divorced from experiencing of things and persons. The poetic speech that receives and articulates the primordial word, calling forth depths of meaning, enriching deadened words and acts--such primordial saying is treated as sentimentality or illusion. Art becomes the preserve of collectors who demonstrate their financial cunning in piling up works that will gain value. The seeing of the artist, the depths to be received and disclosed, these are matters for esthetes. The integrative moment of the public world is likewise degraded when primordial receptivity is suppressed. We have discussed this suppression in politics in another essay; here the integrative moment finds its public, institutional expression. The articulative moment of work, now alienated from any ground in receptivity and become autonomous as the drive to mastery of the world, becomes the single and sovereign expression of human species life. The political, integrative moment that preserves the human in a public space withdraws, becoming a mere instrument of a degraded form of work. This is the deeper meaning of technogenesis--the collapse of receptive and integrative moments into a debased form of articulation, the instrumental manipulation of nature, things, and others for the sake of mastery.

The receptive moment is the way back to our roots, and thus the way back into a proper life of work, a proper poetic, and ultimately a proper political life. This does not mean that a people becomes religious and all these things shall be added. We have indicated at several points that receptive, expressive, and integrative moments are interrelated in the earthly, communal, and historical struggle. The receptive moment is not something apart from work, art, and political life. The receptive moment is decisive in all these realms. We abide within meanings to be disclosed if we heed them, and heeding is the religious moment. In the age of the technogenetic city, the religious summons is a calling back into receptivity, into heeding the natural and human possibilities that surround us. Whether our work be nurture of the young, political action, poetic or artistic expression, industrial work, agricultural labor, or service trades, receptivity is becoming open to possibilities for a more human world. Receptivity does not obviate the difficult task of articulating these possibilities, discovering new styles of work, art or political life. Moreover, we face integrative tasks of fashioning stable human communities and structures of care in which human species life can be cherished and preserved. Yet the religious moment, the receptive moment, is the primary and decisive moment for our age. The endless cycle of meaningless activity can only be broken by receptive appropriation to the open realm of meaning. This open realm, albeit now in distorted form, abides in our foundational symbols.

The religious moment of receptivity extends to every realm of experiencing, for our standing within meanings is our abiding in the giving

of our world. It is likewise suffering the pains of alienated and distorted
giving through the twisted structures of personal and institutional relationships. The invitation to care evoked by a child's pleading smile, the possibilities of creativity disclosed by an unpolished stone, the fun of a task that
calls for completion, the opportunity to share in a thoughtful conversation,
these and endless other openings on a human world beckon to us. This
giving that receives us into a world may be heeded or ignored, attended to
or forgotten, but our working, sharing, creating, and thinking arise from
that receptivity. This can be called religious for it is the beckoning of
life-giving, coming to presence in which human species life abides in the
earth, a beckoning that liberates us to possibilities and binds us to one
another.

Religious symbolization in myth and ritual articulates this receptive
moment. These foundational expressions, however transparently or opaquely
they articulate this receptivity, have their source in this common life-giving
grace. What, then, do we mean by speaking of receptivity as the religious
moment? This is meant in two respects; the primordially religious and
the specifically religious articulation. In the primordial sense, receptivity
is religious for it sets up human species life in the gracious giving of a
world not of its making. This constitution of human species life in grace,
and in the struggle to overcome alienation and deformation of life, sets up
a world in which care about the meaning of things, persons, and existence
takes priority. Where such matters recede into forgetfulness, human
species life is endangered. In this primordial sense, receptivity, heeding,
listening, and caring are not only the beginning of dialogue but the beginning
of wisdom.

But the religious moment always takes concrete form in foundational
symbols and myths as we have indicated above. The religions of the world
bear witness to the receptive moment in different ways with very different
consequences for the course of economic, social, political, and artistic life.
We can plumb any realm of experience for its receptive, religious moment,
but our ways of entering into the receptivity of life are founded for us in
particular religious symbols and rituals. In this sense, our particular
religious heritage, whatever its distortions in recent centuries, is of crucial importance in uncovering the possibilities of life. The receptive
moment in our time is a summons to a new attentiveness to meaning in all
realms of our common life and simultaneously a call to find our way back
into the creative possibilities of our religious heritage.

The peculiar significance of the religious heritage becomes clearer
when we see it in dialogue with political life. The political realm, as we
have observed, brings to expression an integrative vision of human species
life for a people. However distorted the institutionalization of politics, its
essential meaning is to constitute a public space in which human species life
finds voice and continuation. In the structure of language and faith which we

have been discussing, the political realm gives institutional expression to
the promise of futurity, to the promise in which human species life is sustained and summoned to new possibilities. In this respect, the political
always embodies more or less adequately the primordial religious promise.
And here the interplay of religious and political traditions comes to light.
The religious heritage bears an integrative vision of the promise of human
species life. It bears this vision as legitimation and critical challenge to
the political realm. So far as the political embodies the promise, it merits
religious confirmation. By the same token, the deformation of political
institutions finds critique from many realms of life but comes under special
critique where the religious heritage is alive. Thus, the religious spokesman, often the prophet, reawakens the receptive moment within the political
vision, summoning it once again to its own source of promise, challenging
the deformation of its institutional articulation. The political realm seeks
legitimation from religion, yet in this dialogue of legitimation the religious
spokesmen have the task of reawakening the receptive moment of holiness
and grace from which the political derives its true life. Nowhere in our
own religious heritage has this task been more completely articulated than
in the prophetic tradition of the Hebrew Scriptures.[45] And that should be
indication enough that spokesmen of the religious word need not come from
established religious institutions. It is often political spokesmen, upholding
an integrative vision of the human, who have recalled religious institutions
to their proper tasks. This was eminently the case in Abraham Lincoln's
struggle with the abolitionists during the Civil War and with the vendetta of
the North after the war.

  Receptivity to the life-giving powers of earth, community, and
history seems to contrast sharply with the Christian heritage of a completed
history, a once and for all overcoming of the evil powers of history. In the
symbol, Kingdom of God, we perceive the real depths of this tension between a promise of divine presencing in the day to day struggle of liberation
and a proclamation of a completed history. The inner tension between
eschatology and history, a victory won and a struggle engaged, is borne in
the various transmutations of the symbol, Kingdom of God. As Norman
Perrin has indicated in a sketchy but insightful essay on the Kingdom of God
as a biblical symbol, the very term is probably late, perhaps even Christian,
but it roots back in the symbol of Reign or Kingdom referring to the sovereignty of the Mystery.[46] In the Covenant tradition of Sinai, the symbol may
not have prominence, for here the federation of tribes is constituted by the
gracious giving of law and binding in a covenantal community. Certainly in
the Covenant of Zion, of the Davidic Kingship, the Eastern traditions of
divine kingship gain a place in the Hebrew tradition, and we have important
symbolism and mythology of kingship developing.[47] With the collapse of
the Davidic Kingship, the fall of Jerusalem and the Exile, there are centuries of hope and expectation for a restoration. The anticipation of restoration

is temporarily realized at various points only to collapse under another
imperial domination. [48] At the same time, the historical covenant of Sinai
and the prominence of the Law took precedence in the life of the Jewish
people, while kingship became a locus of hope for liberation.

The symbol of the Kingdom became a central concern of radical,
apocalyptic movements in later Judaism, movements of revolutionary
anticipation of a divine overcoming of the imperial forces that held sway
in the land. Thus, in addition to the general notion of divine sovereignty
there was a powerful underground movement of apocalyptic expectation of
a divine intervention, overcoming and terminating history. [49] As Norman
Perrin notes, the so-called War Scroll from the community which is associated with the Dead Sea Scrolls proclaims divine intervention in the overcoming of evil and the Roman oppressors. [50] Moreover, this intervention
had an extra-historical character in the sense that it involved intervention
from another world. This was the context in which Jesus' proclamation of
the Kingdom was appropriated, though it now seems quite clear that his
own preaching had a much more earthly, communal, and historical character; in brief, so far as can be discerned from recent studies, Jesus'
proclamation of the Kingdom blends the historical character of the Sinai
Covenant with promise of release of divine power which draws upon the
foundational symbol of Kingdom. [51] Nevertheless, the apocalyptic context
in which Jesus' message was appropriated took precedence in the Christian
development, and the symbol of the Kingdom bore an accent of finality, an
eschatological sense of the end of the struggle. When the imminent return
of Jesus as heavenly Son of Man to complete history did not materialize,
the tension between the historical and eschatological aspects of the symbolism of Kingdom, between the on-going struggle and the victory already won,
became integral to the integrative vision of Christianity. And, as we noted
earlier, the eschatological vision of the completion of history in the figure
of Jesus Christ became dominant in the struggle of the churches to cope
with earthly responsibilities.

This inner tension in the integrative vision of Christianity between
on-going historical struggle (the tradition of Sinai) and victory already won
(the apocalyptic expression of the tradition of Zion) found new articulation
in the American experience. [52] When the American settlers drew upon
Hebrew imagery of Exodus and Land of Promise they were drawing upon
the tradition of Sinai, a tradition renewed again and again in the work of the
prophets, a tradition which found later institutionalization in Judaism as
people of the Torah. Thus, the historical, earthly, communal aspects of
the covenant heritage and symbolism of the Kingdom found a peculiar renewal
in the American settlement. As we noted, this new articulation of Sinai was
held in tension with the note of finality, so American religious experience
repeatedly underwent apocalyptic awakenings as well as fundamentalist

movements. Nevertheless, a peculiar concern for earthly history informed
the integrative vision of American destiny.

As we confront the devastation of the earth, the dissolution of human
communities, and the eclipse of promise, the symbolism of the Kingdom has
special importance. Our time calls for a critical appropriation to the symbolism of the Kingdom. However, we shall have to draw much more fully upon
Hebrew symbolism of earth, community and history than heretofore. Such
a critical appropriation to our heritage conforms to the historical roots of
Jesus' proclamation and to the continuing struggle of Christianity to recover
its own roots in the Hebrew Scriptures. [53] It means another step in coming
to terms with history and playing down the note of finality which has been
so dominant in Christian history. This is neither arbitrary nor unprecedented,
for the tension between historical and eschatological notes has persisted both
in Judaism and Christianity.

Judaism, as we have implied, accented the historical covenant of
Sinai and the Law, retaining the eschatological note of Kingship in an expectation of a Messiah to come at the end of time. There have been movements
of apocalyptic expectation within Judaism over the course of history, but the
dominant note has been one of covenant community according to the Law and
in faithfulness to the Mystery. The covenants of Sinai and Zion have been
kept in tension within Judaism as well, though the accent has been just the
contrary of the Christian. [54] Whereas Christianity articulated an integrative
vision with an eschatological accent of victory already won, Judaism expressed
an historical vision with the promise of a final victory. This complementarity
of Christianity and Judaism has great importance for appropriation to the symbolism of the Kingdom, for these powerful strands of Western religious
history are now deeply rooted in the American experience. As a consequence
of migrations during the nineteenth and twentieth centuries and the tragic
migration forced by the Holocaust, the United States of America is now an
important locus of Jewish life. The dialogue of history and eschatology which
was embodied anew in the American experience of Exodus now has co-equal
partners in its further appropriation to the Kingdom. The Christian and
Jewish communities of America are rooted powerfully though differently in
this heritage. We should not idealize these possibilities of dialogue and
religious renewal, for both Jewish and Christian communities are immersed
in the forgetfulness of the technogenetic city. Furthermore, Christian communities are still stained with ancient prejudices; consequently much of our
dialogue has to preoccupy itself with basic tasks of mutual respect. Nevertheless, the historical possibilities are present for a renewal of both communities through dialogue, for maintaining a sense of the historical promise
of liberation and justice in this land. The historical character of the Kingdom has been the special burden of Judaism, and perhaps only in dialogue
with the Jewish community can Christianity make another step toward its
earthly responsibilities.

Such a Jewish-Christian dialogue would involve radical appropriation to our heritage. If we consider the symbolism of the Kingdom, we can discern some indications of the direction in which such a dialogue would take us. This is not the place to unfold the implications of such a dialogue, but playing down the eschatological note would mean undergirding our actual concern for earth, community, and history in a wholly new way. This is not a matter of saying that we are in a desperate plight and no resources are available to overcome our difficulties, though this is certainly true. It is a matter of coming to terms once again with the foundational symbols of our common life as our forefathers did again and again in Western history. We are asking about our own identity, our cultural, religious, political, and communal possibilities. These possibilities, as we have indicated above, are not willy-nilly creations of our own imaginations but the constituted possibilities of our symbolic heritage. The presence of a strong and creative Jewish community in the United States of America may be seen as an integral element in the Western development, the emergence of a partnership in dialogue through which these heritages may find critical renewal.

Relocating the symbolism of the Kingdom within its Hebrew matrix would open an entirely new horizon in our understanding of earth, community, and history. This understanding would not be strange to the settlers of this new world, but it is an understanding that has been dimmed in the course of American development. We cannot go back and live in the patriarchal times or ceremonial cities of ancient Israel, but we can make a new beginning on our foundations through such a dialogue of faith.

Our being with the earth takes on a different character under the historical covenant. The command in Genesis to subdue the earth, to bring it under dominion, has sometimes been used to rationalize the modern claim to mastery over nature. However, this passage refers much more to the servanthood of humankind, to its cherishing care of the earth. [55] Dominion in Hebrew Scriptures is the dominion of Jahweh, the Mystery. Humankind holds no dominion, only servanthood, albeit a practical, creative, and collaborative servanthood. The rape of the earth, degradation of natural processes to energy for human exploitation, is a violation of the sovereignty of the Mystery. Americans have always known that the rape of their land was a violation of covenant, yet greed and private profit have repeatedly triumphed over this deeper religious sense. [56]

The history of the churches reflects a strange ambivalence about the earth. We have drawn attention to the severing of bonds with the earth, but monastic and sectarian movements cherished work and cultivation. This is an important part of our religious heritage. It reflects the deeper roots of the Christian story in the Hebrew respect for the earth as divine giving of plenty. The Thanksgiving ritual of Puritan experience reflects this sense of divine giving. It is not merely that the land is under our care. In our struggle with the earth, in respect and cultivation of the earth, we express our servanthood and collaboration with the divine life. Many strands in the monastic and sectarian heritages kept this appreciation of earth alive. [57]

We are so familiar with an individualized notion of Christianity that it almost goes without saying that individualism is the value par excellence of Western Christianity. There is some truth to this. Christianity did cut through the natural bonds of human community--sexual, familial, local, and political. Christianity established an ecumenical community of saved souls transcending peoples and traditions. Moreover, respect for the single soul brought an important value to modern, Western life, however much it was violated in actuality. But the roots of the historical covenant are communal. The Covenant of Sinai is the constituting of a confederation of tribes, the establishment of a community, a people. [58] Whatever place individualism held in this Covenant, and the prophets in their way bear testimony to the importance of the single voice, still the religious reality inheres in a community. In this sense, the individual person and the covenanted community are inseparably conjoined. [59] When individual personhood perishes, when the prophets are scorned and killed, the community perishes as well. And when the community heeds the Word of the Mystery, its life and the life of persons find their place in the economy of the Promise.

In our individualistic tradition we easily lose sight of the communal character of Jesus' ministry. [60] He comes out of a communal life of Israel to address himself to that community for the renewal of its communal faith. The Kingdom is nothing if not a communal symbol. Whatever the eschatological note he sounded, and this is still a matter of much debate, it was an eschatology of a community, of a new covenant community. [61] The individualism that has emerged in America is foreign to this Hebrew context. Once again, the communal character of our religious heritage has been preserved and enriched through monastic and sectarian communities. These strands of Christian history have borne witness to the deeper communal roots of the covenant faith. [62] This does not mean that individual life and personal rights should be eschewed in a recovery of religious roots. Rather the opposite, for individual rights can only be preserved where authentic communal life is sustained. It is precisely the dilemma of the modern world that the destruction of community has led to the erosion of individual life. We oscillate now between oppressive collectivism and anarchic individualism. Neither is a path toward a human world. Neither is consonant with our religious heritage.

The American experience reenacted the Hebrew covenant of Land and Community. The breach of this covenant of Promise led to callous disregard for land, community, and person. We have traced this process. Now we can acknowledge the roots of that American Promise and the possibility of its renewal. Here the authentically historical character of our biblical heritage comes into the foreground. This earth, this land, and these communities constitute the place of disclosure of the divine life. This is the life and responsibility to which we are called, now extended as promise to a global humankind. It is no longer American destiny to bear this promise for mankind. We live in an interdependent world, and the promise of life will be global in character or no promise at all.

The meaning of history has been very ambiguous for Christianity. The issue for Christianity is whether we are living in one history or two. Is the history of saving presence of the Mystery our own history here and now, or do we wait for another history, another eon? If we relocate the symbolism of Kingdom in its Jewish context, we are ready to talk about one history, to recognize that the presencing of the Mystery in our struggles for liberation is that Kingdom in our midst. We are ready to see in the dialogue of the common life a disclosing of divine grace and promise. [63]

In relocating the symbolism of the Kingdom in its Hebrew matrix, we make no claim to do more than suggest a line of thinking and reconstruction which stretches before us. When the effort of such relocation becomes comparable to the effort that was invested in recovering the historical Jesus, we shall be richly endowed with understanding of earth, community, and history. For the moment, we can at least acknowledge that our religious heritage does not support the arrogant claims to sovereignty that the technogenetic city embodies, and indeed it challenges such claims at many points.

In shifting the accent from finality to historical responsibility under the Covenant, we are opening many questions which cannot be treated here. This is the path which our forefathers cut in the wilderness, a path on which we can continue in trust. Religious thought is more and more ready to relocate the eschatological note in the context of our one historical world, seeing in this note of finality a powerful symbol of liberation from human arrogance. The eschatological moment points then, to the hiddenness of Mystery. History is never something in hand. History points to the Sovereignty of divine grace and promise, to the antecedent giving of our world in which our responsibility arises. History conceals its complete meaning even as it bestows particular possibilities. No faith, party, or class possesses the meaning of history.

The eschatological note remains within the historical covenant. It means that American destiny is never manifest. It is hidden. It is held in trust. It means that the earth which we are called to cherish is never transparently gracious or lifegiving yet always hides a divine graciousness. It means that the community in which we find ourselves bears personal and structural distortions that nevertheless conceal possibilities of humanization. And it means that the one history in which we are appropriated to liberating possibilities is an ambiguous and finite responsibility. Eschatology points to the finitude of our responsibility for history. History is the place where the Mystery summons and liberates, where we are being called out of our forgetfulness. The note of finality, the eschatological motif in our religious heritage, points to the completeness of the divine presencing in our actual history, not as something in hand but as gracious care. We do not wait for some other world or history. In recollection, in heeding and care we already participate in that final completeness. Thus, the Cross in the Christian heritage points to that divine presence even in suffering and death, the divine adequacy to all alienations.

The scope of receptivity in our time is almost boundless when we become aware of our forgetfulness. It touches not only our life with earthly processes and human connections but also our symbolic foundations of grace and promise. It touches the history which Christianity has struggled so hard to square with its sense of finality. This receptive moment has its source in the divine life so far as we apprehend that life in our Jewish and Christian traditions. For the Christian heritage the Cross has always been a decisive moment in religious history. Whatever its many other riches in meaning and human possibility, the Cross is a foundational symbol of the divine acceptance of human life in forgiveness and grace.[64] The Cross stands as one of the momentous symbolizations in human history of divine receptivity and graciousness. So long as the Cross remains alive in our technogenetic city, the recollection of forgiveness and grace will penetrate the wasteland. And here the eschatological note sounds again, for this forgiving grace discloses its powers in the scorned, outcast, and despised of the earth. Forgiving grace manifests itself in the uttermost extremity of human alienation.

Divine receptivity forms the background of the Christian story as witnessed in the Hebrew Scriptures. The Exodus which formed the backdrop of the American promise begins with a note of divine receptivity that is repeated again and again in the Scriptures:

> In the course of those many days the King of Egypt died. And the people of Israel groaned under their bondage, and cried out for help, and their cry under bondage came up to God. And God heard their groaning, and God remembered his covenant with Abraham, with Isaac, and with Jacob. And God saw the people of Israel and God knew their condition.   (Exodus 2:23-25)

> And now, behold, the cry of the people of Israel has come to me, and I have seen the oppression with which the Egyptians oppress them. Come, I will send you to Pharoah, that you may bring forth my people, the sons of Israel, out of Egypt. But Moses said to God, "Who am I that I should go to Pharaoh, and bring the sons of Israel out of Egypt?" He said, "But I will be with you; and this shall be the sign for you, that I have sent you: when you have brought forth the people out of Egypt, you shall serve God upon this mountain."   (Exodus 3:9-12)

This is the context of divine receptivity, of the hearing of the cry of the oppressed, that finds its proper response in the Shema, "Hear, O Israel, The Lord your God is One!" This call to hear proceeds from One who hears, and that initiative founds our receptivity in a promise of liberation.

NOTES AND REFERENCES

[1]Robert Bellah has been a leading spokesman of the importance of religious foundations for the West and particularly for America; see his The Broken Covenant: American Civil Religion in Time of Trial (New York, New York: The Seabury Press, 1975).

[2]Robert Heilbroner, An Inquiry Into the Human Prospect (New York, New York: W.W. Norton & Co., 1974) turns to Greek mythology for a symbolism of America's future; William Leiss, The Domination of Nature (Boston, Mass.: The Beacon Press, 1972) reflects a general feeling of the irrelevance of religion to modernity.

[3]See William Leiss, op. cit., for an extreme position on this issue, see Lynn White, Jr., Machina Ex Deo: Essays in the Dynamism of Western Culture (Cambridge, Mass.: The MIT Press, 1968) esp. pp. 88ff.

[4]Ernst Troeltsch, The Social Teaching of the Christian Churches (New York, New York: Macmillan Co., 1931) Two Volumes; the ambiguity of this relationship to secular society is developed by Charles Norris Cochrane, Christianity and Classical Culture (New York, New York: Oxford University Press, 1957, paperback) esp. pp. 509ff on the unifying and transformative impact of Christianity; see also Sheldon S. Wolin, Politics and Vision (Boston, Mass.: Little, Brown and Co., 1960), Chapter Four.

[5]This is a simplification of the multiple theologies already present in the New Testament; see Norman Perrin, The New Testament: An Introduction (New York, New York: Harcourt Brace Jovanovich Inc., 1974), Chapter 3 and passim.

[6]The Post-Constantine period and the work of Augustine could be understood in this sociological context; see Charles N. Cochrane, op. cit., for an exposition of the wrestling of the Church in this period with the meaning of secular society and the state; see also cursory treatment in Robert M. Grant, Augustus to Constantine (New York, New York: Harper & Row, 1970).

[7]See Sheldon Wolin, op. cit., for a summary of this orientation.

[8]This is, of course, the extreme statement of the apocalyptic context in which the teaching and ministry of Jesus were appropriated and gradually modified, see Norman Perrin, op. cit., pp. 74-85.

[9]Jaroslav Pelikan, The Shape of Death (Nashville, Tenn.: Abingdon Press, 1961).

[10]R. L. P. Milburn, Early Christian Interpretations of History (London: Black, 1954) explicates the variety in historical perspective but centered in prophecy and fulfillment, esp. pp. 21ff.

[11]Ernst Troeltsch, op. cit., Introduction.

[12]The most radical expression of this detachment is to be found in the realm of sexuality, see Derrick Bailey, Sexual Relation in Christian Thought (New York, New York: Harper & Bros., 1959).

[13]Augustine's formulation of the cupidity of the earthly city was a decisive expression of this orientation, The City of God, translated by John Healey (London: J.M. Dent and Sons, 1931), esp. Fifteenth Book.

[14]Christianity always stressed the expectation of the coming and thus broke with the cyclical view of human events that characterized the classical world, but "historical" here refers to the meaning in history where the churches struggle; see Gibson Winter, "Human Science and Ethics in a Creative Society," Cultural Hermeneutics, Vol. 1, No. 2, July 1973, pp. 145-176.

[15]See Gerhard Von Rad, Old Testament Theology, translated by D.M.G. Stalker (New York, New York: Harper & Row, Publishers, 1962, 1965) Two Volumes, esp. Vol. II, Chapter G and pp. 105ff and 369-374, where "history" refers not to a linear sequence of events but disclosure events in a saving history and the cultic celebrations of those events.

[16]The eternal, unchangeable character of deity in Christian theism has been attributed primarily to Hellenization of Christian theology as in Leslie Dewart's The Future of Belief (New York, New York: Herder and Herder, 1966); the most telling reconstruction of theism has issued from Charles Hartshorne's work as in Schubert M. Ogden, The Reality of God and Other Essays (New York, New York: Harper & Row, 1963), esp. Chapter I; see also a recent reconstruction along similar lines by David Tracy, Blessed Rage for Order (New York, New York: The Seabury Press, 1975) Chapters 7 and 8; however, the finality of Christ remains a stumbling block for such reconstruction and calls for a similar work in Christology.

[17]This is not to raise the difficult and unresolved question as to whether Jesus made such claims or was fitted into an apocalyptic context, an argument being pursued in post-Bultmann discussions of the historical Jesus; for a review of this discussion, see Reginald H. Fuller, The New Testament in Current Study (New York, New York: Charles Scribner's Sons, 1962) and esp. p. 140 on the post-Easter Kerygma.

[18]For the background of the New Testament eschatology, see Sigmund Mowinckel, He That Cometh (Nashville, Tenn.: Abingdon Press, 1955); for the centrality of this theme, see Hans Conzelmann, History of Primitive Christianity, translated by John E. Steely (Nashville, Tenn.: Abingdon Press, 1973) esp. Chapter IV.

[19]See Robert L. P. Milburn, op. cit., esp. Chapters III and VI; see also Erich Auerbach, Scenes from the Drama of European Literature

(New York, New York: Meridian Books, Inc., 1959) in the essay titled,
"Figura."

[20]John F.A. Taylor, The Masks of Society (New York, New York:
Meredith Publ., 1966) Chapter III.

[21]See Leslie Dewart, op. cit.; on the character of this metaphysical tradition, see Martin Heidegger, An Introduction to Metaphysics
(New York, New York: Doubleday & Co., Anchor Books, 1961); in relation
to the concept of God, see Martin Heidegger, Identity and Difference (New
York, New York: Harper & Row, 1969), "The Onto-Theo-Logical Constitution
of Metaphysics," and Martin Heidegger, The End of Philosophy, translated
by Joan Stambaugh (New York, New York: Harper & Row, 1973) esp.
"Metaphysics as History of Being."

[22]Martin Heidegger, The End of Philosophy, op. cit., pp. 46ff.

[23]For a discussion of this autonomous rationality from a somewhat
different perspective, see David M. Rasmussen, "Between Autonomy and
Sociality," Cultural Hermeneutics I, No. 1, April 1973, pp. 3-45.

[24]A. Wolf, A History of Science, Technology and Philosophy in the
16th & 17th Centuries, Second Edition (New York, New York: Harper Torch-
books, 1959) esp. 35-38.

[25]William Leiss, The Domination of Nature, op. cit., esp. Ch. 4.

[26]Friedrich Nietzsche, Thus Spoke Zarathustra (Baltimore, Md.:
Penguin Books, 191, 69) Part Four, p. 297; this market place scene was
developed earlier by the author, The Gay Science, translated by Walter
Kaufmann (New York, New York: Vintage Books, 1974) Book Three, Section 125.

[27]This is not an argument for a particular religious symbolization;
it simply affirms that the holy or sacred manifests itself in foundational
symbols that bestow a world within particular cultural heritages, integrating
and preserving deep lying elements of human experiencing of space, time,
community, tools, things, and events. Philip Wheelwright speaks of this
dimension helpfully as "man's threshold existence"--"always on the border-
land of a something more" in The Burning Fountain: A Study in the Language
of Symbolism (Bloomington, Ind.: Indiana University Press, 1968) p. 18;
see also Mircea Eliade's treatment of the symbolic disclosures of space,
time, cosmos, and existence in The Sacred and the Profane: The Nature of
Religion (New York, New York: Harcourt, Brace & World, Inc., 1959).

[28]Arthur Koestler, Darkness at Noon (New York, New York:
Macmillan Co., 1941); see also Aleksandr I. Solzhenitsyn, The Gulag
Archipelago: 1918-1956 (New York, New York: Harper & Row, 1974)
Vols. III-IV, Chapter 11 for a more complex discussion of the attitude of
party members in camps after their arrest.

[29]Franz Kafka, The Trial (New York, New York: Knopf, 1959).

[30]This is said as a perspective on the human but a perspective
with broad foundations; see Mircea Eliade, Images and Symbols: Studies

in Religious Symbolism (New York, New York: Sheed and Ward, 1969)--
"It is of the greatest importance, we believe, to rediscover a whole mythology, if not a theology, still concealed in the most ordinary, everyday life
of contemporary man; it will depend upon himself whether he can work his
way back to the source and rediscover the profound meanings of all these
faded images and damaged myths." p. 18.

31Mircea Eliade puts this as follows: "As we have seen, the symbol not only makes the world 'open' but also helps religious man to attain to
the universal. For it is through symbols that man finds his way out of his
particular situation and 'opens himself' to the general and the universal.
Symbols awaken individual experience and transmute it into a spiritual act,
into metaphysical comprehension of the world." The Sacred and the Profane,
op. cit., p. 211.

32See Mircea Eliade, Patterns in Comparative Religion (New York,
New York: Sheed & Ward, 1958) esp. Chapter VIII, Sections 116 and 120.

33See Mircea Eliade, The Myth of the Eternal Return (New York,
New York: Pantheon Books, Inc., 1954).

34Mircea Eliade makes many references to sacrifice in his Patterns
in Comparative Religion, op. cit., but he suggests some of the deeper source
of sacrificial participation in his discussion of the Cosmic Tree and the
sacrificial stake in Vedic, India, which links up to our own mythic history
of the Tree in the Garden and the Place of the Cross in Christianity; see
Mircea Eliade, Images and Symbols, op. cit., pp. 44f.

35Hannah Arendt sets out this structure of forgiveness and promise
in non-religious terms in The Human Condition (Garden City, New York:
Doubleday Anchor Books, 1959) pp. 212-223.

36For a profound discussion of the problem of fault, see Paul
Ricoeur, The Symbolism of Evil (New York, New York: Harper & Row,
1967).

37See Paul Tillich's brief but insightful remarks on this in Love,
Power and Justice (New York, New York: Oxford University Press, 1954)
pp. 84ff.

38The religious symbol is open and creative yet may recede and in
desacralized times fall into the unconscious; thus, the all-powerful sky God
manifests his power in epiphanies of storm and meteorological phenomena,
yet in receding may become objectified in astral calculations; see Mircea
Eliade, The Sacred and Profane, op. cit., on openness of aquatic symbolism,
pp. 136ff, on the sky God, pp. 120ff; on desacralization of the world to the
unconscious, pp. 209ff; the place of repetitiveness was discussed by David
Krieger in Seminar presentation, and note the "repetitiveness" of the impulses arising in the unconscious as the forgotten depths of religion and myth.

39This is, of course, only one aspect of the theologies of hope but
helps to account for their popularity.

[40]See Norman Perrin, "The Interpretation of a Biblical Symbol,"
The Journal of Religion, Vol. 55, No. 3, July 1975, esp. pp. 352ff.

[41]See Conrad Cherry, God's New Israel: Religious Interpretations
of American Destiny (Englewood Cliffs, N. J.: Prentice-Hall Inc., 1971)
esp. pp. 61-81.

[42]Calvin's theology and politics developed in a consistently Christian framework, yet Calvinism is a rediscovery of the institutional dimension
of civil society and an important turning toward the quest for the best society,
a quest with roots deep in Hebrew Scriptures which was enacted in the colonial experience; see Sheldon Wolin, Politics and Vision, op. cit., pp. 179
and 192: the centrality of imagery from Hebrew Scriptures in Calvin's
political formulations comes out clearly in Michael Walzer's The Revolution
of the Saints: A Study in the Origins of Radical Politics (New York, New
York: Atheneim, 1969) esp. Chapter Two.

[43]Ernest Lee Tuveson, Redeemer Nation: The Idea of America's
Millennial Role (Chicago, Ill.: University of Chicago Press, 1968).

[44]Robert Bellah has a balanced discussion of this without the
emphasis on the millennial hope in The Broken Covenant, Chapter II "America
as a Chosen People."

[45]One of the finest expositions of this work of prophecy is given by
R.B.Y. Scott, The Relevance of the Prophets (New York, New York: The
Macmillan Co., 1957) esp. Ch. VIII; see also the penetrating treatment of
prophecy by Abraham J. Heschel, The Prophets (New York, New York:
Harper & Row, 1962) esp. Ch. 27.

[46]Norman Perrin, "The Interpretation of a Biblical Symbol,"
op. cit., fn. 10, p. 352.

[47]The traditions of Sinai and Zion are set forth in their duality and
relations by Coert Rylaarsdam, "Jewish-Christian Relationship: The Two
Covenants and the Dilemmas of Christology," Journal of Ecumenical Studies,
Vol. 9, No. 2, 1972, pp. 249-270: see also, Delbert R. Hillers, Covenant:
The History of a Biblical Idea (Baltimore, Md.: Johns Hopkins Press, 1969)
esp. Ch. 5.

[48]Sigmund Mowinckel, He That Cometh, op. cit., esp. Chapters
IV-VI.

[49]Ibid., Chapters VIII-X.

[50]Norman Perrin, "The Interpretation of a Biblical Symbol,"
op. cit., p. 359.

[51]Norman Perrin, Rediscovering the Teaching of Jesus (New York,
New York: Harper & Row, 1967) Ch. II; also "The Interpretation of a
Biblical Symbol," op. cit., pp. 360ff.

[52]For the basic tension between the Covenants of Sinai and Zion,
see Coert Rylaarsdam, op. cit.

[53]Once it is recognized that the various theologies of the New
Testament transmute the figure of Jesus to apocalyptic vision, new law and

fulfillment, salvation history and other contexts, the upshot of this new
quest for the historical Jesus is to recover his context in Judaism; although
he does not turn in this direction, since he is exploring the emergent theologies of the New Testament, this turn backwards becomes essential to unfolding the symbol of Jesus, see Norman Perrin's lecture, University of
Chicago Divinity School, Autumn 1975, "Jesus and the Theology of the New
Testament."

[54]Coert Rylaarsdam, op. cit.; George Foote Moore, Judaism in
the First Centuries of the Christian Era (Cambridge, Mass.: Harvard
University Press, 1927-30) esp. Vol. I, Part I on historical aspects; Vol.
II, Part VII on Messianic Expectation; Vol. III, fn. I. 4, pp. 17-22 on
continuities in Judaism; also Max Brod, Paganism-Christianity-Judaism:
A Confession of Faith, translated by William Wolf (University, Ala.:
University of Alabama Press, 1970) esp. Chapters 6-8.

[55]Gerhard Von Rad, Old Testament Theology, op. cit., Vol. I,
pp. 146ff.

[56]Perry Miller traces this conflict between covenant obligation
to land and acquisitiveness, between communal unity and social degradation,
to the earliest period of the colonies; see esp. Errand Into the Wilderness
(New York, New York: Harper & Row, 1956) Chapter I.

[57]Discussion of monastic and sectarian movements in Ernst
Troeltsch, Social Teachings of the Christian Churches, op. cit., Vol. I,
pp. 237-245 and 328-372. See also Kenneth E. Kirk, The Vision of God
(London, Engl.: Longmans, Green & Co., 1934) Lectures IV and V for a
discussion of the ambiguities in this disciplined life with respect to worldly
concerns.

[58]See Coert Rylaarsdam, op. cit., pp. 253ff; also George E.
Mendenhall, Law and Covenant in Israel and the Ancient Near East (Pittsburgh,
Pa.: The Biblical Colloquium, 1955).

[59]Walter Eichrodt explicated this interdependence of individual and
people in the covenant calling it Man in the Old Testament (London, Engl.:
SCM Press, 1951) esp. pp. 16ff and 23ff.

[60]Norman Perrin has stressed the table fellowship constituted by
Jesus' message, Rediscovering the Teaching of Jesus, op. cit., passim and
esp. pp. 151ff; at the same time, he continues under the influence of Rudolph
Bultmann's existentialist hermeneutic and stresses the experience of individuals as decisive in the proclamation of the Kingdom by Jesus, The New
Testament: An Introduction, pp. 288ff; "The Interpretation of a Biblical
Symbol," op. cit., p. 360; need this proclamation be understood differently
from the place of person and covenant people in the Hebrew Scriptures as
set forth by Walter Eichrodt, footnote 59?

[61]This eschatological note can be disentangled from the apocalyptic matrix in which the gathered community placed it; see Norman Perrin,
"Jesus and the Theology of the New Testament," op. cit.

[62]The Left Wing of the Reformation was also an important bearer of this communal heritage; see George H. Williams, The Radical Reformation (Philadelphia, Pa.: Westminster Press, 1962).

[63]For an attempt to formulate this notion of one history in liberation theology see Gustavo Gutierrez, A Theology of Liberation (Maryknoll, N.Y.: Orbis Books, 1973) pp. 153ff; whether a "Christofinalized" history can be history, however, remains debatable.

[64]The Cross is not discontinuous with the symbolism of forgiving sacrifice in the Hebrew Scriptures as in the "Suffering Servant" poems of Second Isaiah; see Sigmund Mowinckel, He That Cometh, op. cit., Chapter VII.

NOTES ABOUT THE CONTRIBUTORS

ROBERT BENNE is Associate Professor of Church and Society at the Lutheran School of Theology at Chicago. He is author of WANDERING IN THE WILDERNESS (1972) and co-author of DEFINING AMERICA: A CHRISTIAN CRITIQUE OF THE AMERICAN DREAM (1974).

RALPH WENDELL BURHOE is Editor of ZYGON, JOURNAL OF RELIGION AND SCIENCE and Senior Fellow, Center for Advanced Study in Religion and Science. He is co-editor of EVOLUTION AND MAN'S PROGRESS (1962), editor of and contributor to SCIENCE AND HUMAN VALUES (1971) and contributor to several other books. He has also published numerous papers in scientific, philosophical and theological journals.

J. RONALD ENGEL is Assistant Professor of Social Ethics at the Meadville/Lombard Theological School. He has published several articles in theological journals.

JOHN HALL FISH is on the faculty of the Associated Colleges of the Midwest Urban Studies Program. He is author of BLACK POWER/WHITE CONTROL (1973), co-author of THE EDGE OF THE GHETTO (1968), and author of several papers.

PHILIP HEFNER is Professor of Systematic Theology at the Lutheran School of Theology at Chicago. He is author of FAITH AND THE VITALITIES OF HISTORY (1966) and THE PROMISE OF TEILHARD (1970), co-author of DEFINING AMERICA: A CHRISTIAN CRITIQUE OF THE AMERICAN DREAM (1974), editor and translator of THREE ESSAYS BY ALBRECHT RITSCHL (1972), contributor to several volumes, and author of numerous papers.

JOHN KRETZMANN is on the faculty of the Associated Colleges of the Midwest Urban Studies Program. He is the author of several papers.

W. ALVIN PITCHER is Associate Professor of Ethics and Society in the Divinity School of the University of Chicago and Chairman of the Ethics and Society field. He is the author of numerous papers.

W. WIDICK SCHROEDER is Professor of Religion and Society at the Chicago Theological Seminary. He is author of COGNITIVE STRUCTURES AND RELIGIOUS RESEARCH (1970) and co-author of RELIGION IN AMERICAN CULTURE: UNITY AND DIVERSITY IN A MIDWESTERN COUNTY (1964), WHERE DO I STAND? LIVING THEOLOGICAL OPTIONS FOR CONTEMPORARY CHRISTIANS (1973), and SUBURBAN RELIGION: CHURCHES AND SYNAGOGUES IN THE AMERICAN EXPERIENCE (1974). He has also published numerous papers in both social scientific and theological journals.

FRANKLIN SHERMAN is Professor of Christian Ethics and Director of Graduate Studies at the Lutheran School of Theology at Chicago. He is author of THE PROMISE OF HESCHEL (1970) and THE PROBLEM OF

ABORTION AFTER THE SUPREME COURT DECISION (1974), editor of and contributor to CHRISTIAN HOPE AND THE FUTURE OF HUMANITY (1969), and editor of volume 47 of LUTHER'S WORKS (1971). He has published numerous papers and is editor of the Facet Books Series in Social Ethics.

GIBSON WINTER is Professor of Christianity and Society at the Princeton Theological Seminary. He is the author of numerous books, including ELEMENTS FOR A SOCIAL ETHIC (1966) and BEING FREE: REFLECTIONS ON AMERICA'S CULTURAL REVOLUTION (1970). He has also published many papers in both social scientific and theological journals.

STUDIES IN RELIGION AND SOCIETY

edited by

Thomas C. Campbell, W. Alvin Pitcher,
W. Widick Schroeder and Gibson Winter

Other CSSR Publications in the Series:

Paul E. Kraemer, AWAKENING FROM THE AMERICAN DREAM, 1973

William C. Martin, CHRISTIANS IN CONFLICT, 1972

Victor Obenhaus, AND SEE THE PEOPLE, 1968

Walter M. Stuhr, Jr., THE PUBLIC STYLE: A STUDY
OF THE COMMUNITY PARTICIPATION OF PROTESTANT MINISTERS, 1972

W. Widick Schroeder, Victor Obenhaus, Larry A. Jones, and
Thomas Sweetser, SJ, SUBURBAN RELIGION: CHURCHES
AND SYNAGOGUES IN THE AMERICAN EXPERIENCE, 1974

Thomas P. Sweetser, SJ, THE CATHOLIC PARISH: SHIFTING
MEMBERSHIP IN A CHANGING CHURCH, 1974

Lawrence Witmer, ed., ISSUES IN COMMUNITY ORGANIZATION, 1972

Order from your bookstore or the Center for the Scientific Study of Religion

Other Books in the Series:

Thomas C. Campbell and Yoshio Fukuyama, THE FRAGMENTED
LAYMAN, 1970

John Fish, BLACK POWER/WHITE CONTROL: THE STRUGGLE
OF THE WOODLAWN ORGANIZATION IN CHICAGO, 1973

John Fish, Gordon Nelson, Walter M. Stuhr, Jr., and Lawrence Witmer
THE EDGE OF THE GHETTO, 1968

W. Widick Schroeder and Victor Obenhaus,
RELIGION IN AMERICAN CULTURE, 1964

Gibson Winter, RELIGIOUS IDENTITY, 1968

Order from your bookstore